WATER MANAGEMENT IN INDIA

What Works, What Doesn't

M. Dinesh Kumar

GYAN

Water Management in India : What Works, What Doesn't

Rs. 750

ISBN: 978-81-212-1033-1

Published in 2009 in India by
Gyan Publishing House,
23 Main, Ansari Road, Darya Ganj,
New Delhi-110002
Phones : 23282060, 23261060
Fax : 011-23285914
E-mail: books@gyanbooks.com
Website: www.gyanbooks.com

Lasser Type Setting by: Quick Media, Delhi
Printed at : Young Art Press, Delhi

Contents

Preface

The past couple of decades saw global debates on an impending water scarcity. These debates often focused on problems in countries like India and China and ways to deal with them. Several eminent scholars from India and abroad had contributed substantially to this fascinating debate, many of them mooting solutions, which were argued to be "innovative" and "out of box". Nevertheless, their arguments were less often supported by hard core scientific evidences and more often by rhetoric. Yet, most of them solutions found great appeal among academicians and practitioners alike. This had led to series of research studies, apart from actions on the ground in certain cases.

Some of the big ticket solutions were: rainwater harvesting for domestic water security; rainwater harvesting and groundwater recharge to address water scarcity in rural and urban areas; increasing the use of groundwater in water rich areas; use of micro irrigation technologies to save water in agriculture; virtual water trade from water-rich to water-scarce regions. What is most striking is the lack of inter-disciplinary perspective and rigorous methodology in analyzing the effectiveness of these solutions. Most of these works were limited to the confines of the disciplines of those who undertook them, be it watershed management, water harvesting and local recharge, intensive groundwater use for agricultural growth or virtual water trade.

Some of the scholars pursued these approaches through their writings and speeches on a mission mode and with a crusader's zest. Hence, there were serious knowledge gaps about "what solutions work and under what conditions". Hence, they appeared as easy solutions.

On the other hand, several of the standard and classical approaches to deal with water scarcity and over-exploitation of groundwater such as electricity metering and water/electricity pricing, water rights reforms were rubbished on the ground that there are serious practical difficulties in introducing them and water/energy pricing are politically sensitive issues. The main assumptions which seem to be driving this philosophy are that India has informal water economy and very poor water literacy, making the transaction cost of bringing in any orderly behaviour huge; and farmers want free power and water. But, sadly, this was not supported by any evidence. This made it easy for pushing some of these "innovative" approaches into the policy agenda. One fine example of this is the dug well recharging programme of the government of India.

The country's water policy makers do not seem to be fully aware of the limited opportunities that some of these "quick fix" solutions in the popular parlance offer. More importantly, their likely negative social, economic and ecological impacts are little understood. But, on the other hand, pessimism about the feasibility of implementing the classical approaches is greater than ever before. Meters are taken away from farm wells, and electricity supplied to agriculture was made either free or is heavily subsidized. The policy makers seem to be caught up in the dilemma of making a choice between "what is ideal for the society" and "what is popular and appealing". The result is that some interventions are carried out "lock, stock and barrel" costing the nation its precious resources. This is leading to a colossal anarchy in the water sector, with catastrophic effects on ecology, social welfare and equity.

It is, therefore, the right time to confront some of the most debated, yet unresolved questions regarding water management options for India. In this book, I try to synthesize several pieces of the empirical research carried out in the recent past on some of these most pressing issues. The "received wisdom" about the potential of some of the water management solutions in popular parlance is systematically challenged through various chapters of this book. Also, the "sceptical pessimism" about the feasibility of some of the more classical approaches is questioned.

I am thankful to all those scholars and practitioners who have provoked me through their excellent writings and speeches on these controversial topics, to explore new conceptual frameworks and methodological frontiers for doing empirical work which formed the basis for this book. I am also thankful to Sir Ratan Tata Trust, Mumbai and its Programme Manager, Shri Arun Pandhi for having supported the research through the IWMI-Tata Water Policy Research Program (ITP), which formed the basis for the papers included in this book. I am also thankful to the International Water Management Institute where I worked during 2001-2008, the time when most of relevant studies were written, and several of my colleagues there who provided me the intellectual stimulant for doing most of the work presented in the book.

I owe a lot to my beloved wife Shyma and daughter Archana who constantly provided me the inspiration and motivation to always do "what I wanted to" and write "what I thought is correct and responsible". They had been witness to and victim of several unpleasant incidents, which I had to face because of the strong position I had taken on many sensitive issues. This book is dedicated to them. I am thankful to several of my present and former colleagues, Dr. A. Narayanamoorthy, Dr. R. Indu, Dr. O. P. Singh, Mr. Manoj Kumar Sharma, Dr. MVK Sivamohan, Mr. Avinash Kishore and Mr. Nitin Bassi who encouraged me to take up this task. Last, but not the least, I am also extremely thankful to the new philanthropic organization named "Arghyam" in Bangalore. Their generous support had enabled us set up this new research venture named Institute for Resource Analysis and Policy in Hyderabad which provided me an excellent platform to bring my past work to fusion.

I sincerely hope that book will guide policy makers take informed decisions vis-a-vis the investments in water sector.

M. Dinesh Kumar

1
Introduction

Water Crisis in India

Many regions in the world are already facing severe water shortages, and many more are likely face water crisis in future (Seckler *et al.*, 1998; HDR, 2006). Still, there is an alarming lack of long term policies to target quantity, quality and management problems (Tortajada, 2001). But, the impact of water resource endowment and water environment of a country on its economy cannot be over-emphasized (HDR, 2006; Laurence *et al.*, 2003; Barrios *et al.*, 2004).

Currently, India is the largest irrigation water user in the world (source: based on Seckler *et al.*, 1998). Due to the ability of agriculture sector to reduce poverty, and achieve food sufficiency, there is a growing need to manage water for the same in developing countries (Chaturvedi 2000; Tortajada, 2001: pp. 361). India has 1/6th of the world population. This economy, which is in transition, has sixty per cent of it depending on agriculture for livelihoods. Water plays a big role in its economic growth apart from sustaining agricultural production and food security (Shah and Kumar, 2008). Therefore, what India does to manage its future water needs has great significance for the developing and underdeveloped economies of the world that are still facing problems of food insecurity, malnutrition and high poverty rates.

But, India is facing a major water crisis (Amarasinghe et al., 2005; Kumar, 2003; Phansalkar and Verma, 2005). The origin of this crisis lies in the limited knowledge about the nature and magnitude of water scarcity, the causes and the types of interventions that would be needed to avert it. At the fundamental level, there is little understanding of the way in which the factors such as economy, society, environment, demography, technology and governance forms could drive our water future (Phansalkar and Verma, 2005). The types of impact each one of these drivers would have on water demand would be different. So, is the likely impact of some of them viz., technology, economic growth and environmental changes on our ability to tap the available water resources.

Even, fundamental differences exist on the issue of whether future water scarcity is going to be a reality or not. Little consensus exists on how far the demands for water are going to grow in future (based on GOI, 1999 and Amarasinghe *et al.*, 2008). Even when some argue that water demands are going to grow in future (GOI, 1999; Kumar, 2003), many believe that the available water resources in the country would be more than sufficient to meet these demands, provided we make significant investments in large-scale engineering interventions, considering the great mismatch in water resource availability and demand with respect to space and time. These techno centric views by and large dominate India's water policy debates.

Whereas some others, while foreseeing a major imbalance in future water supplies and demands under a "business as usual scenario", believe that supply-side interventions without efficient pricing of the expensive imported water, would only naturally trigger demand growth, thereby leading to an ecological crisis (Rath, 2003). Some also believe that many soft approaches would come to the rescue of populations in dealing with water crisis, import of virtual water from well-endowed regions being one among them (Iyer, 2008).

A few scholars question the very method of making future demand projections that use the assumption that institutional regimes governing water use and current use ethics and practices would continue. They argue for pro-active steps to ensure that water use becomes more efficient, equitable and sustainable, so as to bring checks on the demand growth. They have harped on the need for institutional interventions—like regulations, water rights reforms and voluntary cuts in water use brought out through water literacy, education and awareness (see Shah *et al.*, 1998). They advocate a soft path to development, discouraging water-intensive economic activities including agriculture, in ecologically fragile and naturally water-scarce regions, and small scale water and hydel projects to meet the moderated demands (see for instance, D' Souza, 2002).

Even the demand projections are often shrouded in controversies. Among those who believe that future water demands are likely to be higher than that at present, differences exist over the source of such demand growth. Some strongly argue that with increasing urbanization and industrialization and changing structure of Indian economy from predominantly agrarian to industrial, much less number of people would be engaged in agriculture, a unique characteristic of many developed economies[1]. Some others argue that with greater adoption of micro irrigation, water saving technologies, other resource conservation technologies and increasing use of wastewater in urban fringes for agriculture, the growth in water demand could be reduced significantly (Amarasinghe and Sharma, 2008). Against these views, some others believe that increased use of modern water supply, use and treatment technologies would ease the pressure on freshwater resources for urban, industrial and environmental sectors.

On the other hand, many others feel it important to assess the type, nature and magnitude of future water scarcity more pragmatically, and then design interventions to mitigate it (see Kumar, 2003; Amarasinghe *et al.*, 2008). The type of scarcity could be physical, economic or demand-supply gap; and the nature of scarcity could be seasonal or perennial. From the above analysis, it is evident that there appear to be fundamental differences in the way future water management problems are being approached, with the result that solutions being advocated to deal with the problems vary widely.

Debates on Water Management Alternatives

Uncertainty exists about the type, nature and magnitude of water problems that India is likely to face in the coming decades due to lack of consensus on the approaches and methodologies (Phansalkar and Verma, 2005). While major demand for water is likely to come from agriculture, particularly the need for growing more food for the growing population, major variations in the assumptions made and therefore the projections of future food demand were seen in recent estimates by scholars and agencies (see Amarasinghe et al., 2008; GOI, 1999; Kumar, 2003). Nevertheless, many scholars continue to paint a grim future based on estimates. For instance, the global water supply and demand balance estimates by Seckler *et al.* (1998), shows that by 2025 India would be hit by severe water scarcity in many parts. The GOI (1999) estimates, which forecasts a heightened future water demand, shows that a combination of supply side and demand side interventions would be able to deal with water scarcity in future under the optimistic scenario of water demand. This scenario considered increase in conveyance efficiency in irrigation systems, field application efficiency and crop yield improvements, and some improvements in yield of rain-fed crops, which in turn means. Whereas on the supply side, inter-basin water transfer was considered in view of the major basin-wise disparities in demand and supplies (see GOI, 1999 for details). The recent analysis by International Water Management Institute of India's water future also support inter-basin water transfer projects to growing urban water demands of cities in water-scarce basins (see Amarasinghe *et al.*, 2008).

The civil society front is characterized by polarized and intense debates on the approaches to deal with water scarcity. Many from water bureaucracies and outside believe that solution to avert an impending future water crisis lies in mega water transfer projects that could take water in bulk from well-endowed areas in the Ganges and Brahmaputra to scarce areas in the west, central and Southern parts of India. They also take the position that the future social tensions and ecological crisis that can be perpetuated by water scarcity would be enormous and widespread that they would justify the localized negative social and ecological impacts of major water transfer projects, which can occur due to deforestation, land submergence, and diversion of water from rivers affecting the ecological health of the rivers downstream[2].

Though over the past 25 years, there have been significant improvements in efficiency of water use in irrigation globally leading to leveling off of water use (source: Gleick (1998) as cited in Sorooshian *et al.* 2002), it has mostly been in developed countries (Sorooshian *et al.*, 2002). Therefore, many from academic and scientific institutions have mooted water demand management to avert a crisis (Amarasinghe *et al.*, 2005; Kumar, 2003; Molden *et al.*, 2003; Seckler *et al.*, 1998; Tortajada, 2001), focusing on improving water productivity in agriculture to make more water available for environment (Molden *et al.*, 2003). They argue that significant improvements in productivity of both rainwater and irrigation water is possible through farm management and on-farm water management (Hussain *et al.*, 2003).

Globally, many advocate rainwater harvesting not only as a means to augment the supplies, but often as a source of irrigation supplement to enhance the productivity of rainwater (Falkenmark, 2004; Fox et al., 2002; Rockström *et al.*, 2002). In India, it concerns roof top water harvesting for domestic water security, runoff harvesting in rural areas for various uses, and artificial groundwater recharge projects to create buffer for tackling droughts and intensifying irrigation (Agarwal and Narain, 1997; Athavale, 2003). Voluntary organizations which work on environment and development strongly advocate the need to exercise control on the use of water in agriculture, domestic sector and pollution assimilation, and lobby for stringent regulations on water withdrawal and use.

A few scholars had mooted the idea of virtual water import in the form of food grains as a solution to water scarcity in water deficit regions and nations (Allan, 1997; Warner 2003; Hoekstra and Hung, 2002; Chapagain and Hoekstra, 2003; Iyer, 2008), suggesting the use of revenue earned from export of more water-efficient cash crops for importing water-intensive cereals like rice and wheat. The underlying rationale in the virtual water trade argument is "global water use efficiency" and "distribution of scarcity". This is based on the assumption that all the humid, water-rich countries are at an advantage in economic terms in producing food grains as compared to the arid and semi-arid countries. In the Indian context, virtual water trade is being pushed as an alternative to large-scale water transfer projects, including the national river linking project, wherein the proponents argue for producing cereals which need large quantities of water in the water rich regions and exporting the surplus to naturally water-scarce regions.

Current Gaps in the Debates on Water Management

Rainwater harvesting is the most significant big ticket solution to water problems in India, which has emerged in the past couple of decades. Its proponents have been successful in projecting "local water harvesting solutions" as a significant alternative to the conventional water projects. NGOs, civil society organizations and local governments alike had implemented local water harvesting and groundwater recharge projects on a large scale in many arid and semi arid parts of the Indian country-side (Kumar *et al.*, 2008).

But, very little systematic and scientific analysis exist to show the potential of rainwater harvesting and groundwater recharging, particularly the extent to which it can reduce the supply-demand imbalances specifically in water scarce regions. More importantly, the extensive documentation available on RWH traditions in India is silent about the economic viability issues[3]. Very little analysis exists about how well the rainwater harvesting projects fare in terms of cost and economics, as compared to large water resource projects (UNDP, 2006). Much of the knowledge generated about rainwater harvesting is about the local hydrological and socio-economic impacts. The scientific accuracy of certain claims about rainwater harvesting such as improved runoff collection efficiency is often subject to questioning. After Perry (2001), before we consider small water harvesting as an alternative to large water projects, the issue to be resolved is how many local interventions would be required to achieve the same productive impact as a single large intervention and their social and downstream environmental impacts.

In the last one decade, the concept of water productivity and "more crop per crop" has gained acceptance in academic and policy circles in India (see Kijne *et al.*, 2003). But, this complex concept is poorly understood, including its relevance in various situations prevailing in India. Very little understanding exists on the drivers of change in water productivity in both physical and economic terms, and the opportunities and constraints in enhancing the same (Kumar and van Dam, 2008).

On-farm water management and farm management can improve crop water productivity (Hussain *et al.*, 2003). But, the degree of incentive farmers would have to carry out on farm water management depends on the opportunity cost of using water itself. Between surface irrigation and groundwater irrigation, it is well irrigation which is most amenable to water productivity improvements through various measures including micro irrigation because of its inherent virtues. Today, nearly 65% of India's irrigation is from wells. In any Indian states, electricity use for groundwater pumping for agriculture is heavily subsidized (Kumar, 2005; Kumar, 2007). The zero marginal cost of electricity used for groundwater pumping and the lack of well-defined water rights means zero opportunity cost of using groundwater (Saleth, 1997; Kumar and Singh, 2001; Kumar, 2005).

Many scholars have advocated introduction of pro rata pricing of electricity (Kumar & Singh, 2001; Moench, 1995; Narayanamoorthy, 1997). But, a few scholars have expressed serious scepticism about the viability of introducing metering of agro wells, and pro-rata pricing of electricity on socio-economic viability (Saleth, 1997; Shah, 1993; Shah et al., 2004) and political feasibility grounds (Shah *et al.*, 2004). The huge transaction cost of metering electricity use by hundreds of thousands of agro wells in rural areas (Shah *et al.*, 2004), and the high tariff levels at which the energy demand start responding to tariff changes (Saleth, 1997) are some of the concerns. Nevertheless, there is some empirical work available recently which question the validity of the arguments about socio-economic viability of power tariff reforms (see Kumar, 2005). After Saleth (1997), there are theoretical issues associated with fixing power tariff that encourage efficient, equitable and sustainable use of groundwater also cannot be ignored. Large-scale empirical work, which argue for or against power tariff reforms are absent.

Use of drip irrigation is advocated by government of India in naturally water-scarce regions, as a technology to improve water use efficiency and water saving. The Task Force on Micro Irrigation constituted by government of India estimates the area that can be brought under micro irrigation systems at an astronomical 97 million hectares. But, little attention has been paid to the constraints facing the farmers in adopting this system such as: erratic power supply conditions; and lack of clear economic incentives for saving water and energy[4] due to inefficient pricing of electricity and water. The water saving benefits of MI systems are often over-played. The existing cereal dominated cropping systems and the small sizes of land holding of farmers are other physical constraints. Leaving aside the issue of water saving benefits and economic incentives, the estimates were found to be far higher than what is physically and technically possible.

As regards virtual water argument, the operational aspects of virtual water trade have not been studied. It is important to know whether the much-talked about virtues of global water use efficiency and distribution of scarcity are really achieved through virtual water trade between nations and regions. Given the fact that our country is characterized by regional imbalance in water availability and demand, the virtual water trade option needs to be weighed against physical transfer of water between water-rich and water-scarce regions. There is discussion at the policy level on the use of economic principles in water allocation decisions (Alagh *et al.*, 1995). But, there is very little empirical work on economic valuation of water in India that compares water-scarce and water-rich regions. Conventional economic theory suggests that the value generated from the use of a resource would be high in regions where it is scarce. But, this had rarely found application in planning and designing water transfer projects.

Improving economic conditions alone is not the objective of ensuring water security. It is also needed for social advancements. The recent years have seen renewed interest in understanding how growing threats to water security affects future progress in human development and economic growth of nations. The underlying concern is that water insecurity could decouple economic growth and progress in human development (HDR, 2006). Such concerns are very valid for India, which still has low levels of investment in water infrastructure and institutions, and low progress in human development and poor economic conditions. The international development discourse is, however, characterized by unhealthy debates with divergent views. Though scholars have provided robust evidences to the effect that water security catalyses human development and economic growth (Braga *et al.*, 1998; Briscoe, 2005), number of regions for which these evidences are available is too limited for a global consensus on this issue. An alternative view suggests that countries would be able to tackle their water scarcity and other problems relating to water environment at advanced stages of economic development (Shah and Koppen, 2006).

Thus, there are significant gaps in the debates on water management alternatives for India. The country's water policy makers do not seem to be aware of the constraints and challenges in implementing the solutions that are in the popular parlance, be it micro irrigation, "more crop per drop" or water harvesting and groundwater recharging, or virtual water trade. Over and above, the likely outcomes and impacts of these policy choices are little known.

Purpose and Scope of the Book

The purpose of this book is to guide policy makers take informed decisions vis-à-vis the investments in water sector. While doing this, we challenge the "received wisdom" about the scope and potential of some of the most popular and widely talked-about water management solutions for water-scarce regions of India. It also challenges the "sceptical pessimism" about adopting some of the more classical approaches to water management. The water management solutions being investigated are: roof water harvesting; local water harvesting and groundwater recharge; virtual water trade; micro irrigation; pricing of electricity for groundwater pumping; and creating large water storages. The book is based on a large body of research undertaken by the author in different parts of India during the pasty 3-4 years, but most of w hich quite recent.

The issues being investigated are: roof water harvesting for domestic water security; rainwater harvesting and local groundwater recharge schemes for reducing water scarcity and improving groundwater regimes in over-exploited areas; virtual water import as an economic instrument for dealing with water scarcity in water-deficit regions; potential of micro irrigation for reducing water demand in agriculture in India; and socio-economic viability of introducing power tariff reform for improving the efficiency, equity and sustainability in groundwater use. This is done by systematically identifying the physical, socio-economic, institutional and policy settings under which these options succeed or fail, and subsequently seeing how far the conditions are favourable or unfavourable in India. The viability of each option is analyzed from hydrological or physical, technical, socio-economic/economic, institutional and policy perspectives. Lastly, the nature of linkage between water security, human development and economic growth, and the role of large storages in achieving the same are also investigated.

The first option being examined in the book, which is covered in chapter 2, is roof water harvesting for domestic water security in rural and urban areas of naturally water scarce regions. The hydrological opportunity, physical feasibility and economic viability and the actual impact on equity and sustainability in water use are analysed in the face of the current pricing regimes for domestic water supplies in rural and urban areas. It discusses the hydrological opportunity, physical feasibility, cost and economics of roof water harvesting for different types of housing stocks under different rainfall regimes, geographical settings, and socio-economic conditions. The potential equity impact of subsidizing RWHS is also analyzed.

The third chapter looks at the rainwater harvesting efforts for their effectiveness in improving water situation in naturally water-scarce river basins. The hydrological opportunity, i.e., the reliability of water supplies from rainwater harvesting; effectiveness of groundwater recharge through local recharge activities; the economics of water harvesting/recharge for improving agricultural productivity; the impacts of intensive water harvesting on basin water economy; and the equity impacts are analyzed. Macro level hydrological data on rainfall, rainy days, inter-annual variability, geo-hydrology, and climate, and data from five selected river basins on rainfall and evapo-transpiration and water demand for agriculture, and detailed hydrological observation from one of the water-scarce river basins in Saurashtra are presented to illustrate the point.

The fourth chapter looks at the socio-economic viability of introducing pro rata electricity pricing in the farm sector, and its efficiency, sustainability and equity impacts. It challenges the deep-rooted notion that raising power tariff would reduce the economic prospects of irrigated farming and hence would be highly unpopular. The analysis was done using primary data from 600 farmers from three states, viz., Gujarat, Uttar Pradesh and Bihar. For analyzing efficiency impacts, the cropping pattern, irrigation water dosage and irrigation water productivity (at the field level and farm level) values for farmers who are confronted with differential marginal costs of energy and water used for irrigation are compared. The sustainability impact is analyzed by comparing the groundwater use per unit of irrigated land. The equity impacts of introducing pro rata pricing are analyzed by comparing the price at which water is traded by electric well owners and diesel well owners. The different categories of farmers whose farming systems are compared are: (1) farmers who are confronted with zero marginal cost of using water and energy; (2) farmers who are confronted with low marginal cost of using water (water buyers from electric well owners); and farmers who are confronted with high marginal cost of using water (diesel pump owners and water buyers from diesel pump owners) from Uttar Pradesh and Bihar. The overall socio-economic viability of raising power tariff is examined by comparing the impacts on net returns from farming.

The fifth chapter looks at the potential for micro irrigation systems in India, and the amount of reduction in water requirement for agriculture possible through it. It challenges the available estimates of the ultimate potential of MI systems in India, on the premise that they are not based on any proper assessment of the constraints facing their adoption in different regions from physical, socio-economic, institutional and policy angles. The chapter discusses the conditions under which MI systems can provide the much-talked about benefits of water saving, yield enhancement, water productivity improvement and incremental income; and examines as to what extend those conditions are favourable for MI adoption in India. First, a state of the art review of the research on micro irrigation systems in India for their physical and economic benefits/impacts are presented. The chapter then critically analyzes the potential contribution of MI adoption in India by: assessing the constraints and opportunities for their adoption and then arriving at the crop area that can be brought them; the field level impacts of MI adoption; and the aggregate level impacts of adoption.

The sixth chapter looks at the operational feasibility of virtual water trade as an economic instrument to deal with water shortages experienced by water-deficit countries and regions. This can be studied by examining whether the much-talked about virtues of "global water use efficiency" and "distribution of scarcity" are achieved through virtual water trade.

In order to do this, virtual water trade through agricultural commodities across the globe was analyzed, and the factors that govern virtual water flow were identified. For this data from 145 countries on renewable water availability, gross and net cultivated area, irrigated area, ppp adjusted GDP and net virtual water export in per capita terms are used. Here, we identify the key constraints in virtual water trade between nations and between regions with differential water endowments. Finally, we weigh the virtual water trade option against regional water transfers between regions in India that are characterized by imbalances in availability and demand for water in agriculture.

In the seventh chapter, the author confronts the most difficult question of "what India's investment priority in the water sector should be" if it has to realize the goals of economic growth and social development through water management. This chapter attempt the following: (i) analyzing the nature of linkage between water situation of a country, comprising improved water access and use, water environment and institutional capacities in the water sector, and economic growth of a nation; and (ii) assessing the role of large water storages in boosting economic growth and changing human development indicators of countries which fall in hot and arid, tropical climates.

There are three main propositions. First: improving the water situation through investments in water infrastructure, institutions and policies would help ensure economic growth through the human development route. Second: nations can achieve reasonable progress in human development even at low levels of economic growth, through investment in water infrastructure, and welfare policies. Third: countries need to invest in building large water storages to support economic prosperity, and ensure water security for social advancements. The hypotheses are: (1) improved water situation supports economic growth through the human development route; and (2) countries, which are in tropical climates with aridity, can support their economic growth through enhancing per capita reservoir storage that improves their water security.

In order to realistically assess the water situation of a country, which can capture the crucial attributes like access to water for various uses; level of use of water in different sectors; condition of the water environment; and technological and institutional capacities in water sector, a new index named Sustainable Water Use Index was derived from WPI. In this chapter, we first analyze the nature of linkage between water situation of a country, vis-à-vis access and use, water environment and institutional capabilities in the water sector on economic growth. For this, data on sustainable water use index derived from WPI; human development and per capita GDP (ppp adjusted) for 145 countries, and data on global hunger index (GHI) for 117 countries are analyzed. In order to illustrate how creating water storages supports economic growth of countries which fall in hot and arid, tropical climates index, data on per capita dam storage are analyzed for 22 countries.

A summary of the key findings, policy directions and emerging issues is presented in Chapter 8.

References

Agarwal, Anil and Sunita Narain (1997) *Dying Wisdom: Rise and Fall of Traditional Water Harvesting Systems*, Centre for Science and Environment, New Delhi.

Alagh, Y. K, R. D. Desai, G. S. Guha and S P Kashyap (1995) *Economic Dimensions of Sardar Sarovar Project,* New Delhi: Har-Anand Publications.

Allan, J. A. (1997) Virtual water: A long term solution for water short Middle Eastern economies?' Paper presented at the 1997 British Association Festival of Science, University of Leeds, 9 September 1997.

Amarasinghe, Upali, Bharat R. Sharma, Noel Aloysius, Christopher Scott, Vladimir Smakhtin, Charlotte de Fraiture, A. K. Sinha and A. K. Shukla (2005) *Spatial Variation in Water Supply and Demand across River Basins of India*, IWMI Research Report 83, Colombo, Sri Lanka.

Amarasinghe, Upali, Tushaar Shah and Peter McCornick (2008) Seeking Calm Waters: Exploring policy options for India's Water Future, *Natural Resource Forum*, 32 (4): 305-315.

Amarasinghe, U.A.; Sharma, B.R., eds. (2008) *Strategic analyses of the National River Linking Project (NRLP) of India, series 2.* Proceedings of the Workshop on Analyses of Hydrological, Social and Ecological Issues of the NRLP. Colombo, Sri Lanka: International Water Management Institute, 500p.

Athavale, R. N. (2003) *Water Harvesting and Sustainable Supply in India*, Centre for Environment Education, Ahmedabad, Jaipur and New Delhi: Rawat Publications.

Barrios, Salvador, Luisito Bertinelli and Eric Strobl (2004) Rainfall and Africa's Growth Tragedy, research paper.

Bastiaanssen, Wim, Mobin-ud-Din Ahmed and Zubair Tahir (2003) Upscaling Water Productivity in Irrigated Agriculture Using Remote-sensing and GIS Technologies, in Jacob Kijne and others (Eds.) *Water Productivity in Agriculture: Limits and Opportunities for Improvement*, Comprehensive Assessment of Water Management in Agriculture. UK: CABI Publishing in Association with International Water Management Institute.

Braga B., O. Rocha and J. Tundisi (1998) Dams and the Environment: The Brazilian Experience, *International Journal of Water Resources Development*, 14 (2).

Briscoe, John (2005) "India's Water Economy: Bracing up for a Turbulent Future," key note address at the 4th Annual Partners' Meet of IWMI-Tata Water Policy Research Program, Institute of Rural Management Anand, 26-29 February, 2005.

Chapagain A.K. and A.Y. Hoekstra (2003) Virtual water trade: A quantification of virtual water flows between nations in relation to international trade of livestock and livestock products, Virtual water trade, proceedings of the international expert meeting on virtual water trade, edited by Hoekstra, A. Y., Value of water research report series # 12.

Chaturvedi, Mahesh C. (2000) Water for Food and Rural Development, Developing Countries, *Water International*, 25 (1): 40-53.

D'Souza, Dilip (2002) *Narmada Dammed: An Enquiry into the Politics of Development*, New Delhi: Penguin Books India.

Gallopin, Gilberto C. and Frank R. Rijsberman (2000) Three Global Water Demand Projections, *International Journal of Water*, 1 (2000).

Falkenmark, Malin (2004) Towards Integrated Catchment Management: Opening the Paradigm Locks between Hydrology, Ecology and Policy Making, *International Journal of Water Resources Development*, 20 (3).

Fox, P., J. Rockström and J. Barron (2002) Risk Analysis and economic viability of water harvesting for supplementary irrigation in semi arid Burkina Faso and Kenya, *Agricultural Systems*, 83 (3): 231-250.

Glieck, P. H. (1997) "Human Population and Water: Meeting Basic Needs in the 21st Century," in R. K. Pachauri R.K and Lubina F. Qureshi (eds.) *Population, Environment and Development*, 357p.

Government of India (1999) Integrated Water Resource Development: A Plan for Development, Report of the National Commission for Integrated Water Resources Development Vol. I, Ministry of Water Resources, Government of India, New Delhi.

Hoekstra, A.Y. and P. Q. Hung (2002) Virtual water trade: A quantification of virtual water flows between nations in relation to international crop trade, Value of Water Research Report Series No.11, IHE, Delft, the Netherlands.

Hussain *et al.* (2003) Land and Water Productivity of Wheat in the Western Indo-Gangetic Plain if India and Pakistan: a Comparative Analysis, in Jacob Kijne and others (Eds.) *Water Productivity in Agriculture: Limits and Opportunities for Improvement*,

Comprehensive Assessment of Water Management in Agriculture. UK: CABI Publishing in Association with International Water Management Institute.

Iyer, R. Ramaswamy (2008) Water: A Critique of Three Basic Concepts, *Economic and Political Weekly*, 43 (1): 15-17.

Kumar, M. Dinesh (2003a) "Demand Management in the Face of Growing Water Scarcity and Conflicts in India: Institutional and Policy Alternatives for Future," In Kanchan Chopra, CH Hanumantha Rao and Ram Prasad Sengupta (Eds.) *Water Resources, Sustainable Livelihoods and Ecosystem Services*. Published by Indian Society for Ecological Economics, New Delhi: Concept Publishing Company.

Kumar, M. Dinesh, Shantanu Ghosh, Ankit Patel, O. P. Singh and R. Ravindranath (2006) Rainwater Harvesting in India: Some Critical Issues for Basin Planning and Research, *Land Use and Water Resources Research*, 6 (1): 1-17.

Kumar, M. Dinesh, Ankit Patel, R. Ravindranath and O. P. Singh (2008) Chasing a Mirage: Water Harvesting and Artificial Recharge in Naturally Water-scarce Regions of India, *Economic and Political Weekly*, 43 (35): 61-71.

Kumar, M. Dinesh and Jos van Dam (2008) Improving Water Productivity in Agriculture in Developing Economies: In Search of New Avenues, proceedings of the 7th Annual Partners Meet, IWMI-Tata Water Policy Research Program "Managing Water in the Face of Growing Scarcity, Inequity and Diminishing Returns: Exploring Fresh Approaches," ICRISAT Campus, Patancheru, 2-4 April, 2008.

Laurence, Peter, Jeremy Meigh and C. Sullivan (2003) Water Poverty Index: International Comparisons, Keele University, and Centre for Ecology and Hydrology, Wallingford, United Kingdom.

Molden, David, Hammond Murray-Rust, R. Sakthivadivel and Ian Makin (2003) A Water Productivity Framework for Understanding and Action, in Jacob Kijne and others (Eds.) *Water Productivity in Agriculture: Limits and Opportunities for Improvement*, Comprehensive Assessment of Water Management in Agriculture. UK: CABI Publishing in Association with International Water Management Institute.

Narayanamoorthy, A. (1997) Impact of Electricity Tariff Policies on the Use of Electricity and Groundwater: Arguments and Facts. *Artha Vijnana*, XXXIX (3): 323-340.

Perry, Chris J. (2001) World Commission on Dams: Implications for Food and Irrigation, *Irrigation and Drainage*, 50: 101-107.

Phansalkar, Sanjiv and Shilp Verma (2005) India's Water Future 2025/2050, research highlight, IWMI-Tata water policy research program, Anand, India.

Rath, N. (2003) Linking rivers: some elementary arithmetic, *Economic and Political Weekly*, 39 (29): 3033.

Rockström, J., Jennie Barron and Patrick Fox (2002) Rainwater management for improving productivity among small holder farmers in drought prone environments, *Physics and Chemistry of the Earth*, 27 (2002): 949-959.

Saleth, R. Maria (1997) Power Tariff Policy for Groundwater Regulation: Efficiency, Equity and Sustainability. *Artha Vijnana*, XXXIX (3): 312-322.

Sorooshian, Saroosh, Martha P. L. Witaker and Terri S. Hogue (2002) Regional and global hydrology and water resource issues: The role of international and national programmes, water policy article. *Aquatic Sciences*, 64 (2002) 317-327.

Seckler David, Upali Amarasinghe, David Molden, Radhika de Silva and Randolph Barker (1998) *World Water Demand and Supply 1990-2025: Scenarios and Issues*, Research Report 19, Colombo, Sri Lanka: International Water Management Institute.

Shah, Tushaar (1993) *Groundwater markets and Irrigation Development: Political Economy and Practical Policy*, Bombay: Oxford University Press.

Shah, Tushaar, Christopher Scott, Avinash Kishore and Abhishek Sharma (2004) *Energy Irrigation Nexus in South Asia: Improving Groundwater Conservation and Power Sector Viability*, IWMI Research Report # 70, Colombo, Sri Lanka.

Shah, Tushaar and Barbara van Koppen (2006) Is India Ripe for Integrated Water Resources Management? Fitting Water Policy to National Development Context, Special Articles, *Economic and Political Weekly*, August 5, 2006.

Shah, Zankhana and M. Dinesh Kumar (2008) In the Midst of the Large Dam Controversy: Objectives, Criteria for Assessing Large Water Storages in the Developing World, *Water Resources Management*, 22: 1799-1824.

Singh, O. P. (2004) Water-intensity of North Gujarat's Dairy Industry: Why Dairy Industry Should Take a Serious Look at Irrigation?, paper presented at the second International Conference of the Asia Pacific Association of Hydrology and Water Resources (APHW 2004), Singapore, June 5-9, 2004.

Tortajada, (2001) First Meeting of the Club of Tokyo for a Global Water Policy Dialogue, Tokyo, 25-26 September, *Water Policy*, 3(5): 359-362.

United Nations Development Programme (2006) *Human Development Report- 2006*, New York: United Nations.

Warner, J. 2003. Virtual water – virtual benefits? Scarcity, distribution, security and conflict reconsidered, Virtual water trade, proceedings of the international expert meeting on virtual water trade, edited by Hoekstra, A. Y., Value of Water Research Report Series # 12.

Footnotes

1. They moot future emergence of phenomena like diversification, modernization and commercialization of agriculture, with a greater need for reliable supplies in that sector. They expect significant growth in demand to come from urban and industrial (Amarasinghe, Shah and McCormick, 2008).
2. Key note address at the national seminar on Sustainable Management of Water Resources, Junagadh Agriculture University, Junagadh, by V. B. Patel, Former Chairman, Central Water Commission, Government of India.
3. For instance, Agarwal and Narain (1997) and Athavale (2003) which have extensively documented rainwater harvesting systems in different parts of India are silent on the cost and economic viability issues.
4. This is not to say that it is always possible to save energy use in irrigation through MI system adoption.

2

Can Roof Water Harvesting Ensure Domestic Water Security?

ABSTRACT

Roof water harvesting is being widely promoted as a panacea for the growing drinking water crisis in India. In this chapter, we analyse the scope, hydrological opportunity, physical feasibility and economic viability of roof water harvesting systems across classes and under different physical and socioeconomic situations. The author argues that the roof water harvesting systems are not alternative to public systems in urban and rural areas of regions receiving low rainfall. Hydrological opportunities for RWHS are very poor in urban and rural areas under low rainfall conditions. The systems offer very little scope in ensuring domestic water security for urban housing stocks of low and middle-income groups. At the same time, they offer tremendous potential for independent bungalows having large roof area. However, their physical feasibility is very poor in urban areas. Their economic viability as a supplementary source of domestic water supply seems to be poor in urban areas, when compared to augmenting the supplies from the existing public systems.

The incredibly low rates charged for domestic supplies by urban water utilities, and government subsidies for RWHS would only lead to urban elite increasing their access to water supplies, while the burden on water utilities would remain unchanged. This will lead to greater inequities in access to water supplies. At the same time, in rural areas with dispersed populations and hilly areas, they may be economically viable as a supplementary source to already existing public water supply schemes. But as its impacts are not likely to be uniform across classes, government subsidies are not desirable. In hilly regions receiving high rainfalls, government investment for conventional public water supply schemes could be replaced by heavy subsidies for installation of RWHS which appear to be economically more viable.

Key words: *Per Capita Roof Area, Roof Water Harvesting System (RWHS), Rainfall-Runoff Harvesting System (RRHS), High Income Group (HIG), Low Income Group (LIG), Middle Income Group (MIG)*

1. Growing Drinking Water Crisis in India

The problems and constraints posed by population growth and improving economic conditions in managing fresh water supplies for human survival has been a major theme in the discussions on water in the recent decades (Rosegrant *et al.*, 1999). Within that, sustaining water supplies to maintain community health and hygiene in fast growing urban and rural areas has been a topic of major interest.

Population growth impacts on water demand in two ways. First of all, the demand for water for drinking and sanitation increases proportionally, provided the economic conditions and poverty rates remain constant. In urban areas, faster growth rate in population will impact demand rates positively. This is due to the implications urban population growth has on waste disposal (WRI, 1995).

In 2001, the urban population in the country was 285 million, recording a phenomenal rise from a modest of 25.8 million in 1901. Urban population is growing at a rapid rate, much faster than the rural population. According to the projections of the UN populations division, India's urban population will touch 600 million-mark by the year 2025, making it nearly 45 per cent of the country's total population (WRI, 1995). Along with the rapid growth in aggregate urban population, there has been simultaneous concentration of the population in a few cities (TERI, 1998). This adds to urban population growth rates and per capita demand for water (Kumar, 2003).

Similarly, economic condition and poverty rates are two important parameters that can significantly impact on water use practices and use patterns, causing an overall increase in the demand for water in the domestic sector (Rosegrant et al., 1999). Economic growth increases the demand for a wide variety of environmental services related to water (Pearce and Warford, 1993). During the last five to six decades, India has made substantial progress on the economic front, and the percentage population living below the poverty line declined from 45 percent in 1951 to 35 per cent in 1993-94 (Datt, 1997). Such trends are also drivers of change in the per capita water requirement. The net result is an exponential growth in urban water demand.

Simultaneously, there will be exponential growth in the demand for water to assimilate pollution of water bodies in cities. Faster growth in population increases the waste disposal requirements in cities more than proportionately, which in turn adds to the per capita water demand for pollution assimilation (WRI, 1995). But, very little importance is given to water quality management in India (Biswas, 1992; Kumar and Shah, 2004). According to Central Pollution Control Board, while about 22,600 mld of wastewater was generated from Indian cities in 2003, only 5,900 mld (26%) was treated before disposing off into natural streams (source: Central Pollution Control Board website, newsletter on sewage pollution).

The fact is that cities dump their untreated and toxic effluents and domestic waste into the river. But, a large section of the urban and rural populations, still depend on the natural flows in rivers for meeting their sanitation needs, and a variety of other uses such as bathing of cattle, etc. source: NSSO survey on water and sanitation). Pollution of rivers can permanently jeopardise the ability of the poor people living in the urban and rural areas to access the minimum water supplies essential for their survival (Kumar and Ballabh, 2000). It is important to maintain minimum flows in the rivers and flush out pollution load to secure the larger goals of public health and environmental management. The government and the quasi-governmental agencies have to invest in providing extra flows in rivers or to treat effluents as a social welfare measure.

Another important issue is the competition drinking water use is facing from irrigation and industrial uses in urban and rural areas (Kumar, 2003). Depletion of groundwater resources caused by excessive pumping for agriculture (Kumar, 2002) and pollution of surface and groundwater bodies due to indiscriminate disposal of industrial effluents and municipal waste are posing threat to drinking water sources. The industrial water demand in India has been growing exponentially over the last one or two decades (Kumar, 2003). The water requirement for water consuming industries such as agro-based industries, petrochemicals, fertilizers, refineries, and industrial chemicals industries increased 40 times from just 100 million litres a day in 1947-50 to 4000 million litres a day in 1997 (TERI, 1998). This has direct positive impact on the extent of pollution of water bodies, in addition to the negative impact on availability of water for domestic uses (Kumar, 2003).

Problems relating to groundwater quality such as high levels of fluorides, total dissolved solids (TDS), nitrates and arsenic are also emerging in many rural and urban areas of the country (Kumar, 2007). According to a 2005 report of the Central Ground Water Board, incidence of excessive fluorides in groundwater occur in 14 Indian states, namely, Andhra Pradesh, Bihar, Gujarat, Haryana, Karnataka, Kerala, Madhya Pradesh, Maharashtra, Orissa, Punjab, Rajasthan, Tamil Nadu, Uttar Pradesh and West Bengal affecting a total of 69 districts, according to some estimates. Some other estimates place 65% of India's villages exposed to fluoride risk. Incidence of high levels of salinity in groundwater are reported from all these states except West Bengal and also the NCT of Delhi, and affects 73 districts and three blocks of Delhi (source: http://wrmin/resource/cont.gw/htm). Intensive use of fertilizers cause nitrate contamination (Moench and Metzger 1992; WRI 1995). This has serious implications as nearly 80 per cent of the rural domestic needs and 50 per cent of the urban needs are met from groundwater sources (TERI, 1998; World Bank/GOI, 1998).

The water supplies in many large urban centres are being stretched beyond their capacities in order to cope with the rapidly growing demand for several of the consumptive uses. The result is the declining per capita supplies. Increasing inequity in distribution is a growing concern in urban water supplies in many big cities (TERI, 1998). The studies in two cities of Gujarat, namely, Rajkot and Bhuj, show that during droughts when overall water supply from public systems shrinks, access to water for domestic uses become highly inequitable across classes (IRMA/UNICEF, 2001). Thus, water security has already become a growing concern in both urban and rural parts of many regions of India.

2. Roof Water Harvesting

India has a great and long tradition of water harvesting. These water-harvesting systems were in vogue both in urban areas and rural areas of some of the most arid and water stressed regions of the country such as Kachchh and Saurashtra in Gujarat and Western Rajasthan (Agarwal and Narain, 1997). For the people of this region, water harvesting was not a technique, but a part of their culture (Mishra, 1995) and was deep rooted in the socio-cultural fabric.

There were several different kinds of water harvesting techniques in vogue and were used for different purposes (Agarwal and Narain, 1997). They included: (a) roof water harvesting for domestic uses; (b) water harvesting for agricultural uses, especially supplementary irrigation in arid and semi-arid and drought prone areas; (c) water harvesting for reclamation of alkaline and saline soils and water harvesting for community health and hygiene; and (d) water harvesting for groundwater recharging (*Down to Earth* 1995: 49-50; Kamra *et al.* 1986; Mishra, 1995).

Roof top water harvesting is recommended in areas of high intensity rainfalls, well distributed over the years. But in the Middle East and in Sub-Saharan Africa, roof water harvesting is widely practised (Ilyas, 1999). In Sri Lanka, roof water harvesting was practised by households having permanent roofs either with tiles, asbestos or tin. In most difficult situations, in remote villages, people have even used thatched roofs, though not for drinking (Ariyabandu, 1999). In Australia, nearly 17% of the population use rainwater tanks as a source of water to meet their daily water needs for indoor and outdoor uses (Marsden Jacob Associates, 2007). In Japan, use of roof water tank is mainly for car washing, whereas in urban Thailand, rainwater tanks are used as measure to reduce peak urban floods.

Roof water harvesting systems was one of the most common water harvesting practices adopted by individual households in urban as well as rural area to meet with their domestic water supply needs in many arid and drought prone regions of India. The changing social and cultural milieu and the introduction of modern piped water supply systems delineated the communities from the traditional water harvesting systems they used to depend on for their basic needs (Agarwal and Narain, 1997). On the other hand, the changing demographic patterns, specifically concentration of population in small geographical areas and development of large metropolitan cities forced public water utilities to go for import of exogenous water. More often, this has been at the cost of reallocation of water meant for irrigation in rural areas. While the demand on exogenous sources increased from multiple sectors, increasing reallocation of water due to political economic considerations leads to social tensions, and often conflicts (Kumar, 2003). Kumar (2003) and Kumar *et al.* (2008) cited examples of some well-documented conflicts reported in Gujarat between farmers and municipalities and between drinking water users in rural areas and municipalities.

The ability of urban areas to increase its water supply potential is further limited due to depletion of groundwater resources—falling groundwater levels and deteriorating groundwater quality—and pollution of surface water bodies. In such circumstances, urban water utilities are severely strained to maintain the supply levels. They are increasingly coming under pressure to find alternative sources of water that would reduce water imports. Roof-water harvesting is being promoted as a viable alternative to water supply systems based on exogenous water that has long-term social, environmental and political ramifications.

The recent past has seen a lot of media hype about the role of roof water harvesting in mitigating urban water crisis and achieving domestic water security. Several public advocacy institutions and NGOs have been engaged in promoting this system in urban and rural areas of the water scarce regions.

The Corporations of Chennai city had introduced amendments in its building bylaws to make it mandatory for every housing stock to have its own roof water harvesting system. The Central Ground Water Board has been consistently pursuing roof top rainwater harvesting and recharge as a method to arrest groundwater depletion in urban areas.

Very little empirical work, however, exists to actually assess the impact of roof water harvesting on urban and rural water supply situation. Three critical factors seem to be missed out in the already available estimates based on back of the envelope calculations. *First*: the inter-annual variability in the rainfalls is quite significant in many arid and semi-arid regions, and it can pose serious limitations on the amount of water that could be captured. *Second*: the roof area per capita that is available for capturing rainwater is quite limited and this can be a serious constraint on the amount of water that could be captured. *Third*: there has been no systematic analysis of the cost and economics of roof water tanks against the alternative sources of water supply, for the kind of hydrological regimes that exist in India.

3. The Scope and Impact of Roof-water Harvesting

There are two sets of inquiry in this. First: how much water could be captured using roof water harvesting technique in different types of housing stocks and in typical rainfall years, or in other words what are the hydrological opportunities for roof water harvesting? Second: what is the scale at which this technique can be adopted in the urban and rural environments? Or in other words, what are the constraints in adopting this system in typical urban/rural setting, if water is available? How far roof water harvesting systems are economically viable and what are the considerations involved in economic evaluation of roof water harvesting systems?

Analysis of hydrological opportunities for roof water harvesting in a particular region or locality involves a reasonably good understanding of the rainfall characteristics, viz., magnitude of rainfall, number of rainy days, and year to year variations in rainfall and rainy days. Analysis by Pisharoty (1990) showed that the variability in rainfall is higher in areas of low rainfall, as compared to high rainfall areas. Further, after

Pisharoty (1990), the high rainfall regions get the annual rains in much larger number of days as compared to low rainfall regions (source: Characteristics of Indian Rainfall, monograph, Physical Research Laboratories, 1990). Analysis carried out recently for the state of Gujarat with annual rainfall data for a large number of rain gauge stations shows that the coefficient of variation in rainfall is inversely proportional to the mean annual rainfall values (see Figure 1 based on Kumar 2002). The year-to-year variation in rainfall is very high in low rainfall regions. Therefore, in a low rainfall year, the absolute value of rainfall available in such regions will be extremely low.

Therefore, the hydrological opportunities for roof water harvesting to meet domestic water needs would vary significantly from year to year, as well as from location to location. We need to closely look at the implications of the phenomenon of "rainfall variability" for the scope of roof water harvesting as a domestic water supply source. Unlike irrigation, a high level of dependability or reliability is required in domestic water supplies. Therefore, what is important is the performance of RWHSs in years when extremely low rainfalls occur. For the purpose of analysis, we can take the lower and upper values of rainfall that has a probability of occurrence of once in six years (mean+/-standard deviation). Going by Figure 1, in low rainfall areas, the difference between the mean annual rainfall and the magnitude of rainfall (lower and upper) corresponding to $1/6^{th}$ probability of occurrence would be extremely high. In high rainfall areas, the "difference" would be comparatively lower. Therefore, for low rainfall area, the impact of RWHS is analysed for typical rainfall years (mean rainfall & mean rainfall +/- standard deviation), where as in the case of high rainfall areas, only the mean annual rainfall figures are used for analysis.

3.1 Hydrological Opportunities for Roof Water Harvesting in Urban Areas

For the purpose of analysis, the city of Ahmedabad, which falls within the semi-arid tropic of India, is chosen. The mean annual rainfall is 688.2 mm (based on data provided by GAU). The highest and lowest rainfalls which have a probability of occurrence of once in six years are estimated as 1060 mm and 316 mm respectively. The runoff coefficients for different types

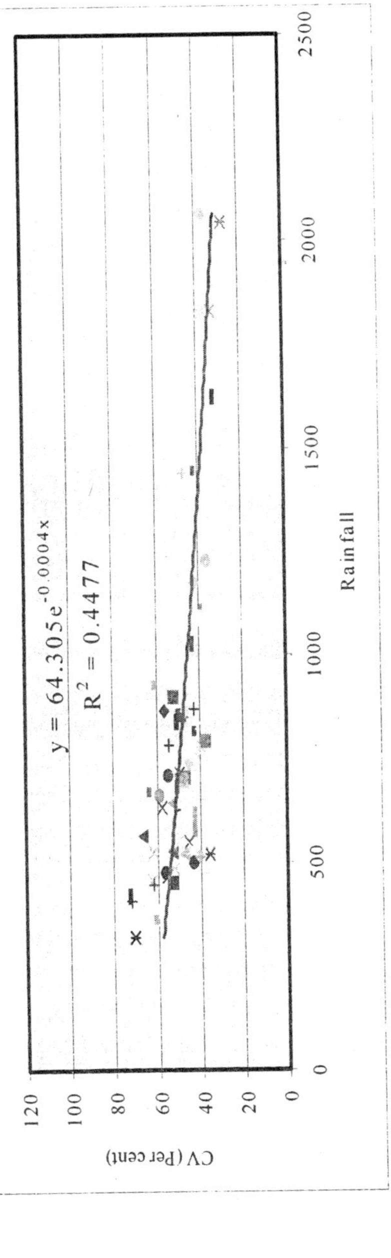

Figure 1: Correlation between Rainfall and Coefficient of Variation

of roof (source: AFPRO undated) are provided in Table 1. Subsequently, the runoff values were estimated on the basis of the runoff coefficient of 0.70 (for concrete roof).

Table 1. Coefficient of Runoff for different Roof Types

Type of Roof	*Runoff Coefficient*
Galvanised Iron Sheet	0.90
Asbestos Sheet	0.80
Tiled Roof	0.75
Concrete Roof	0.70

Source: Manual on Construction and Maintenance of Household Based Rooftop Water Harvesting Systems, Report prepared by AFPRO (Action for Food Production) for UNICEF.

The analysis shows that there can be major variations in the volume of water that could be captured across housing stocks (Table 2). In the case of large individual bungalows (300 sq. m roof area), it can vary from 44.5 m^3 to 13.2 m^3. If we assume the per capita water requirement for the upper class family as 500 litres per day, the water stored would be sufficient to meet the domestic water requirements for three months in a good year to 26 days in a bad year. For small bungalows, a per capita domestic water requirement of 300lpcd is assumed. For planning of water supply schemes, normally an average supply requirement of 140lpcd (at the demand site) is assumed. However, it is known that the income elasticity of domestic water demand is high at low levels of water use (Rosegrant *et al.* 1999). For bungalows, extra water is required for watering lawns and gardens and washing automobiles and floors[2]. Besides this, the rate of water use for the regular requirements such as drinking & cooking, washing clothes and utensils, washing vegetables and meat, flushing toilets will be much higher compared to the normal rates for lower income families. For a small bungalow (200 sq. m roof area), the amount of water that could be stored varies from 29.7 m^3 in a good year to 8.8 m^3 in a bad year. The stored water would be sufficient to meet the requirements for 99 days in a good year to 29 days in a bad year.

Table 2. Impacts of Roof Water Harvesting for Bungalows and Different Types of Housing Stocks

Type of Housing Stock	*Precipitation (mm)*	*Per capita water harvested (m^3) for terrace areas (m^2)*					*Remarks*
		300.0	**250.0**	**200.0**	**150.0**	**100.0**	
Independent Bungalow	1060	44.5	37.1	29.7	22.2	14.8	
	688	28.9	24.1	19.3	14.4	9.6	
	316	12.3	11.1	8.8	6.6	4.4	
		600.0	**480.0**	**400.0**	**360.0**	**320.0**	Eight flats
3-Storeyed Apartment	1060	4.6	3.7	3.1	2.8	2.5	in Single
	688	3.0	2.4	2.0	1.8	1.6	Floor
	316	1.4	1.1	0.90	0.80	0.75	
		700.0	**600.0**	**500.0**	**400.0**	**320.0**	Four flats
10-storeyed Apartment	1060	3.3	2.8	2.3	1.9	1.5	in a Single
	688	2.1	1.8	1.5	1.2	1.0	Floor
	316	0.94	0.82	0.70	0.60	0.44	

Note: The average family size in flats systems is assumed as four and that in independent bungalows as five.

Source: The author's own estimates.

In the case of a 3-storeyed housing stock (of the middle income groups with 600 sq. m roof area), the volume of water that could be captured varies from a maximum of 4.6 m^3 to a minimum of 1.4 m^3. For the lower income groups (320 m^2 roof area), it can vary from 2.4 m^3 to 0.75 m^3. If we assume that the per capita water requirement of middle income group as 200 litres per day, the stored water would be sufficient to meet the requirements for 23 days in a good year to one week in a bad year. At the same time, for the lower income group, with a per capita water requirement of 150 litres per day, the stored water would be just sufficient for 16 days in a good year to just five days in a bad year. If we assume that the stored water is used for basic survival needs alone in a bad year (with a per capita requirement of 50 litres per day going by Glieck (1997)), it would be sufficient for only 15 days. Therefore, the water will not be adequate even for taking care of basic survival needs.

In the case of multi-storeyed apartments for HIGs (with a roof area of 700 sq. m), the volume of water per capita varies from a maximum of 3.3 m^3 to a minimum of 0.94 m^3. At the same time, for the middle-income groups (with a roof area of 320 sq. m), it can vary from 1.5 m^3 to 0.44 m^3. If we take the per capita water requirement of the HIGs living in multi-storeyed flats as 200 litres per day, the stored water would be sufficient to meet the requirements for less than 17 days in a good year, to 5 days in a bad year. If we take the per capita water requirement of MIGs as 150 litres per day, the stored water could be sufficient to meet their requirements for 10 days in a good year to 3 days in a bad year. If we assume that the stored water is used for basic survival needs alone in a bad year, like in the earlier case, it would be sufficient for just 9 days.

The analysis clearly shows that roof water harvesting can only help improve the domestic water security of those who are living in bungalows and flat systems in dry seasons, provided the available per capita roof area is more than 6.0 sq. m. Its contribution to meeting water supply needs become quite insignificant for multi-storeyed flat systems with per capita roof area less than 2.0 sq. m and for 3-storeyed flats with per capita roof area less than 3.0 sq. m. In sum, urban roof water harvesting systems are best suited to the higher and middle-income groups. It cannot have any role in meeting the survival needs of slum dwellers in view of the fact that slum dwellings most often lack good roofs. Therefore, roof water harvesting is not a substitute for urban water utilities that are engaged in distributing water from centralised water systems.

3.2 Hydrological Opportunities for Roof Water Harvesting in Rural Areas

Now in rural areas, the situation changes drastically. Every family has its own individual dwellings. But the roof area of the dwelling ranges from 20 m^2 to 50 m^2 only. Now let us analyse the situation in one of the talukas in Banaskantha district of Gujarat, named Radhanpur, which is facing one of the most acute water scarcity problems. The mean annual rainfall in Radhanpur is 495.77 mm and standard deviation is 295.42 mm. Therefore, in 1/6th of the years, the rainfall would be more than 791.2 mm (495.77+295.42) and in another 1/6th of the years, rainfall would be 200.3 mm (495.77-295.42). Let us take the mean annual rainfall +/- standard deviation for estimating the probable runoff. Let us assume that houses with large roof area (more than 50 m^2) having concrete roofs (with runoff coefficient of 0.70) and those having smaller roof area (less than 50 m^2) having roof made of galvanized iron sheets (runoff coefficient 0.90).

Here also we find that the per capita water availability is extremely low for houses having small roof area (20 m^2). Even in a high rainfall year (that will occur once in 6 years), the amount of water that could be made available from the system would be only 2.2 m^3 per person. If we take 70 litres per day as the per capita water need for domestic purposes (going by the government norm for adequate supplies for domestic needs in rural areas), the available water would be sufficient for only 32 days. If we consider 50 litres per capita as the amount of water required to meet the basic survival needs of the people in rural areas in a low rainfall year, the available water would be just sufficient for 11 days. In sum, in a low rainfall region, the absolute value of annual rainfall would be extremely low in a bad year, and hence the amount of water that can be captured by the roof water harvesting system. It is in bad years, domestic water security becomes crucial as public systems collapse in such years. The ability of roof water harvesting systems to provide adequate quantities of water during the periods of crisis is highly questionable.

At the same time, in high rainfall areas, which experience low year-to-year variations in the annual rains, and where it rains in larger number of days, roof water harvesting systems can become a significant contributor to the overall domestic water supply. For instance, in the Dangs district of Gujarat, which receives a mean annual precipitation of 2000 mm (IRMA/UNICEF, 2001), the amount of water that can be stored by a family having a roof area of 20 m^2 would be 30 m^3 for tiled roof. This will be sufficient to take care of basic survival needs of a family of five for 120 days. If the family goes for storage tank of 6m^3 capacity, the water stored would be sufficient to cover the drinking and cooking requirement (5 litres per day) of a 6-member family for 200 days. The Western Ghats, and the northeast, which experience heavy rainfall (GOI 1999: pp 13) are ideal for roof water harvesting. These hilly regions face acute water shortages soon after the rainy season as natural storage of runoff water and groundwater recharge are extremely poor and taking water to high elevations would be prohibitively high.

4. Physical Feasibility for Roof Top Water Harvesting in Urban and Rural Areas

In RWHS, physical feasibility is as important as hydrological opportunity. The issue of scalability is directly linked to this. First of all, RWHSs require underground storage tanks. For an apartment with a roof area of 320 sq. m, the maximum volume of water that would be captured would be 237 m^3 for a rainfall of magnitude 1060 mm. The capacity of existing storage tanks in a typical 10-storeyed apartment will be 30-40 m^3. Most urban housing stocks are not going to provide the kind of land area required for building such large tanks, which is necessary for storing the water for the lean seasons. In that case, we now need to examine alternatives, i.e., the possibility of collecting the entire rainwater in the existing storage tanks. The possibility

Table 3. Impact of Roof water Harvesting Systems on Different Housing Stocks in Low Rainfall Rural Areas

Type of Housing Stock	*Precipitation in Radhanpur, Banaskantha (mm)*	*Per capita water harvested (m^3) for roof areas (m^2)*				
		75.0	**50.0**	**40.0**	**30.0**	**20.0**
Independent House	791.0	8.30	5.50	4.43	3.32	2.21
	495.0	5.20	3.50	2.77	2.08	1.38
	200.0	2.10	1.40	1.12	0.84	0.56

of this is decided by the rate of inflow of water into the tank and rate of outflow of water from the tank. Rainfall is the source of inflow of water and the withdrawal of water for domestic uses is the outflow. Now the actual rate of inflow of rainwater depends on the number of rainy days besides the total quantum of rainfall.

First of all, the low rainfall regions such as most parts of western India including Gujarat, Rajasthan, and parts of Madhya Pradesh and Maharashtra experience monsoon rains in very few rainy days. In Kachchh, for instance, the average mean annual rainy days are 16 (Kumar 2002: pp 12). Again, analysis of mean annual rainy days and its CV for Gujarat shows that in areas where the mean annual rainy days are smaller in number (these are areas having low rainfall also), the variability in number of rainy days is very high (Figure 2). For instance, going by the chart in Figure 2, the CV in rainy days in a region, which has mean annual rainy days equal to 10, is close to 50 per cent. This means, in 1/6th of the years, number of rainy days in that region would be less than five. In Bhuj (with a mean point rainfall of 350 mm and a CV of 68%, the CV in annual rainy days is 47 per cent.

Therefore, in a low rainfall region, during a bad year, the entire rain occurs in a very few days. Again, even in areas that receive medium rainfalls, large chunk of the rainfall occurs during 3-4 days. With a 200 mm rainfall occurring in one day, for a roof area of 700 sq. m (for a HIG), the total water collected would be 98 m^3. The daily demand for water in a 10-storeyed apartment (with 40 families) is only 32 m^3 if we consider a daily per capita requirement of 200 litres. In a 3-storeyed apartment (with 24 families) the daily demand would be only 14.4 m^3 if we consider a per capita requirement of 150 litres per day. In a wet spell of 200 mm magnitude, the amount of water collected would be approximately 44.8 m^3. This means, if the rainwater is to be fully utilized, additional storage would be required. The actual size of additional storage would depend on the magnitude and pattern of rainfall.

The actual size of the new storage tank would depend on the time duration between two large wet spells, given the

Figure 2: Correlation between Rainy days and Coefficient of Variation

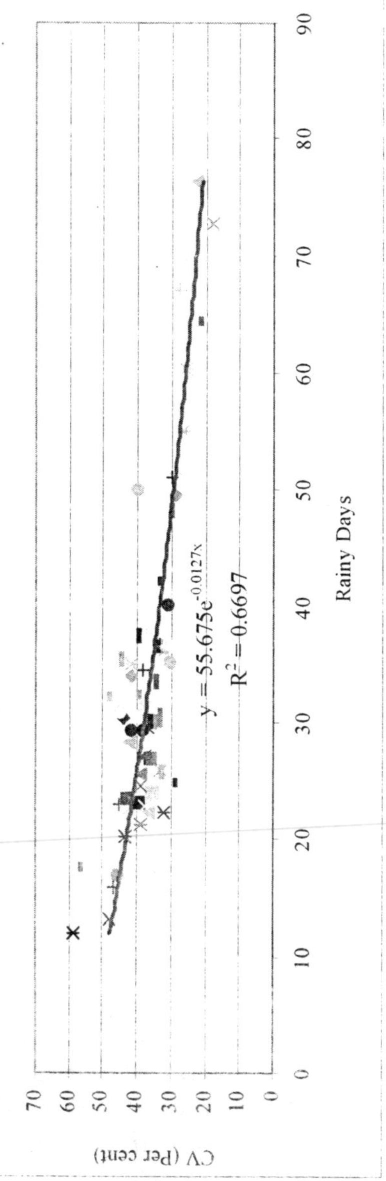

rainfall magnitude and the roof catchment. If there is good number of non-rainy days between two large wet spells, the capacity requirement would come down, provided water from the new storage tank is used up during this period. For this to happen, two operational requirements have to be met. First: when rainwater is available, the public system will have to cut down its supplies. Therefore, it is inevitable that the operation of the decentralized RWHS and the centralized public water supply system are synchronised. Second: rainwater stored in the new tank will have to be lifted and put in the old storage tanks as and when it gets empty space. Hence, the operation of the roof water harvesting system for optimum level of use of rainwater poses a complex management problem in the case of large housing stocks with several users under a single roof.

The independent bungalows, on the other hand, will be able to provide a storage space equivalent to the minimum of the volume of water that falls on their roof, and the quantum of water, which is required to meet their basic requirements of 150 lpcd throughout the year. The following examples illustrate this. In the case of a large bungalow (600 sq. m roof area), the storage requirement would be 270 m^3. In the case of a small bungalow, the storage space would be only 120 m^3. This is a viable proposition. For rural areas storage would not be a problem as the water that has to be stored for independent households is small and there is sufficient area available for construction of the storage tanks. The storage requirement would be much less in high rainfall regions as the annual rains are spread over a long period of time with large number of rainy days. For instance, hills of Dangs get rains in 75 days (source: GAU 1997).

5. Cost and Economics of Roof Water Harvesting Systems

We have seen that roof water harvesting does not ensure domestic water security to all types of households either in rural or in urban situations in low rainfall areas and can only supplement other water supply systems. We will discuss what those systems are in the coming paragraphs. In that case, roof water harvesting as an option for domestic water supply has to be evaluated purely in relation to economic performance. We should know whether RWHS could produce and supply water at a cost lower than that of conventional systems, and other water supply options (Marsden Jacob Associates, 2007). However, this aspect does not seem to have received adequate attention from those who have been promoting roof water harvesting systems.

There are two different types of RWHS systems in practice in India. The first system captures rainwater from the roof and stores in an underground storage tank. In the second one, rainwater collected from the roof is used to recharge groundwater in the premise using artificial recharge systems. Experiments across India with roof water harvesting cum recharging systems showed varying unit costs. They include those in Indian Institute of Technology, Delhi, the office of Central Ground Water Board, Faridabad and Jaipur and Office of Narmada Water Supply Project, PHED Colony, Indore, Madhya Pradesh.

Table 4 shows that the cost per unit volume of water in four different situations ranges from a lowest of US$ 0.15 per cubic metre to a highest of US$ 0.66 per cubic metre. In all these four cases, instead of storage tanks, recharge tube wells are installed, and the life of the system was taken as 20 years. Under such a situation, the cost of production of unit volume of water depends on the physical condition with regard to the roof area, rainfall, and the geo-hydrological setting. For a building with a large roof area located in a high rainfall area, the cost of production of unit volume of water will be much less when compared to a building with a smaller roof area and located in a low rainfall area, with similar geo-hydrological setting.

The annualized unit cost of RWHS depends on the cost of the water collection system; the cost of the storage system; and the effective storage and system life. For a given gross or effective storage, the storage space required, and therefore the cost of the storage system, is determined by the rainfall pattern (Marsden Jacob Associates, 2007). If water can be withdrawn during the times of inflow into the tank, the effective storage can be enhanced. But, in India, areas receiving low to medium rainfall receive almost all the rains in a few rainy days (see Map

Table 4. Cost of Production of Water through Roof Top Rainwater Harvesting and Recharge (US Dollars)

Sr. No	*Cost of Roof Top Water Harvesting & Recharge Structure (US$)*	*Total Volume of Water Captured (m^3)*	*Cost of Harvesting Water (US$/$m^3$)*	*Normal Annual Rainfall (mm)*	*Location of the Structure*
1	7188.00	544.00	0.66	668.00	Central Ground Water Board, Jaipur
2	16,417.00	2142.00	0.38	930.00	PHED, Indore
3	8542.00	2900.00	0.15		Shram Shakti Bhawan, New Delhi
4	5146.00	830.00	0.31	712.20	Indian Institute of Technology, Delhi

Sources:http://www.cgwa.india.com/iitdelhi.htm;
http://www.cgwa.india.com/rajasthan.htm;
http://www.cgwa.india.com/newdelhi.htm;
http://www.cgwa.india.com/madhyapradesh.htm

Note: In the case of Shram Shakti Bhawan, the cost figures are estimated based on the estimate of cost per cubic metre of water provided and the volume of water recharged. In other cases, the cost per cubic metre was estimated on the basis of the cost of the system, volume of water captured and a 20-year life of the system considered.

1 based on Pisharoty, 1990); major rainfall events are lesser; and the distribution of rainfall is non-uniform, concentrated in a short time period during which the withdrawal of water would be negligible. Hence, the system requirement would be same as the gross storage. While the cost effectiveness of RWHS can be improved by optimal design, while estimating the unit cost we have considered that the system storage is just equal to the total inflows it can receive from the roof. The cost of production of water through RWHS with water storage facilities works out to be in the range of Rs. 40/m^3 (US$ 0.8/m^3), if we consider the life of the system as 40 years. Now let us look at the alternatives for providing water supplies in situations where local sources either become unsustainable or are non-existent. The most sought after alternatives are regional water supply schemes involving import of water from long distances. The normal unit cost of regional water supply schemes is estimated as Rs. 13.5/m^3. This figure is arrived at on the basis of the figures provided in Kumar (2000) and adjusted to an annual inflation rate of 7 per cent, for a supply level of 40lpcd and a system life of 20 years. Therefore, RWHS is more expensive than a regional water supply scheme.

The cost of RWHS is even comparable with the cost of desalination, indicative of the poor economic performance of the technology. Data available from sources show that cost of desalination using Reverse Osmosis technology reduces with increasing capacity of the plant (based on Shah *et al.* 1997 as cited in Table 5.9 of GOG (1999)), and was estimated to be Rs. 45/m^3 for plants having a capacity of 100 m^3/day (IRMA/ UNICEF 2001). In the case of three desalination plants (reverse osmosis) operated in Delhi, the cost of production of water worked out to be Rs. 40/m^3 and was less than the cost of tanker water supply (GOI 1999: pp. 168).

The data available from Central Salt and Marine Research Institute (CSMRI), Bhavnagar, India shows that if the salinity of the raw water is below 6000 ppm, the Reverse Osmosis process of desalination will be more cost effective. The cost of installation of the plant with a capacity of 10m^3/ day works out to be Rs.1.8 lac to Rs. 2.5 lac, i.e., US $ 3600 to 5000. The

Table 5. Unit Cost of Production of Water through RWHS in High Rainfall Areas

Roof Catchment Area (m^2)	*Storage Capacity Required for Different Rainfall Regimes*			*Cost per Cubic Metre of Water Harvested (Rs/m^3)*		
	2000 mm	*2500 mm*	*3000 mm*	*2000 mm*	*2500 mm*	*3000 mm*
40	42	54	52.5	28.00	27.6	22.4
50	51	65.75	75	26.07	26.9	24.4
60	60	77.5	97.5	24.44	25.3	26.5
80	75	97.5	123.75	22.92	23.8	22.9
100	90	117.5	150	22.00	21.9	21.1
120	90	120	157.5	18.33	17.8	18.5
150	105	141.25	187.5	17.11	15.9	16.7

Note: 1] It was assumed that the families having roof area of 40 m^2 would draw 60lpcd of water a day during times of inflow; the withdrawal would grow gradually to 100lpcd for 60 m^2; those with 80 m^2 roof area would draw 150lpcd of water; 100m^2 would draw 200lpcd of water; 120 m^2 would draw 300lpcd and 150 m^2 would draw 400lpcd of water. 2 It was further assumed that the cost of the underground tank of RWHS would reduce with increasing size from Rs. 1600/m3 (US$ 320) for a 37.5 m^3 tank to Rs. 1200/m^3 for a 175 m^3 plus capacity tank, and with that a minor economy of scale could be obtained with large-sized roof water tanks.

electricity required for running the plant is 50 HWH for 10 m^3 of water. The annual operation cost therefore works out to be Rs. 73000, i.e., US$1440 if we consider the cost of electricity as Rs. 4/KWH or 8 cents/KWH. The cost of one cubic metre of water produced from the plant would be Rs. 27-30, i.e., 54 cents to 60 cent. If we consider the unit cost of electricity as Rs.6/KWH or 12 cents/KWH, then the unit cost would be in the range of Rs. 37-Rs. 40/m^3 of water, i.e., 72 cents to 80 cents. The cost does not include the cost of distribution and delivery, as it is anticipated that the desalination plants would be decentralized for every village and that people would come and collect water from the plant itself.

As provision of adequate quantities of water for all domestic uses is considered as a social responsibility, this method of comparing unit costs, for making choices between various technological alternatives, is quite inadequate. The underlying premise is that there are limits on the scope of RWHS imposed by hydrological factors. In most situations the RWHS at best remain as a supplementary source of public water supply, and the communities have to depend on public water supply schemes for meeting a lion's share of their domestic needs. Exceptions are areas, which receive excessively high rainfall.

Where both RWHS and conventional systems have the ability to contribute to the water supply in physical terms more or less at the same level, economic evaluation should compare unit cost of production of water through RWHS with unit cost of production through conventional systems. Where RWHS can only supplement the conventional system in physical terms (for a supply quantum of "y"), it is understood that the investment decision should go in favour of the conventional system for a supply level of "x-y". Then the marginal cost of production of water through conventional system (beyond "x-y" level) should be compared with unit cost of production of water through RWHS.

The actual unit cost and the marginal cost of production and supply of water through public systems would vary according to the situation with regard to: availability of local resources; topography; and, how concentrated are the demands for domestic water supply. In hilly areas, both the marginal cost and the average unit cost would be high, and hence the average unit cost will not decline with increase in supply level. The high unit cost is owing to high pumping costs required, which adds to the average unit cost of Rs. 4300/capita[3]. Our estimates show that to supply water to a hill population (of size 5000) at an elevation of 500 m, the unit cost would be Rs. 30/m^3, for a supply level of 50lpcd, whereas for raising the supply level to 100lpcd, the marginal cost would be around Rs. 25/m^3. The high marginal cost is owing to proportional increase in cost of pumping equipment and energy used for pumping, which form a significant component of the capital cost and O & M costs, respectively.

In regions where the beneficiary communities are fairly dispersed, the unit cost of supplying water would be considerably higher than the figures provided early (i.e., Rs.13.5/m^3). This normal unit cost figure is more applicable to normal terrain conditions and concentrated populations. Nevertheless, in most situations, the marginal cost of additional supplies is likely to be much less than the unit cost when production and supply of water is maintained at the previous level. It would keep declining with increase in level of aggregate supplies at the end user level to almost zero, and so the average unit cost. The situations include water supplies in scattered populations as well as in urban agglomerates and villages where population lives in large clusters, except hilly regions. This is because there would not be any significant increase in: the cost of water supply infrastructure (distribution and delivery system); and the operation cost, covering the cost of pumping water, with the marginal increase in the quantity of water to be supplied.

But, in the case of roof water harvesting in low to medium rainfall areas, where inflow is distributed over very short time periods, and simultaneous use of water from the storage during inflows is insignificant, the unit cost (Rs. 40/m^3) remains more or less the same. Now, the marginal cost production of water through roof water harvesting system also works out to be very close to the unit cost. This is because the cost of the system heavily depends on the storage capacity of the roof water collection tank and starts from nearly thousand rupees (for the channel and gutter pipe). Therefore, the marginal cost works out to be Rs. 40/m^3 of water production capacity.

Having discussed the unit and marginal costs for different water supply systems, let us examine how economics of RWHSs work out in different situations. Let us take a low rainfall area and consider a regional water supply scheme to act as the conventional system. Here, the maximum amount that can be supplied by RWHS ("y") is much smaller in comparison to the total domestic water demand ("x"). Therefore, up to a supply level of (x-y), the government can justify investments in regional water supply scheme, even if the cost of production of unit volume of water works out to be higher than that of RWHS. But interestingly, the normal unit cost of production of water (Rs. 13.5/m^3) is much lower for Regional Water Supply Schemes when compared to RWHS (Rs. 40/m^3). Under such a scenario the RWHS will not be economically viable even as a supplementary source. This is because the unit cost of production of water to meet the required additional supplies (Rs. 40/m^3) would be much higher than the marginal cost of providing the same amount through the regional water supply scheme, which would work out to be even far less than Rs. 13.5 m^3.

Thus, in nutshell, RWHS, as a supplementary source, for water supply would not pass the scrutiny for economic feasibility in areas, which receive low to medium rainfalls and where populations are concentrated like cities. At the same time, in hilly terrain, which suffers from lack of natural storage of water, roof water harvesting systems can be economically viable proposition for supplementing conventional water supply systems. The Centre for Science and Environment (a Delhi based environmental NGO) has been rigorously persuading the authorities of large Municipalities and Corporations to make roof top water harvesting mandatory for housing stocks and commercial buildings.

Unfortunately, the concept of urban demand management has not found place in the discourses on strategies to address the growing urban water scarcity problems. Dr. S. Arlosoroff, an international expert on water technology and management, argues that it could lead to demand reduction in both household and utility levels and, if applied on a large scale, could reduce the cost of saving every unit volume of water. Demand management efforts using water conservation kits in Israel, Singapore, and California, the Boston area and other areas have achieved demand reduction of 10-20 per cent and sometimes 20-40 per cent, at an approximate cost of US$ 0.1-0.15 per cubic metre (Arlosoroff, 1995). In Israel, in spite the substantial increase in per capita GDP, standard of living, introduction of modern appliances and area under parks and gardens, urban water consumption per capita has declined over a period from nearly 110 litres per capita per day to nearly 70 litres per capita per day during 1984-91 (deduced from source: The department of Urban Water, Water Commission, Israel as cited in Figure 6 of Arlosoroff 1995). Thus, in urban areas, roof water harvesting systems score low not only in terms of cost of production per unit volume of water, but in terms of the extent to which it could contribute to meeting the gap between demand and supplies.

Now, the hilly regions in India receive excessively high rainfall in the range of 2000-3000 mm such as the Western Ghats and the hilly northeast (source: water management perspective as cited in Table 2.1 of GOI 1999: pp 13). In such regions, roof water harvesting systems will be able to take care of a large chunk of the needs of the communities with much low inter-annual variability as shown in Section 3.2. The analysis shows that the unit cost of production of water through RWHS in such areas would be far less than that in low rainfall areas (see Table 5). The real cost advantage comes from the fact that the effective storage of water would be much higher than the actual storage space, which determines the cost of the system.

Analysis is based on the assumption that the average number of rainy days ranges from 60 for an area with mean annual rainfall of 2000 mm to 70 for 2500 mm to 75 for 3000 mm, and the households would be able to draw water for a minimum of as many days as the number of days of inflow from the roof catchment stops[4]. Table 5 also shows that the unit cost is lower for RWHS with larger roof catchments, though the total amount harvested would be higher. It also shows that the unit cost reduces drastically when the households increase the daily withdrawal in proportion to the greater inflows available from the larger catchments.

As there is a paucity of natural water storage and sparse population in such regions, the cost of provision of water supply through conventional systems would work out to be prohibitively high due to high cost of infrastructure for water conveyance and distribution and cost of energy used for lifting water. Under such a scenario, investment in RWHS can be justified if its unit cost works out to be less than the cost of provision of water through long distance pipelines. We have seen that the unit cost of water supply through conventional pipeline schemes depends heavily on the amount of lift. To meet the shortfall, government can invest in the cheapest of the alternatives.

Now, let us examine coastal areas of Kachchh and Saurashtra of Gujarat, which receive low to medium rainfalls. Roof water harvesting systems are strongly advocated by NGOs, scientific institutions and social activists for coastal areas affected by salinity of groundwater and also areas, which lack freshwater sources locally[5]. This is mainly based on the premise that regional water supply schemes are prohibitively expensive, and will not able to adequately cater to the sparse population of these regions. In many coastal areas of India such as coastal Saurashtra and Kachchh, quality of local groundwater is extremely poor that it cannot be used for uses such as cleaning, bathing, washing and cattle drinking. The entire demand, therefore, has to be met by public water systems. Hence, the decision-making with regard to investment in water supplies should involve considerations such as the maximum amount of water that the system can supply in comparison to the overall domestic needs. The above set of analysis shows that the RWHS cannot meet those needs.

In such situations, desalination would be a viable alternative to many of the conventional systems involving transport of water over long distances and the non-conventional systems such as RWHS. The reason being that poor quality groundwater characterized by salinity in the range of 4000-6000 ppm is available in abundance in these coastal regions. Also, the distance between the source of production and the supply points could be minimized to a great extent with decentralized desalination plants, thereby reducing the cost of transport of water, and chances for technical and non-technical losses. Desalination would be economically more efficient than a combination of RWHS and desalination plant as its average cost would be only Rs. 27-Rs. 30/m^3 for a plant size of 10m^3/day against Rs.40/m^3 for RWHS. For a village with a population of 1000 persons, the total water requirement would be 50 m^3 to meet the basic survival needs and hence a plant with a capacity of 50 m^3/day could be planned. Hence, the unit cost will drop further.

6. Practical and Policy Implications

In low rainfall areas, the RWHSs are only suited to only those classes, which have access to large roofs and storage space. For majority of the urban dwellers and rural households, they offer very little scope in augmenting domestic water supplies and poor technical feasibility. It benefits regions, which receive high rainfalls, especially rural areas. In rest of the cases, RWHSs can only help augment the basic supplies where public water distribution systems are already in place and that too marginally. From economic point of view, the systems will be unviable in areas with concentrated populations and will be viable in rural areas with scattered populations and hilly terrains. In regions which do not have freshwater sources, and have easy access to seawater or saline groundwater, the desalination systems will be economically more viable than RWHS.

The urban dwellers will not have any incentive to invest in individual RWHS. This is because they are quite expensive, given the cost of plastering terraces for creating slopes, installing gutters and down pipes, storage tanks and accessories such as filters and first flush devises and water extraction devises, where as urban water utilities charge flat rates for domestic water supplies in many cities, and even when metered the pro rata charges are very low (ADB, 2007). Here also, the rich families, which have individual tap connections to municipal water supply, manage to access greater quantities of water, and corner lion's share of the subsidy benefits. Even if the individuals invest in RWHS, especially those who are economically rich, they may continue to use the services of existing water utilities. The consequence will be that urban elite will increase their access to water supplies in terms of per capita supplies, while the pressure on water utilities will remain unchanged. This also means greater inequities in access to water supplies.

The government agencies engaged in drinking water supply are now contemplating introduction of subsidies for installation of roof water harvesting systems, while many Corporations have already made it mandatory for urban dwellings and commercial buildings to install RWHSs through building byelaws. If we assume that urban households decide to install RWHS due to proper enforcement of the law, going by the cost of saving water using water saving technologies, RWHS would turn out to be more expensive in terms of cost per unit volume of water. NGOs also subsidise RWHS built in rural areas through their project funds. At the same time, a blanket subsidy, with no changes in the pricing structures for water utility services would mean that the rich cornering lion's share of the benefits.

Only pricing urban water supplies on volumetric basis using incremental block rates can help negate such inequities. The unit rates can be kept nominal for certain minimum levels of use. This would help the lower income groups, as they will be able to access water supplies at low prices. Higher unit rates could be levied for higher volumetric uses. One of the important considerations for urban water pricing can be that the unit price of water at higher levels of use to be higher than the cost of harvesting unit volume of water from RWHS. This would create incentive among the higher income groups, having higher per capita consumption levels, to reduce the dependence on public water utilities and depend more on roof water harvesting. Incentives on building taxes can also be provided to those who install RWHSs. All these can lead to reduced pressure on public systems, making more water available for poor sections of the community.

Therefore, a complete rethinking on pricing of urban water supplies is essential from the point of view of ensuring sustainable water use and equity in access to water for basic needs. Urban building bylaws and the existing Acts/laws concerning municipal or corporation taxes also might require several amendments. Buildings having roof water harvesting systems installed can be given tax deductions. Amendments may be required in the building bylaws on the minimum terrace area available per housing unit, the minimum compound area etc. to encourage installation of roof water harvesting devises. In recent times, regulations on urban house construction are being tried to Australia to encourage the urban dwellers to go for rainwater tanks in their housing stocks (Marsden Jacob Associates, 2007). These apart, subsidies on domestic water saving technologies such as low volume flush toilets, low head showers, flow regulators in kitchen and bathroom sinks, could be thought about.

In low rainfall regions with scattered populations or hilly terrains, public investments in RWHS in the form of subsidies can be justified from a macro economic point of view. But, at the micro level, it would not only fail to ensure desired physical results, but also fail to yield equitable societal benefits. Therefore, the government should invest in ensuring provision of water for basic survival needs at highly subsidised rates in these areas. Theoretically, the price of water for higher levels of use should be higher than the cost of water produced through RWHS in order that it reflects the higher marginal cost of producing and supplying water. Since metering of water use will be extremely difficult and expensive in the rural context, regulated supplies to meet the basic needs would be a workable strategy.

On the other hand, in hilly regions receiving high rainfalls such as the tribal regions of the Western Ghats and North Eastern States, RWHS can not only produce sufficient water for domestic purposes at very low cost, but are economically sound. In such regions, government should provide subsidies for RWHS. This would not only be economically viable, but also would lead to larger societal benefits.

7. Concluding Remarks

RWHS appears to be only one among the several strategies for mitigating the growing urban water crisis in arid and semiarid regions with low to medium rainfalls from the point of view of hydrological opportunity (scope). The physical feasibility of RWHS also appears to be poor in urban areas. Economic viability of roof water harvesting as a supplementary source of domestic water supply will be poor in urban areas. Hence, government subsidy for roof water harvesting is not desirable. It may be economically viable as a supplementary source in rural areas with dispersed population. But as this is not likely to generate uniform impacts across classes, government subsidies are not recommended. In hilly regions receiving high rainfalls, RWHS will not only have hydrological viability, but also will have good economics. In those areas, government investment for community water supply schemes could be replaced by subsidies for installation of RWHS. In villages of coastal regions facing acute shortage of freshwater, desalination can prove to be better alternative than RWHS to regional water supply schemes involving large scale water import from far off regions. The government investments in this sector should be encouraged with improvements in operational and managerial skills.

Along with roof water harvesting, other supply based-approaches such as rainfall-runoff water harvesting (RRWH) can be tried out in cities having large impervious areas under parking plots and industrial and commercial complexes. The water captured from this RRWH can be used for inferior uses such as gardening, washing and cleaning. Also, indirect options for managing the demand such as water pricing and pollution taxes should be thought about rather than trying to meet the growing demands, and this will also help reduce the financial and environmental costs of creating new supplies. Policies aimed at promoting urban water harvesting, including water pricing policies, should be carefully designed and implemented. This should be supported by appropriate legal and institutional framework.

References

AFPRO (Undated) Manual on Construction and Maintenance of Household Based Rooftop Water Harvesting Systems. Report prepared by AFPRO (Action for Food Production) for UNICEF.

Arlosoroff, Saul (1995) The Water Sector in the Middle East- Potential Conflict Resolutions (Israel and its Neighbours)," The Truman Institute for the Advancement of Peace, Hebrew University, Jerusalem, Israel.

Asian Development Bank (2007) *2007 Benchmarking and Data Book of Water Utilities in India*, a partnership between the Ministry of Urban Development, Government of India and the Asian Development Bank, November.

Agarwal, A. and Sunita Narain (eds.) (1997) *Dying Wisdom: Rise, Fall and Potential of Traditional Water Harvesting Systems in India,* 4th Citizen's Report. New Delhi: Centre for Science and Environment.

Ariyabandu, S. de. R. (1999) "Development of Rainwater Harvesting for Domestic Water Use in Rural Sri Lanka," *Asia Pacific Journal of Rural Development*, IX (1), July.

Biswas, Asit. K. (1992) "Water for Sustainable Development: A Global Perspective," *Wasteland News*, 7 (2), November 1991- January 1992.

Central Pollution Control Board (1988) Status of water supply and wastewater collection, treatment and disposal in Class 1 and Class 2 cities, New Delhi: CPCB.

Down to Earth (1996) "Arsenic Down Under," 5 (10), October 15.

Datt, G. (1997) *Poverty in India and Indian States,* International Food Policy Research Institute, Washington D.C.

Government of India (1999) *Integrated Water Resource Development: A Plan for Action*. Report of the National Commission on Integrated Water Resources Development- Volume I, New Delhi: Government of India.

Glieck, P. H. (1997). Human Population and Water: Meeting Basic Needs in the 21st Century. In R. K. Pachauri and Lubina F. Qureshi (Eds.) *Population, Environment and Development*. New Delhi: Tata Energy Research Institute. pp. 105-121.

Government of India (2005) Dynamic Ground Water Resources of India, Central Ground Water Board, Ministry of Water Resources, Government of India, August.

Gujarat Agriculture University (1997) Agro-climatic Atlas of Gujarat, Department of Agricultural Meteorology, B. A. College of Agriculture, Gujarat Agricultural University, Anand Campus.

Ilyas, S. M. (1999) "Water Harvesting towards Water Demand Management and Sustainable Development," *Journal of Rural Reconstruction*, 32 (2).

IRMA/UNICEF (2001) *White Paper on Water in Gujarat*, report prepared for the government of Gujarat.

Kamra, S. K and others (1986) "Water Harvesting for Reclaiming Alkaline Soils," *Agricultural Water Management*, 11.

Kumar, M. Dinesh and Vishwa Ballabh (2000) *Water Management Problems and Challenges in India: An Analytical Review*, Working Paper 140, Anand: Institute of Rural Management Anand.

Kumar, M. Dinesh, Shashikant Chopde, Srinivas Mudrakartha and Anjal Prakash (1999) "Addressing Water Scarcity and Pollution Problems in Sabarmati Basin, Gujarat: Local Strategies for Water Supply and Conservation Management," in Marcus Moench, Elisabeth Caspari and Ajaya Dixit (eds.) *Rethinking the Mosaic: Investigations into Local Water Management*. Kathmandu and Boulder: Nepal Water Conservation Foundation and Institute for Social and Environmental Transition.

Kumar, M. Dinesh (2002) Reconciling Water Use and Environment: Water Resource Management in Gujarat, Resource, Problems, Issues, Strategies and Framework for Action, report prepared for State Environmental Action Project supported by the World Bank, Gujarat Ecology Commission.

Kumar, M. Dinesh (2003) "Demand Management in the Face of Growing Water Scarcity and Conflicts in India: Institutional and Policy Alternatives for Future," In Kanchan Chopra, CH Hanumantha Rao and Ram Prasad Sengupta (Eds.) *Water Resources, Sustainable Livelihoods and Ecosystem Services*. Published by Indian Society for Ecological Economics, New Delhi: Concept Publishing Company.

Kumar, M. Dinesh (2007) *Groundwater Management in India: Physical, Institutional and Policy Alternatives*, New Delhi: Sage Publications.

Kumar, M. Dinesh and Tushaar Shah (2004) Groundwater Contamination and Pollution in India: Emerging Challenges, *Hindu Survey of the Environment 2004*, Kasturi & Sons.

Kumar, M. Dinesh, Ankit Patel, R. Ravindranath and O. P. Singh (2008) Chasing a Mirage: Water Harvesting and Artificial Recharge in Naturally Water-scarce Regions of India, *Economic and Political Weekly*, 43 (35): 61-71.

Marsden Jacob Associates (2007) The Economics of Rain Water Tanks and Alternative Water Supply Options, a report prepared for Nature Conservation Council of NSW, Australian Conservation Foundation and Environment Victoria.

Pearce, David and Jeremy Warford (1993) *World Without End, Economics, Environment, and Sustainable Development*, published for the World Bank, London and New York: Oxford University Press.

Pisharoty, P. R. (1990) Characteristics of Indian Rainfall, Monograph, Ahmedabad: Physical Research Laboratories.

Mishra, Anupam (1999) "Water harvesting here is not a technique, but a culture," Interview, *Down to Earth*, 4 (14) December 1995.

Moench, M. and H. Metzger (1992) *Groundwater Availability for Drinking in Gujarat: Quality, Quantity and Health Dimensions.* Monograph. VIKSAT-Pacific Institute for Studies in Environment, Development and Security, VIKSAT, Ahmedabad.

Rosegrant, M. W. C. Ringler and R. V. Gerpacio (1999) "Water and Land Resources and Global Food Supply," in G.H. Peters and Joachim Von Braun (eds.) *Food Security, Diversification And Resource Management: Refocusing The Role of Agriculture?* Ashgate.

Shah, V.I., Desai, N.V. and Joshi S.V. (1997) Control of Brackishness in Drinking Water. A Base Paper presented by Central Salt and Marine Chemicals Research Institute, Bhavnagar.

TERI (1998) *Looking Back to Think Ahead Growth with Resource Enhancement of Environment and Nature,* Tata Energy Research Institute, New Delhi, March.

World Bank/GOI (1997) "Groundwater Regulation and Management," World Bank-Government of India, India Water Resources Management Sector Review, Volume I-Main Report, New Delhi.

World Resources Institute (1995) *World Resources 1994-95: People and the Environment, Report prepared by World Resource Institute in collaboration with United Nations Environment*

Programme and United Nations Development Programme. Bombay: Oxford University Press.

Footnotes

1. This is a heavily revised version of a paper Kumar, M. Dinesh (2004) Roof Water Harvesting for Domestic Water Security: Who gains and Who Loses, *Water International*, 29 (1):43-53.
2. A total of 200m3 of water is assumed to be the requirement for watering loan (of 100 m2 with a total watering depth of 2 m over the year); a total of 73 m3 of water for washing automobiles (@200 litres per day); and a total of 73 m3 of water for washing the floors (@200 litres day). This alone increases the per capita domestic water requirement by 190 litres a day.
3. This is the cost figure provided in Kumar, 2000 adjusted to the inflation rate.
4. The average number of rainy days in a region is a function of mean annual rainfall, and the mean of number of days for which rains occur in the high rainfall regions in India is about 75 (Pisharoty, 1990).
5. The most prominent among them are AKRSP (I), Ambuja Cement Foundation (ACF) and Self Employed Women's Association, Gujarat. The AKRSP (I) and ACF are promoting these systems in coastal Saurashtra, and SEWA in its project areas in different rural areas of Gujarat.

3

Rainwater Harvesting and Groundwater Recharge in Water-Scarce Regions of India : Potential and Pitfalls

ABSTRACT

In this chapter, we analyses micro and macro level hydrological and geo-hydrological data to examine the potentials and pitfalls in rainwater harvesting in water scarce regions of India. The data include: rainfall magnitudes, variability in rainfall, rainy days and its variability, runoff, infiltration and geology. It also reinforces the rigour in this analysis by using primary data collected from two small river basins in India where intensive water harvesting activities were undertaken. The primary data used include daily rainfall, stream flows, number and capacity of water harvesting structures and groundwater level fluctuations.

The analysis presented in this chapter shows that in water-scarce regions of India, runoff harvesting does not offer any potential for groundwater recharge or improve water supplies at basin scale. The issues can be summarized as follows. First of all, it lacks emphasis on potential local supplies and the demand it has to cater to. While local supply potential is low in most water scarce regions, compounded by poor reliability, demand far exceeds the supply potential. Secondly, there are complexities involved in economic evaluation of RWH, due to lack of scientific data on inflows, runoff collection and storage efficiency, beneficiaries, value of the incremental benefits generated and scale considerations. A rigorous analysis of data available from pilot projects of CGWB shows that artificial recharging using methods such as percolation tank, check dam, sub-surface dyke and recharge shaft is prohibitively expensive. Also, the cost of using a cubic metre of recharge water for irrigation is much higher than the expected gross returns per cubic metre of the water, making irrigated crop production unviable.

With higher degrees of basin development, the marginal benefit from water harvesting at the basin level reduces, while marginal cost increases. Third: in many basins, there is a strong "trade off" between maximizing hydrological benefits and improving cost effectiveness. Fourth: many water-scarce basins are characterized by wide disparity in demand between upper catchments and lower catchments, due to which there is a trade off in maximizing benefits of upstream water harvesting with optimizing basin-wide benefits. Fifth: in many water-scarce basins, local water harvesting only divides the hydrological benefits rather than augmenting. Finally, lack of integration between surface water system and groundwater system reduces the potential of artificial recharging in hard rocks which also coincide with water-scarce regions.

1. Introduction

The roof water harvesting systems, discussed in the previous chapter are meant for domestic water use, and the concept itself is rather new in many parts of India. Whereas every part of India has a tradition of water harvesting from natural catchments for uses ranging from domestic to cattle use to irrigation and fisheries. Over the years, many of the traditional water harvesting systems have either gone under disuse due to a variety of physical, social, economic, cultural and political factors which have caused their deterioration and decline of institutions which have nurtured them (Agarwal and Narain, 1997) or have lost their relevance in the modern day context due to their inability to meet the desires of the communities. While the first dimension of the decline in water harvesting tradition has been well researched and documented, the second dimension is much less understood and appreciated. The lack of resistance to appreciate the fact that different periods in history are marked by genesis, rise and fall of some new water harvesting tradition (Pandey et al., 2003), is also very clear.

In India's water sector history, the past two decades are characterized by a boom in water harvesting. They are markedly different from the traditional ones in two ways; first from the context; and second from the purpose. As regards the context, they are able to use recent advancements in soil, geosciences and hydro-sciences; and modern day techniques and technologies in survey and investigation, earth moving and construction; and management tools such as hydrological and hydraulic modeling. While the traditional ones represented the best engineering feat of those times, in terms of water technology used for water harnessing and distribution (Agarwal and Narain, 1997); and the volume of water handled, the modern water harvesting systems are at best miniatures of the large water resource systems that use advances in civil engineering and hydrology. As regards the purpose, they are employed as resource management solution, and not as resource development solutions. For instance, many water harvesting structures were built for improving aquifer storages and groundwater quality.

The limited Indian research on rainwater harvesting (RWH)/ artificial recharge so far had focused on engineering performance of individual structures (see Muralidharan and Athawale, 1998; Patel, 2002). While a lot of anecdotal evidences on the social and economic gains exist, there is little understanding based on empirical work of: (1) the impacts of water harvesting activities on local hydrological regime in terms of net water gain; (2) basin level impacts on overall basin water balance; and (3) economic imperatives from a long term perspective. Of late, researchers had raised questions of the possible unintended impacts of water harvesting (see Bachelor *et al.*, 2002; Kumar et al., 2006). In the previous chapter, we have also seen that investments in RWHS in most regions of India will not be economically sound.

One of the reasons for the little or lack of empirical research on the hydrological and economic aspects of water harvesting systems is the lack of ability to generate accurate scientific data on various parameters, mostly hydraulic, hydrological and meteorological, governing the performance and impact of water harvesting. Analysis of water harvesting systems also misses the influence of "scale factor".

2. Objectives and Approach

In this chapter, we begin with the basic premise that scale considerations are important in analyzing the impact of water harvesting and groundwater recharging; i.e., one has to move from local watershed level analysis to the river basin level analysis and that basin level impacts are not always aggregates of local impacts. We first discuss the critical issues in rainwater harvesting and groundwater recharging from micro and macro perspectives. The macro level analysis is strengthened by primary data on hydrological variables collected from two small river basins. The scope of this chapter is to discuss the physical—hydrological, geo-hydrological and meteorological—, socio-economic and purely economic considerations for decision making with regard to water harvesting investments or analyzing the impact of RWH systems, and how these considerations limit the scope of water harvesting and groundwater recharge projects.

3. Critical Issues in Rainwater Harvesting and Groundwater Recharging

One of the most important underlying values in rainwater harvesting is that it is a benign technology (Bachelor *et al.*, 2002) and cannot create undesirable consequences. Water harvesting initiatives are driven by firm beliefs and assumptions, some of which are: (1) there is a huge amount of monsoon flow, which remain un-captured and eventually ends up in the natural sinks, especially seas and oceans, supported by the national level aggregates of macro hydrology; (2) local water needs are too small that exogenous water is not needed; (3) local water harvesting systems are always small, and therefore are cost effective; (4) since the economic, social and environmental values of water is very high in regions hit by water shortages, water harvesting interventions are viable, supported by the assumption that cost effective alternatives that can bring in the same amount of water do not exist; (5) incremental structures lead to incremental benefits; and (6) being small with low water storage and diversion capacities, they do not pose negative consequences for downstream uses.

3.1 Lack of Emphasis on Local Water Demand and Potential Supplies

Rainwater harvesting ignores a few critical parameters that govern the potential of RWHS in meeting local water demand. First is the hydrological regime of the region/locality. Second is the reliability of the supplies, governed by the reliability of rainfall. Third is the constraint imposed by local geological and geo-hydrological settings on recharge potential. Fourth is the aggregate demand for water from various sectors within the local area.

Some basic hydrological phenomena, which make the above mentioned parameters very critical in deciding the scope of rainwater harvesting and groundwater recharging, are:

- For runoff harvesting, the rainfall has to exceed a threshold to generate runoff, though the threshold would vary according to the nature of soils and land cover. The estimated runoff based on regression equation arrived at from observed flows in Hathmati sub-basin of Sabarmati basin ($R=0.00193*X^{2.022}$) in western India (source: GOG, 1994) shows that for the runoff to cross 100mm, the minimum rainfall required is 682 mm. Whereas in the case of Kabani sub-basin of Cauvery, runoff starts when the rainfall crosses 366 mm[1]. However, the actual runoff rates would depend on how strong us the correlation between rainfall and runoff in a given basin, and this relation weakens if year to year change in rainfall intensity and pattern is major.
- Regions with lower mean annual rainfall experience higher variability and vise versa (Pisharoty, 1990). Hence, in regions with lower mean annual rainfalls, rainwater harvesting as a dependable source of water is likely to be low.
- Generally, it has been found that larger magnitude of annual rainfall means more number of rainy days and smaller magnitude of annual rainfall means less number of rainy days spread over the rainy season (Pisharoty, 1990). The examples of Gujarat further illustrate this

(see Kumar, 2002b; Kumar, 2004). Lesser rainy days also means longer dry spells and thus greater losses from evaporation for the same region.

- High intensity rainfalls are common in semi arid and arid regions of India (Garg, 1987 as cited in Figure 24; Athawale, 2003). Higher intensity of rainfall can lead to high intensity runoff occurring in short durations, limiting the effective storage capacity of rainwater harvesting systems to almost equal to its actual storage size.
- High evaporation during rainy season means losses from surface storage structures. It also means faster rate of soil moisture depletion through both evaporation from barren soils and evapo-transpiration, increasing the rate and quantum of soil infiltration. This reduces runoff generation potential. Among the seven locations in Gujarat for which ET_0 (reference evapo-transpiration) data are available, ET_0 during monsoon (June to September) varies from a lowest of 543mm in Vadodara to 714mm in Rajkot. As percentage of annual ET_0, it varies from a lowest of 33% in semi humid Surat to 37.3% in Bhuj, Kachchh (source: authors' analysis based on data from IMD, Ahmedabad). In the case of Rajasthan, ET_0 during monsoon ranges from 433 mm in the hill station of Mt. Abu to 967.7 mm in Jaisalmer in the Thar Desert. In percentage terms, it varies from a lowest of 32% of the total annual ET_0 in Sawaimadhupur to a highest of 49.3% in Anupgarh (GOR, 1992). Among the 10 locations selected along Narmada basin in Madhya Pradesh, the values range from 429 mm to 600 mm, with it as a percentage of total ET_0 ranging from 31.3% in Betul to 35% in Mandla (source: GOMP, 1972).
- Soil infiltration capacity can be a limiting factor for recharge. In sandy and sandy loam soils, the infiltration capacity of the recharge area can be sustained through continuous removal of soils. But clayey soils have inherent limitation. Results obtained from short term

infiltration test carried out in dug wells in Andhra Pradesh in two different soil conditions show that the infiltration rate becomes negligible (< 0.60 mm/hr) within 10 minutes of starting the test in the case of silty clay, whereas infiltration stabilizes at a rate of 129.1 mm/hour within the first 25 minutes in the case of sandy loam (NGRI, 2000). If the infiltration rate approaches to zero fast, it will negative affect the recharge efficiency of percolation ponds. As thin soil cover has low infiltration (Muralidharan and Athawale, 1998), the extent of the problem would be larger in hard rock areas (ideal for percolation ponds) with thin soil cover. Dickenson (1994) based on several infiltration studies shows that rate of infiltration declines to a minimum value within 4-5 days of ponding. This also will have adverse effects on the performance of structures built in areas experiencing flash floods and high evaporation rates, solutions for which would be wetting or drying of pond beds through regulation of inflows.

- For artificial recharge, the storage potential of the aquifer is extremely important. The storage potential of an aquifer vis-à-vis the additional recharge is determined by the geological formation characteristics, and the likely depth of dewatered zone.
- In hilly watersheds, the area available for cultivation is generally very low, keeping agricultural water demand low. At the same time, the surface water potential available for harvesting is generally high due to high rainfall and runoff coefficients. On the contrary, towards the valleys and plains, the area available for cultivation increases, raising agricultural water demand. At the same time, the surface water potential available for harnessing is generally low due to the lower rainfall, and low runoff coefficients owing to mild slopes, high PET and deeper soil profiles.

The implications of some of these factors on the potential of rainwater harvesting systems are analyzed in the following two sections, i.e., 3.1.1 and 3.1.2.

Figure 1: Infiltration Rate in Sandy Loam and Siltyclay Soil at the botton of dug well

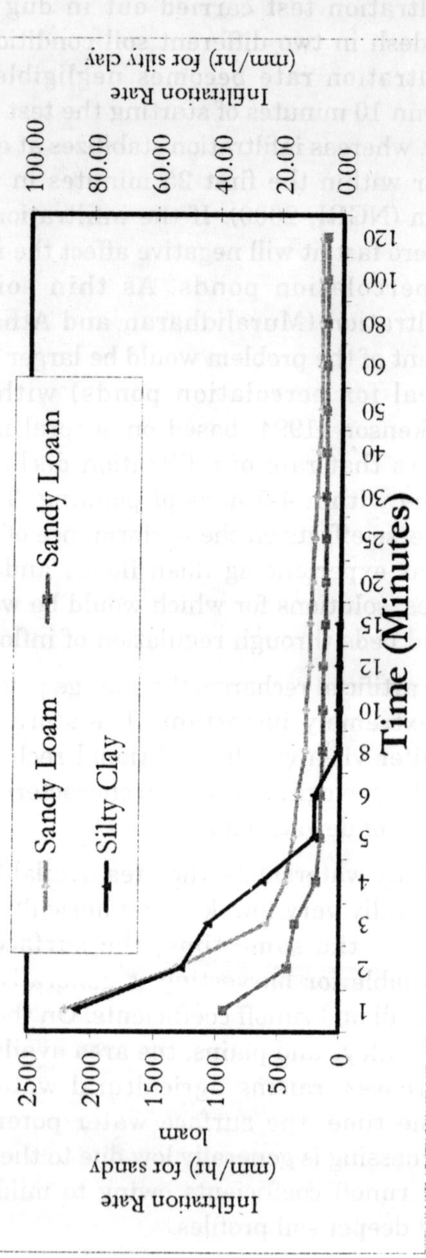

3.1.1 Limitations Imposed by Hydrological Regimes

Local water management interventions are often based on very little understanding of the local hydrological regimes, which govern the potential supplies of water for harvesting. They are rather based on deep-rooted belief that higher the size of water impounding structure, higher would be the hydrological benefit in terms of water storage and recharge. The best example is the participatory water conservation movement launched by the government of Gujarat. The government implemented large-scale work of excavation of thousands of village ponds, irrespective of the nature and size of catchments (Kumar, 2002a). Part of the reason is the lack of availability of data on inflows, determined by stream-flows; and outflows, determined by evaporation rates, for small rainwater catchments. While runoff harvesting is most suited to areas with high "runoff catchment area" to "run on" area ratio (Lalljee and Facknath, 1994), this is also ignored. Higher the aridity, larger would be the required catchment area to the cropped area required for the same water yield (Prinz, 2002). Often, encroachment of catchments of water harvesting systems for crop cultivation is very rampant, reducing the runoff prospects.

The states, which have taken up rainwater harvesting and groundwater recharge programmes on a large scale, are Gujarat (north Gujarat, Saurashtra and Kachchh), Rajasthan, Maharashtra, Tamil Nadu, Karnataka, Andhra Pradesh, Madhya Pradesh, Orissa and Chattisgarh. A major part of these regions is covered by six water-scarce river basin systems, namely, Sabarmati, rivers of Kachchh and Saurashtra, Pennar, Cauvery, east-flowing rivers between Mahanadi and Godavari, east flowing rivers between Pennar and Kanyakumari, which have less than 1,000 m^3 of renewable water per annum (Gupta, 2000: p. 116). Now let us look at the hydrological regime existing in these regions.

For this, we first examine the percentage area of each state falling under different rainfall regimes (<300 mm, 300-600 mm, and 600-1000 mm, 1000-1500 mm, 1500-2500 mm and >2500 mm); and different PE regimes (< 1500 mm, 1500-2500 mm, 2500-3500 mm and >3500 mm). It is understood that regions with relatively low rainfall have higher potential evapo-transpiration due to relatively low humidity, higher number of sunny days (Pisharoty, 1990). Lower rainfall, coupled with higher PE reduces the runoff potential and high evaporation from the impounded runoff, thereby increasing the dryness (Hurd *et al.*, 1999). The analysis shows that Gujarat and Rajasthan have 11% and 42% area, respectively, fall under extremely low rainfalls (< 300 mm); and 39% and 32%, respectively under low rainfall (300-600 mm). The other states by and large fall in the medium rainfall (600 mm-1000 mm) and high rainfall (1000-1500 mm) regimes. In the case of Maharashtra, MP, AP, Karnataka and Tamil Nadu, a lion's share (85% and above) falls in medium rainfall regime, and in case of Orissa and Chattisgarh, 45% and 40% respectively fall in high rainfall regime (see Map 1).

Map 2: Average Mean Annual Rainfall

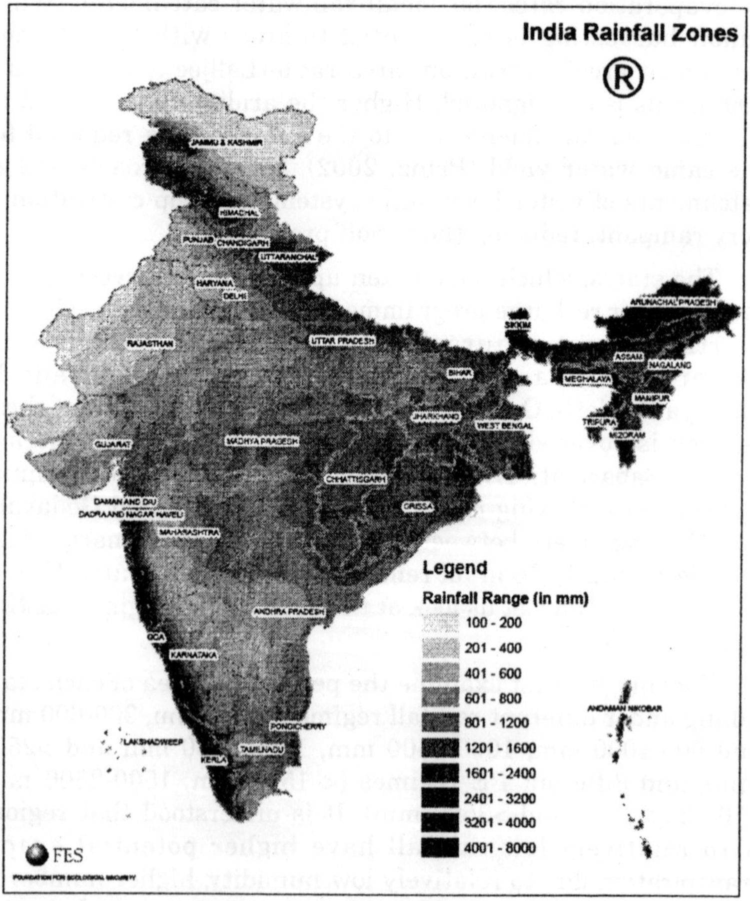

As regards PE, lion's share of Gujarat and Rajasthan fall under high evaporation (2500-3000 mm); nearly 35-56% of the geographical area of other states (except Orissa and Chattisgarh) fall under high evaporation regimes; the area of these states falling in the medium evaporation regime (1500-2500 mm) is in the range of 38-65%. The entire Orissa and Chattisgarh fall in medium evaporation regime. Overall, a large section of the area (of the 9 states considered) has medium rainfall, and medium to high evaporation. A significant portion of the area (of Gujarat and Rajasthan) has very low to low rainfalls and high evaporation (see Map 2).

Map 2: Average Annual Evaporation

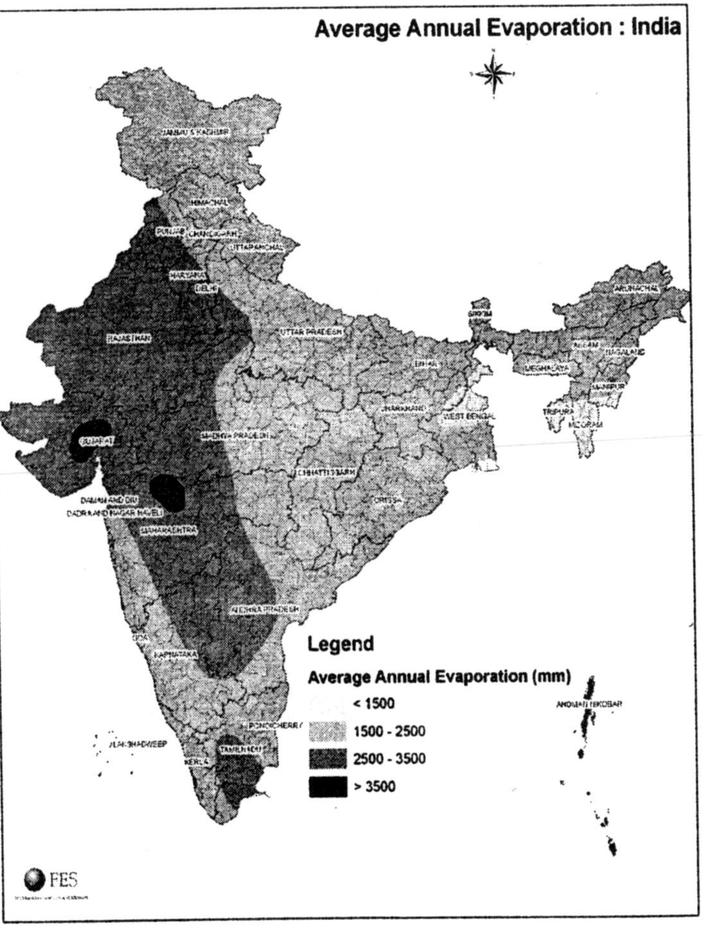

Table 1. Rainfall and PE Regimes of States Having Water Harvesting Programmes

Name of State	*% Area with Rainfall below*						*% Area with Evaporation (PE)*			
	<300 mm (very low)	*300-600 mm (low)*	*600-1000 mm (medium)*	*1000-1500 mm (High)*	*1500-2500 mm (Very high)*	*>2500 mm (Extremely High)*	*<1500 mm (low)*	*1500-2500 mm (medium)*	*2500-3500 mm (high)*	*>3500 mm (Very High)*
Gujarat	10.88	39.08	47.27	2.77					88.53	11.47
Rajasthan	41.80	32.45	25.75						100.00	
Maharashtra			85.86	6.93	7.21			37.96	56.23	5.81
Madhya Pradesh			95.71	4.29				56.94	42.89	0.17
Andhra Pradesh			97.83	2.17				52.70	47.30	
Karnataka			88.01	3.65	5.67	2.67		62.82	37.18	
Tamil Nadu			96.52	2.98	0.50			64.56	35.44	
Orissa			54.01	45.99				100.00		
Chattisgarh			59.39	40.61				100.00		

Source: authors' own estimates based on Pisharoty (1990) using GIS.

In the next step, we analyze: the proportion of the geographical area from each of these regions/states falling under different rainfall variability classes like > 25%, 25-30%, 30-40%, 40-50% and 50% and above. Higher the magnitude of PET during monsoon, higher will be the negative impact on hydrological variables such as surface storage and recharge. While it reduces surface storage through evaporation, higher PET during monsoon also means higher crop water requirement during the season and increased soil moisture depletion leading to reduced recharge from rainfall. In barren soils, higher evaporation rates leads to faster soil moisture depletion perpetuating higher rate of infiltration of the incoming precipitation and lower runoff.

As Table 2 indicates, a large percentage of the total geographical area of Gujarat and Rajasthan (72% and 68%, respectively) has high to very high (30-40% and above) variability in rainfall. Significant parts of the geographical area of the states 3 to 7 (37% to 92%) experience medium variability in rainfall; the rest of the area experiences low variability. The entire Orissa and Chattisgarh experience only low variability in rainfall. In nutshell, more than 50% of the total geographical area of all the states put together experience medium variability; nearly 25% experience "high to very high variability"; and nearly 20 per cent experience "low variability" in rainfall (see Map 3). They coincide with "medium rainfall-medium to high evaporation", "low rainfall-very high evaporation" and "high rainfall- medium evaporation" regimes, respectively.

It can be seen from Map 1, 2 and 3 that regions with high variability in rainfall coincide with those with low magnitudes of rainfall and high PE, which also have high dryness ratio. In such areas, a slight variation in precipitation or PE can substantially magnify the water stress on biological systems as compared to humid regions (Hurd *et al.*, 1999). Higher the variability in rainfall, lower would be the reliability of local water harvesting/recharge systems. This is because chances of occurrence of low rainfalls and extremely low runoff would be higher under such circumstances, and at the same time, the demand for water would be high due to environmental stressed caused by poor soil moisture storage, low runoff and high temperature.

Map 3: Average Coefficient of Variation of Rainfall

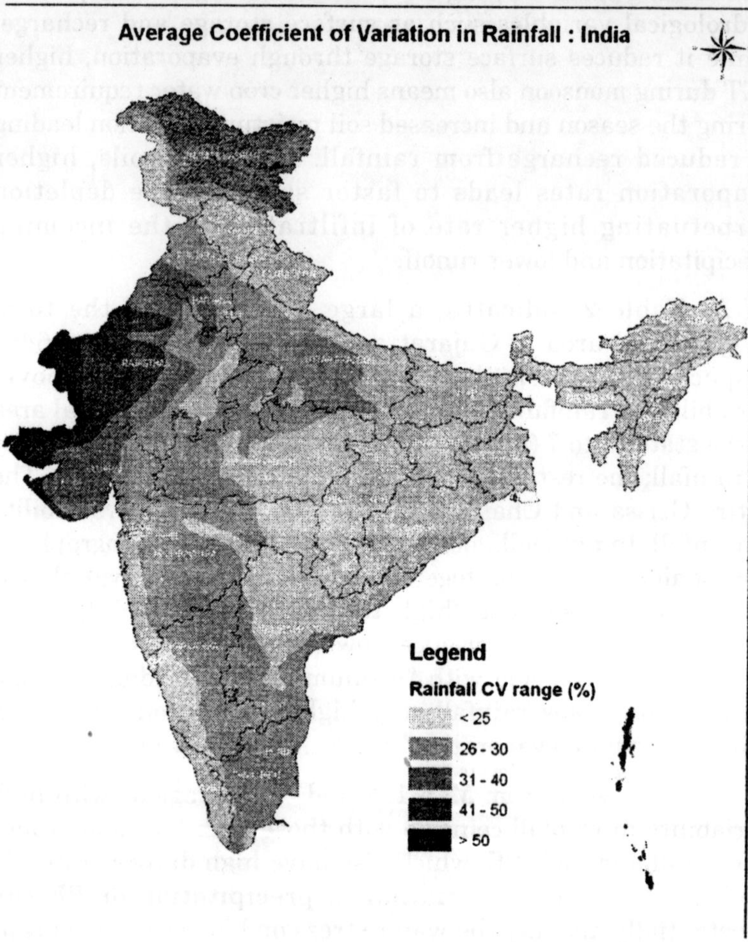

Table 2. Rainfall Variability Regimes of States Having Water Harvesting Programmes

Name of State	*% Area with Rainfall Variability in the range of*				
	<25% (low)	*25 - 30% (medium)*	*30 - 40% (high)*	*40 - 50% (very high)*	*> 50%*
Gujarat	0.24	27.12	44.30	17.11	11.22
Rajasthan	8.33	24.08	23.04	30.71	13.84
Maharashtra	37.67	62.33			
Madhya Pradesh	49.71	50.29			
Andhra Pradesh	62.64	37.36			
Karnataka	29.15	70.85			
Tamil Nadu	7.73	92.27			
Orissa	100.00	0.00			
Chattisgarh	100.00	0.00			

Source: Authors' own estimates based on Pisharoty (1990) using GIS.

In the third step, we analyze the average number of rainy days and its variability across regions. We attempt to find out the percentage of geographical area of each region, falling under different rainy day (say <20 days, 20-30 days, 30-40 days, 40-50 days, 50-75 days, and 75 and above days). We also analyze the implications for the quantum of rainfall in each rainfall event and the maximum and minimum daily rainfalls under different rainfall regimes.

The analysis shows that Gujarat and Rajasthan fall in regions which experience monsoon rains in a fewer days. To elaborate: nearly 21% of Gujarat and 45% of Rajasthan state receive less than 20 days of annual rains; nearly 51% of Gujarat and 70% of Rajasthan fall in areas which experience less than 30 days of rain in a year; nearly 1/3rd of both the states receive 30-40 days of rain. As regards the states 3-7, the area which receives 30-40 days of rain ranges from 9 to 27%; 40-50 days of rain ranges from 29-39%; 50-75 days of rain ranges from 27-58%. The Western Ghat in Maharashtra and Karnataka receive heavy rains spread over many days (> 75). As regards Orissa and Chattisgarh, both the states receive 50-75 days of rain in a year. To sum up, the regions which receive fewer days of rain (erratic rains) coincide with those experiencing low rainfall and high evaporation and high variability in rainfall. The regions which experience many wet days coincide with those which experience high and reliable rainfall and medium evaporation (see Map 1, 2, 3 and 4).

Synthesizing the results of the spatial analysis of rainfall, PE, rainfall variability and number of rainy days that are provided in Maps 1-4, the following trends can be established: the inter-annual variability in rainfall increases with reducing rainfall; the number of wet spells reduces with lowering magnitude of rainfall; the PE increases with lowering magnitude of rainfall. The implications of this trend on the potential of water harvesting in a region needs to be understood. Lower the rainfall, coupled with higher potential evaporation and inter-annual variability in rainfall and fewer rainy days, lower would be the potential of water harvesting. This is due to the following processes. First: the runoff potential by and large would be low

Table 3. Distribution of Rainy Days in States Having Water Harvesting Programmes

Name of State	*% Area with Rainy Days in the Range of*					
	<20 days	*20-30 days*	*30-40 days*	*40-50 days*	*50-75 days*	*>75 days*
Gujarat	20.57	30.87	32.30	6.15	10.11	
Rajasthan	45.31	24.38	28.19	2.12		
Maharashtra			22.57	29.17	43.24	5.01
Madhya Pradesh			21.17	33.26	45.57	
Andhra Pradesh			12.17	29.80	58.03	
Karnataka			26.55	38.79	27.13	7.53
Tamil Nadu			9.35	35.78	54.86	0.01
Orissa					98.77	1.23
Chattisgarh					100.00	

Source: authors' own estimates based on Pisharoty (1990) using GIS.

Map 4: Average Rainy Days in India

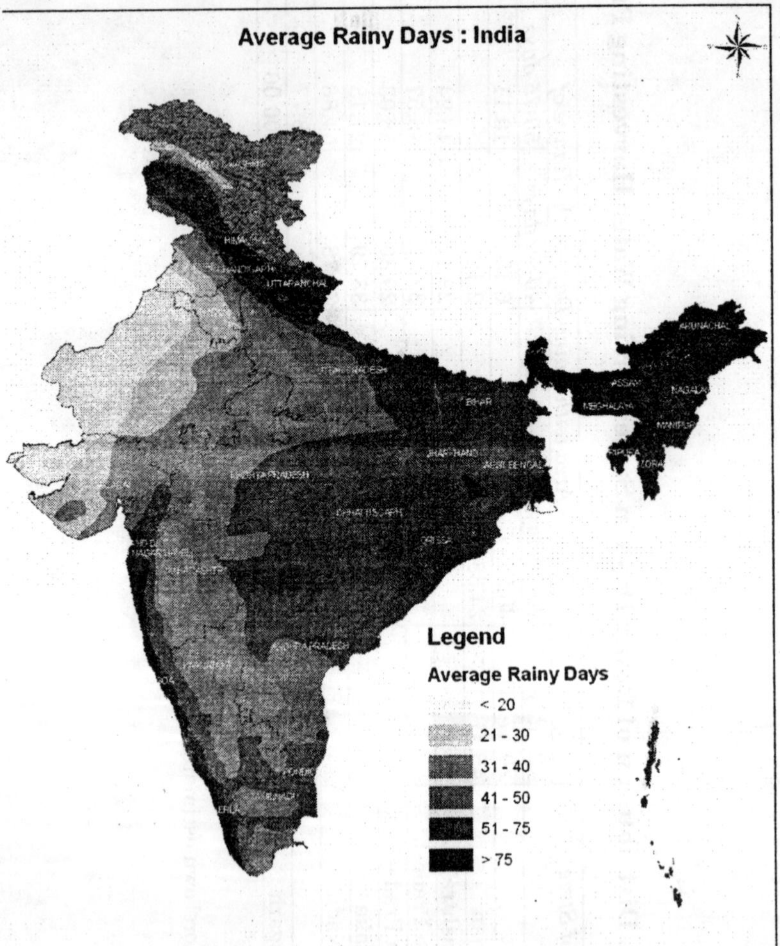

in low rainfall regions with high dryness ratio. Second: evaporation from surface storage would be high due to high PE. Third: the probability of occurrence of very low rainfalls, causing heavy reductions in runoff, would be high, with consequent hydrological stresses.

3.1.2 Limitations Imposed by Socioeconomic System

Water harvesting arguments totally misses on the water demand-availability perspective at micro level. Ideally, the RWHS would work if the area which has uncommitted flows to harness has "un-met demand". This is unlike large water resource systems where provisions exist for transfer of water from "surplus" areas to "scarce" areas.

From an anthropogenic perspective, water-scarce regions are those where the demand for water for various human uses far exceeds the total water available from the natural system, or the technology to access it is economically unviable. This includes the surface water, water stored in the aquifers, and that held in the soil profile. Water scarcity can also be felt when the resources are available in plenty in the natural system in a particular region, but adequate financial resources to access it are not available with the populations living in there. The former is called physical scarcity, and the latter economic scarcity. North Gujarat in India and Israel are ideal examples of physical scarcity, whereas Ethiopia in eastern Africa and Bihar in eastern India are ideal examples of economic scarcity of water. In this article we are concerned with regions facing physical scarcity of water.

Physical scarcity of water occurs in regions which experiences low to medium rainfalls and high evaporation rates. Most parts of Western, North-western Central and Peninsular India fall under this category. They have low to medium rainfalls and high potential evaporation rates (source: based on Pisharoty (1990) as provided in Kumar et al., (2006)) The mean annual rainfall ranges from less than 300 mm to 1000 mm, where as the PE ranges from less than 1500 in some pockets in the north east to more than 3500 in some pockets in Gujarat and Maharashtra.

We would explain the process which determine the supplies and demand for water, which in turn induces water scarcity in those regions, in the subsequent section. As regards natural water supplies, the runoff available from rainfall precipitation and groundwater recharge from a unit land area in such regions is generally low. This is because runoff is the amount in excess of the soil moisture storage and infiltration. Since evaporation rates are high, soil moisture generated from precipitation gets depleted during the rainfall itself, increasing infiltration of water which fulfills the soil moisture deficit. This leaves much less chance for water to runoff.

As regards the demand for water, crop evapo-transpiration mainly determines the requirement of water for agriculture, as agriculture is the largest source of water demand for human uses in all major river basins in India.

Table 4 gives the reference evapo-transpiration against the effective renewable water resources from surface runoff and replenishable groundwater in five important river basins.[2] It shows that for all the five basins, annual reference evapo-transpiration is many times more than effective renewable water resources. But, what is available for crop production includes the soil moisture storage as well. But since the soil moisture storage is a small fraction of the rainfall even in very high rainfall regimes, the potential evapo-transpiration (PET) for the entire year would be much higher than the sum of soil moisture storage—which is a fraction of rainfall—, and effective renewable water resources.

In that case, the imbalance between effective water availability and water demand for agricultural uses is very high for all the five basins. In addition to the agricultural water, there are demands for water from other sectors such as domestic and industrial uses. But, for the time being, we can ignore this. This gap between demand and renewable supplies can be reduced if we have very little arable land, and very large amount of land serving as natural catchments for supplying runoff water. But, unfortunately, the amount of virgin catchment left out in water-scarce regions of India is very small. It varies from 58.6% in case of Pennar basin to 28% in case of Sabarmati basin.

The increasing intensity of crop production in the rich upper catchments of river basins and watersheds has two major negative impacts on available renewable water resources. *First*: it captures a share of the runoff generated from the area, and therefore reduces the available surface water supplies. *Second*: increase in cultivated land increases the water requirement for irrigation. This way, large regions in India are facing shortage of water to meet the existing demands. The recent report on groundwater resource assessment and irrigation potential in India clearly shows that the regions facing problems of groundwater over-exploitation are mostly in Gujarat, Rajasthan, Maharashtra, MP, AP, TN and parts of Karnataka, and coincide with the naturally water-scarce regions (GOI, 2005).

3.2 Costs and Economics of Water Harvesting and Recharge Schemes

In the planning of large water resource systems, cost and economics are important considerations in evaluating different options (Perry, 2001). But unfortunately, the same does not seem to be applicable in the case of small systems, though concerns about economics of recharge systems in certain situations were raised by authors such as Phadtare (1988) and Kumar (2004).

Part of the reason for lack of emphasis on "cost" is the lack of scientific understanding of the hydrological aspects of small scale interventions, such as the amount of stream flows that are available at the point of impoundment, its pattern, the amount that could be impounded or recharged and the influence area of the recharge system. Even though simulation models are available for analyzing catchment hydrology, there are great difficulties in generating the vital data at the micro level on daily rainfall, soil infiltration rates, catchment slopes, land cover and PET which determine the potential inflows; and evaporation rates that determine the potential outflows. Further for small water harvesting project, implemented by local agencies and NGOs with small budgets, cost of hydrological investigations and planning is hard to justify. Often, provision for such items is not made in small water harvesting projects.

Table 4: Average Reference Evapo-transpiration Against Mean Annual Rainfall in Selected River Basins in Water-Scarce Regions

Sr. No	*Name of the Basin*	*Mean Annual Rainfall (mm)*		*Average Annual Water Resources[1] mm*	*Effective Annual Water Resource[2] (mm)*	*Reference Evapo-transpiration[3] (mm)*	
		Upper	*Lower*			*Upper*	*Lower*
1	Narmada basin	1352.00	792.00	444.70	937.60	1639.00	2127.00
2	Sabarmati basin	643.00	821.00	222.84	309.61	1263.00	1788.80
3	Cauvery basin	3283.00	1337.00	316.15	682.80	1586.90	1852.90
4	Pennar basin	900.00	567.00	193.90	467.80	1783.00	1888.00
5	Krishna basin	2100.00	1029.00	249.16	489.15	1637.00	1785.90

Sources: 1. The average annual water resources was estimated by taking the sum of annual utilizable runoff (GOI, 1999: Table 3.6) and the dynamic groundwater resources from natural recharge in these basins (GOI, 1999: Table 3.9) and dividing by the geographical area of the basin.

2. The effective renewable water resources were estimated by dividing the average renewable water resources for the basin by the fraction of total cultivated land to the total basin drainage area. The basin-wise total cultivated land considered was for the year 1993-94 (GOI, 1999: Annexure 3.2, pp 422).

3. Reference evapo-transpiration values were estimated using meteorological data from FAO CROPWAT model, except for Pennar basin and upper Krishna. For Pennar and upper Krishna, the data were obtained from IWMI climate atlas.

Map 5: Major Aquifers in India

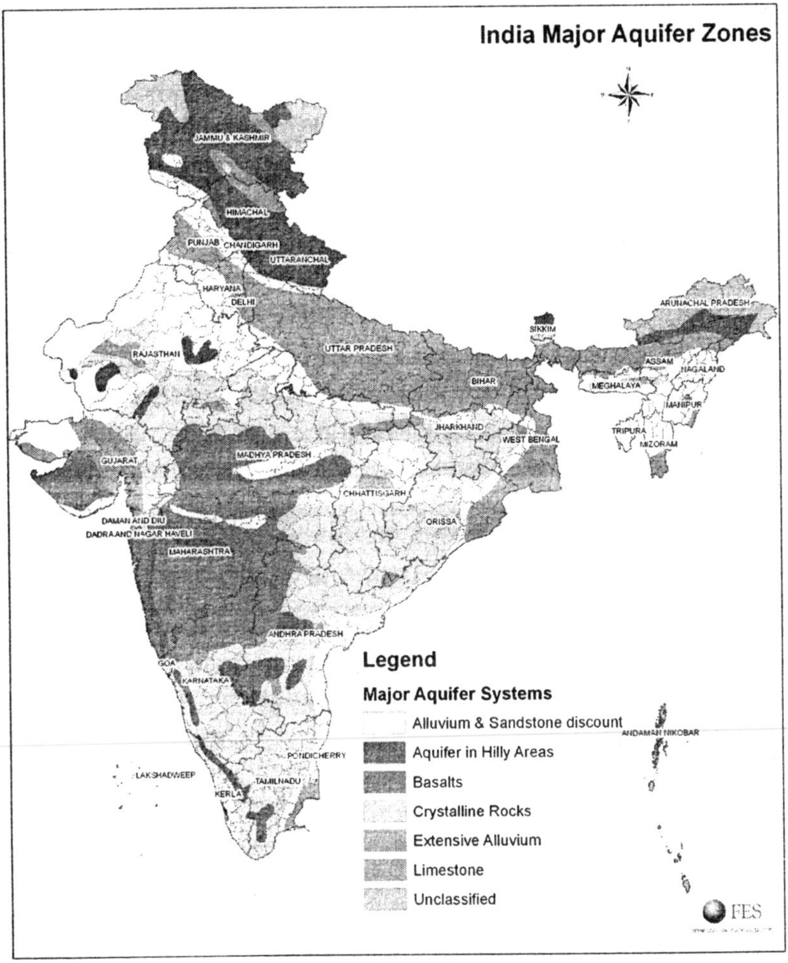

That said, the amount of runoff which a water harvesting structure could capture, depends not only on the total quantum of runoff, but also on how it occurs. A total annual runoff of 20 cm occurring over a catchment of one sq. km. can generate a surface flow of 0.20 MCM. But the amount that could be captured depends on the pattern. As Garg (1987) points out, in arid and semi arid regions in India, high intensity rainfalls of short duration are quite common (source: Garg, 1987 as cited in Athawale, 2003: Figure 24). These runoffs generate flash flood[3]. If the entire runoff occurs in a major rainfall event, the runoff collection efficiency would reduce with reducing capacity of the structures built. If large structures are built to capture high intensity runoff thereby increasing the runoff collection efficiency, that would mean inflating cost per unit volume of water captured. In fact, authors such as Oweis, Hachum and Kijne (1999) have argued that runoff harvesting should be encouraged in arid area only if the harvested water is directly diverted to the crops for use.

Given the data on inflows and runoff collection efficiencies, predicting the impacts on local hydrological regime is also extremely complex, requiring accurate data on geological and geo-hydrological profiles, and variables.

In lieu of the above described difficulties in assessing the effective storage, unit costs are worked out on the basis of the design storage capacity of the structures and thump rules about number of fillings. The recent book by Dr. R. N. Athawale on rainwater harvesting in India though had covered a gamut of technical aspects of water harvesting in different regions of India, does not deal with economics issues (see for instance Athawale, 2003). In order to get projects through, proponents show them as low cost technology, under-estimating the costs and inflating the recharge benefits. The best example is the government of India report on groundwater management and ownership (GOI, 2007), and recently-sanctioned government of India scheme for recharging aquifers in hard rock districts of South India, with an investment of 1,800 crore rupees.

Table 5. Estimated Unit Cost of Artificial Recharge Structures Built under Pilot Scheme of CGWB

Sl. No	*Type of Recharge Structure (Life in years)*	*Expected Active Life of the System*	*Estimated Recharge Benefit (TCM)*	*Capital Cost of the Structure (in Lac Rs.)*	*Cost of the Structure per m^3 of water (Rs/m^3)*	*Annualized Cost* (Rs/m^3)*
1.	Percolation Tank	10	2.0-225.0	1.55-71.00	20.0-193.0	2.00-19.30
2.	Check Dam	5	1.0-2100.0	1.50-1050.0	73.0-290.0	14.60-58.0
3.	Recharge Trench/Shaft/	3	1.0-1550.0	1.00-15.00	2.50-80.0	0.83-26.33
4.	Sub-surface Dyke	5	2.0-11.5	7.30-17.70	158-455.0	31.60-91.00

Source: GOI, 2007, Table 7: p. 14.

*Estimated by dividing the capital cost by the life of the system.

The government of India report (GOI, 2007), which strongly advocates artificial recharge structures of various types as a mid term measure for tackling groundwater scarcity, base its arguments on the pilot experiments conducted by CGWB in different parts of India using five different types of structures (see GOI, 2007: pp 13-15 for details). While the estimated costs per cubic metre of water were one-time costs (see Column 6 of Table 5), the report assumes that the structures would have a uniform life of 25 years. Two things in these figures are very striking. First: the costs widely vary from location to location and from system to system, and the range is wide, which the report duly acknowledges. Second: even for a life of 25 years, the upper values would be extremely high, touching Rs. 7.7/m^3 of water for percolation tank and Rs. 18.2/m^3 for sub-surface dyke.

But, such a long life for recharge system is highly unrealistic. The life of the system depends on the type, and also a variety of complex hydrological and hydraulic parameters. In regions receiving flash floods, and where the silt load in flood water is high, the technical efficiency of recharge structures drastically reduces after every major rainfall event. Percolation tanks would require de-silting continuously year after year, cost of which is quite significant when compared to the capital cost of the system. Filters attached to recharge shaft become dysfunctional very fast, after one or two years of rains. So is the case with the recharge tube wells fitted with sub-surface dykes. Considering an active life of 10 years for a percolation tank, 5 years for check dam and sub-surface dyke, and 3 years for recharge shaft, we have worked out the unit cost of recharging using these systems.

The results are provided in Column 7 of Table 3. It shows that the costs are prohibitively high for sub-surface dyke and check dam, and very high for percolation tanks. Only in the case of recharge shafts, the lower values are reasonably low. Added to the cost of recharging, would be the cost of pumping out the water from wells. The size of returns from crop production should justify such high investments. A recent study in nine agro-climatic locations in Narmada river basin showed that the gross return ranged from Rs. 2.94/m^3 to Rs.13.49/m^3 for various crops in Hoshangabad; Rs. 1.9/m^3 to Rs. 10.93/m^3 for various crops in Jabalpur; Rs. 2.59/m^3 to Rs. 12.58/m^3 for crops in Narsingpur; Rs. 1.33/m^3 to Rs. 17/m^3 for crops in Dhar; and Rs. 3.01/m^3 to Rs. 17.91/m^3 for crops in Raisen (Kumar and Singh, 2006). The lower values of gross return per cubic metre of water were found for cereals, and high values were for low water consuming pulses, and cotton. This means that the net returns would be negative if recharge water is used for irrigating such crops. Contrary to this, the report argues that the costs are comparable with that of surface irrigation schemes (GOI, 2007: pp 13). Such an inference has essentially come from wrong assumptions of the productive life of the recharge structures.

Scale considerations are extremely important in evaluating the cost and economics of water harvesting/groundwater recharge structures because of the hydrological integration of catchments at the level of watershed and river basins. The cost and economics of water harvesting systems cannot be performed for individual systems in isolation, when the amount of surplus water available in a basin is limited. This is because incremental structures do not result in proportional increase in the hydrological benefits (Kumar, 2000a), as interventions in the upper catchments reduce the potential hydrological benefits from the lower systems. What is important is the incremental hydrological benefits due to the new structure. A system in itself may be cost effective and economically viable if evaluated independently, but, if evaluated as a part of a large-scale water-harvesting intervention at the level of river basins, the system may not be justifiable from cost angle when compared against the additional benefit it brings in.

In any basin, the marginal benefit from a new water harvesting structure would be smaller at higher degrees of basin development, while the marginal cost higher (see Figure 2). The reason being: 1] higher the degree of basin development, lower would be the chances for getting socially and economically viable sites for building water impounding structures, increasing the economic and financial cost of harvesting every unit of water, and 2] with higher degree of development, the social and environmental costs of harvesting every unit of water increases (Frederick, 1993), reducing the net economic value of benefits. Therefore, the cost and economic evaluation should move from watershed to basin level. As Figure 1 indicates, the level at which basin development can be carried out depends on whether we consider the flows in a wet year or dry year or a normal year. Nevertheless, there is a stage of development (marked by O in the chart) beyond which the negative social, economic and environmental benefits starts accruing, reducing the overall benefits. Here, O is the optimum level of water resource development.

But, it is important to keep in mind that the negative social and environmental effects of over-appropriation of basin's water resources may be borne by a community living in one part of the basin, while the benefits are accrued to a community living in another part. Ideally, water development projects in a basin should meet the needs and interests of different stakeholders living in different parts. Therefore, optimum level of water development should not aim at maximizing the net basin level benefits, but rather optimizing the net hydrological and socio-economic benefits for different stakeholders and communities across the basin. Hence, it is basin-wide optimization. That said, in certain situations, the local economic benefits from RWH against the economic costs themselves may be questionable. But, such interventions could be justified if there are potential social benefits of changing patterns of water availability and use, in terms of increasing water availability to poorer farmers with low capability land holdings. But such decisions should be based on evaluation of alternative strategies to meet the local water needs of the poor.

Now the ability to derive economic benefit of recharge depends on where the recharged water ends up. In regions underlain by hard rock geology, the groundwater flow patterns are quite complex. Often, the benefits are recharge structures extend up to a few kilometers downstream or upstream depending on the pattern of occurrence of geological structures such as lineaments, fractures and dykes (source: based on Muralidharan and Athawale, 1998). Tracing the recharge water in such situations would require sophisticated studies involving isotopes. This is a common problem in the hard rock areas of Saurashtra, Kachchh, north Karnataka and Tamil Nadu where large-scale water harvesting/groundwater recharge interventions are taken up through check dams, ponds and percolation tanks. Often the communities, for whom investment for recharge system are made, do not get the benefit (Moench and Kumar, 1993). In certain other situations, the recharge water could end up in saline aquifers.

The economics of RWH would also be a function of the incremental value of benefits accrued from the use of newly-added water. Apart from the recharge volume, the value of the use to which the additional water is put is extremely important in determining the incremental benefits, an issue often ignored in the project planning. Often, the benefits of RWHS are not clearly identified or understood. While the cost of water harvesting is significant, it is critical to divert the new water to high-valued uses. Phadtare (1988) pointed out that recharge projects would be economically viable in alluvial north Gujarat if the water is diverted for irrigation, as structures are expensive. Yield losses due to moisture stress are extremely high in arid and semi-arid regions and that providing a few protective irrigations could enhance yield and water productivity of rain-fed crops remarkably, especially during drought years (Rockström et al., 2003). The available extra water harvested from monsoon rains should therefore be diverted to supplementary irrigation in drought years.

There are regions where human and cattle drinking become high priority demands. North western Rajasthan, which is arid and dominated by pastoral communities, named *Gujjars*, is one such example. The social and economic value realized from the use of water for human drinking and livestock use, respectively, would be much more than the economic value realized from its use in irrigating crops. In such situations, water should be diverted for such uses where the opportunity costs are low and net value products are high. But proper water use planning to realize maximum value from the added water is largely missing in water harvesting efforts.

Figure 2: Marginal Cost and Benefits of Water-harvesting with different degrees of Basin Development

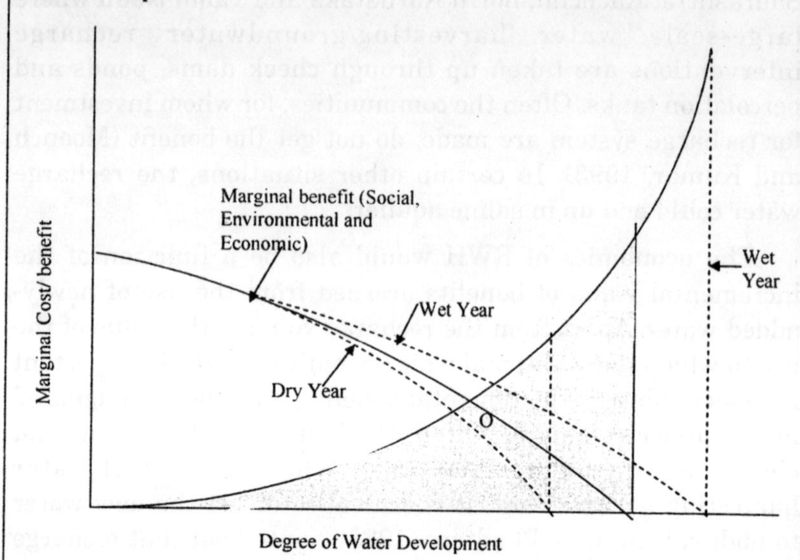

3.3 Lack of Integrated Approach

In many river basins, the surface water systems and groundwater systems are often inter-connected. Any alterations made in one of them could change the availability of water in the other (Sohiquilo, 1985; Llamas, 2000). In many hilly areas, especially in the Western Ghats, the water levels rise steeply after monsoon, and groundwater contributes significantly to the stream flows downstream during lean seasons due to the steep groundwater flow gradients. In that case, any water harvesting intervention to store water underground may not make much sense as it would get rejected and appear as surface flows (Mayya, 2005). On the other hand, in regions with deep water table conditions like in north Gujarat, the runoff directly moves into the groundwater systems of the plains through the sandy river bed as dewatering of the upper aquifers increases the rate and cumulative percolation (Kumar, 2002b).

With 2/3rd of the country's geographical area underlain by hard rock formations, storage capacity of aquifers poses a major challenge for artificial recharge. Most parts of water-scarce states, viz., Gujarat, Madhya Pradesh, Maharashtra, Karnataka, Andhra Pradesh, Orissa, Chhattisgarh and Tamil Nadu are underlain by hard rocks ranging from basalt, crystalline granite, hill aquifers and sandstone. A small areas in Gujarat has extensive alluvium, Narmada valley and (Cambay basin) (see Map 5). The hard rock aquifers have no primary porosity and have only secondary porosity. The constraints imposed by hard rock geology in recharge efforts through percolation tanks are: high depth to water table below and around the recharge structure due to occurrence of recharge mount and shallow bed rocks, which prevent percolation of water (Muralidharan, 1990 as cited in Muralidharan and Athawale, 1998); and low infiltration capacity of the thin soils overlaying the hard rock formations. Due to low specific yield (0.01-0.03), sharp rise in water levels is observed in aquifers during monsoon, leaving little space for infiltration from structures. While harnessing water for recharge is extremely important during normal and wet years, the natural recharge in hard rock formation is high during such years as it is a function of seasonal rainfall (based on regression equations shown in Figure 7 in Athawale, 2003), further reducing the scope for artificial recharge.

In Saurashtra, in spite of the poor potential offered by low rainfalls, high variability, and high evaporation rates (see Map 1-3), significant recharge efforts were made. But, the biggest constraint in storing water underground during high rainfall years is the poor storage capacity or specific yield of the basalt formations. During good rainfall years, the aquifers get saturated with natural recharge immediately after the rains, leaving no space for entry of water from the recharge systems (Kumar, 2000a). An estimated 20,000 check dams built in the region to capture the rainwater and recharge the aquifers are able to store only small fraction of the surplus runoff. In such situations, proper water use programming is required to achieve effective utilization of the available surplus water, where in water from aquifers is pumped out and used during the rainy season itself thereby creating storage space for the incoming flows (Muralidharan and Athawale, 1990; Shah, 2002).

The groundwater level fluctuation data obtained from Ghelo river basin in Saurashtra illustrate this. The basin had experienced intensive water-harvesting since 1995. The data were collected from open wells located inside the basin periodically during and after the monsoon rains. The wells located close to the water harvesting structures and those away from the structures are demarcated. The water level fluctuation in the wells in relation to the rainfall events was analyzed and presented in Figure 3. The time series data shows that the wells close to water harvesting structures get replenished faster than those located away from the structures. But, these wells start overflowing after the first major wet spell, while the second category of wells show similar trends after the second wet spells. Another interesting observation is the steep rise in water levels in wells located both close to and away from the water harvesting structures soon after the first wet spells. It is in the order of 35-40 feet. The steep rise in water levels is indicative of the poor specific yield of the aquifer in the area[4], as the magnitude of cumulative rainfall that had caused this fluctuation is quite small (nearly 200 mm).

Figure 3: Water Level Fluctuation in Wells in Fulzar, Ghelo River Basin

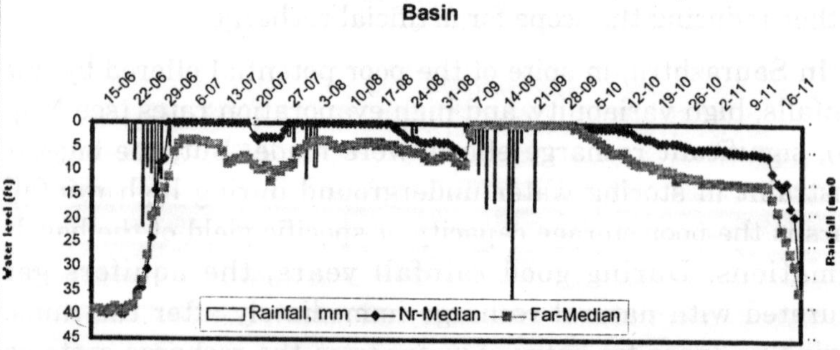

3.4 Trade off between Local Vs Basin Impacts in Closed Basins

Due to lack of integration between plans for water harvesting at the local level and basin level water resource development, RWH often leads to over-appropriation of surface water in river basins. While planning of conventional water development projects is based on dependable yields from the catchments, the plans for WH which happen subsequently do not take into account the "committed flows" for downstream reservoir/water diversion systems.

Also, there is an increasing tendency to believe that because these structures are too small that they are benign (Bachelor *et al.*, 2002) though present in large numbers in most cases. The primary reason for this is that the agencies which are concerned with small water harvesting (in the upper catchment) and those which are concerned with major head- works are different and they do not act in coordinated fashion at the level of the basin. Building of small water harvesting systems such as tanks, check dams is often the responsibility of minor irrigation circles of irrigation department or district arms of the rural development departments of the states concerned. This ad hoc approach to planning often leads to over-appropriation of the basin water, with negative consequences for large schemes downstream (Kumar *et al.*, 2000).

Data collected from Ghelo river basin shows that the inflows into Ghelo-Somnath reservoir had significantly reduced after intensive water harvesting work was undertaken in the upper catchment. Figure 4 shows the catchment rainfall and runoff in Ghelo-Somnath. After 1995, the year which saw intensive water harvesting work, the reservoir overflowed only in 2005 when the rainfall recorded was 789 mm. While reduction in runoff could be attributed to rainfall reduction as well, rainfall-runoff regressions were carried out for two time periods i.e., 1969-1995 and 1995-2005. The regression equations clearly show that the relationship between rainfall and runoff had changed after water harvesting interventions (see Figure 5). For the same amount of rainfall, the runoff generated is now low. Or in other words, the amount of rainfall required for filling the reservoir had now increased from 320 mm to 800 mm. While this is theoretically true, the actual runoff received by the station might actually differ as there are many factors other than just rainfall magnitude which determines the runoff rates. Though the curves intersect, at high magnitudes of rainfall, this is not a problem as such high rainfall does not occur in the basin, and the curve needs to be considered only for the rainfall regime of the basin.

Figure 4: Ghelo-Somnath Rainfall and Reservoir Inflows

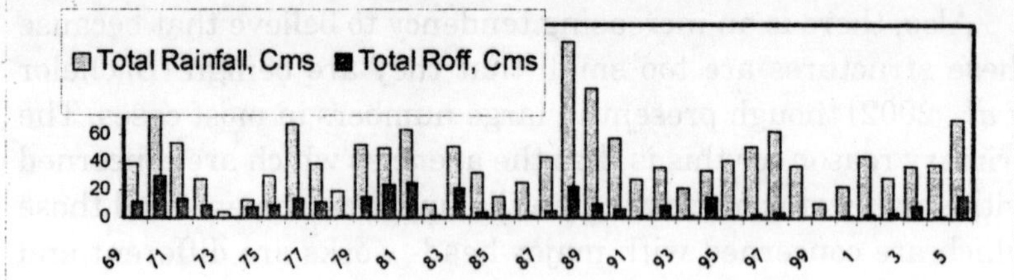

Many large and important river basins in India, which are also facing water scarcity, are now "closed" or do not have uncommitted flows that are utilizable through conventional engineering interventions. Some of them are Pennar, Cauvery and Vaigai in the South (based on GOI 1999: pp 472-477), and Sabarmati, Banas in the west, which are closed. In addition to these, all the west-flowing rivers in Saurashtra and Kachchh in Gujarat are also closed (Kumar, 2002). While Krishna basin is on the verge of closure, some of the basins which are still "open" are Godhavari and Mahanadi in the east (based on GOI 1999: pp. 466-469).

Sabarmati basin, for instance, having a drainage area of 21,678 sq. km, has a utilizable surface flow of 1513.4 MCM allocated to Gujarat (Kumar and Singh, 2001), where as the total live storage capacity of irrigation schemes built in the basin, estimated to be 1470 MCM (GOI, 1999) is still slightly below this. But the basin has many water diversion structures including weirs and a barrage. Actually, the dependable runoff upstream of the reservoirs/diversion structures in the basin is far below the planned water utilization (estimated to be 1560 MCM as per Kumar and Singh (2001)) leaving no spill over. At the aggregate level, the basin is over-appropriated. At the sub-basin level, the scenario is different. Two of the sub-basins, viz., Dharoi and Hathmati are heavily over-appropriated (Kumar *et al.*, 2000). Still, one of the sub-basins, named Watrak, has

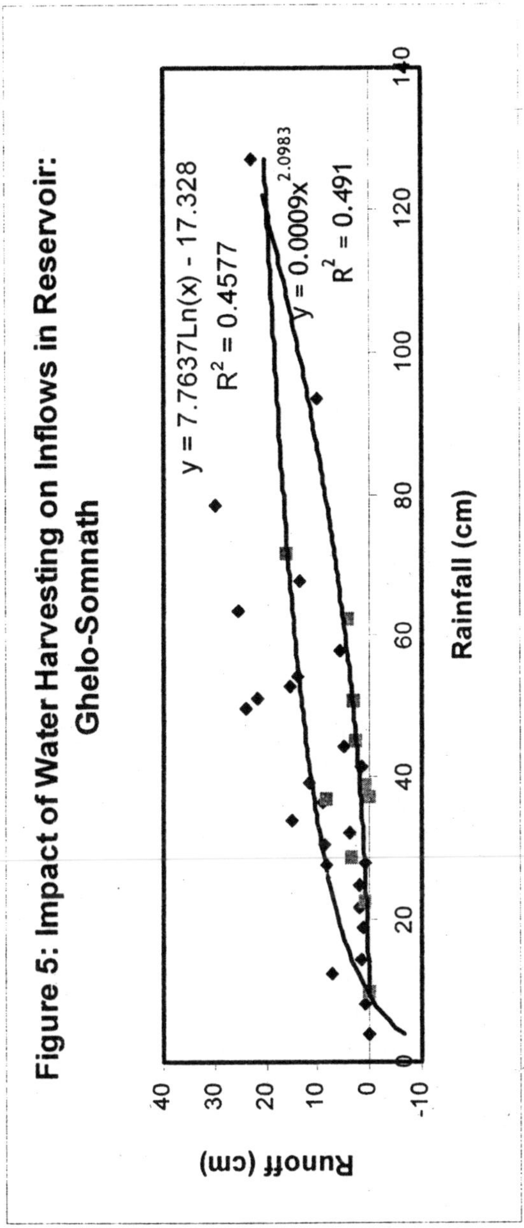

Figure 5: Impact of Water Harvesting on Inflows in Reservoir: Ghelo-Somnath

uncommitted flows (Kumar and Singh, 2001), which eventually end up in the Gulf of Cambay.

It is hard to judge whether a basin is closed or open on the basis of the storage capacity of reservoirs and the dependable flows, as many reservoirs also divert a lot of water during monsoon season, making the effective water utilization more than the live storage capacity. A look at the ratio of total live storage of reservoirs (built, being built and proposed) in 17 major river basins in India against the dependable runoff in these basins shows that for many basins, the ratio is far less than 100 per cent, leaving the impression that there is much more uncommitted flows in the basin for future harnessing. But this is not correct. Take for instance Narmada basin. The total live storage volume of all terminal dam built in Narmada, i.e., Sardar Sarovar, is 5800 MCM, where as the total water utilization from this reservoir is 11, 200 MCM. All the 30 large and 135 medium reservoirs together would divert a total of 30,588 MCM of water for irrigation and various other purposes (NWDA, 2004). But the total live storage of these reservoirs would be much less, i.e., 23,790 MCM (GOI, 1999: pp 36). This is because a significant amount of water would be diverted from these reservoirs for kharif irrigation within the basin and outside, particularly from Sardar Sarovar reservoir. Again the estimates of stage of development do not take into account the reservoirs having live storage capacity of less than 10 MCM.

3.5 Trade off between Economics and Hydrological Opportunity

Regions with semi arid and arid climate experience extreme hydrological events (Hurd *et al.*, 1999). As we have seen in section 4.1.1, high inter-annual variability in rainfall is a common phenomenon in most parts of these water-scarce regions. Rainfall variability induces higher degree of variability in runoff. Such high variability is found even in the high rainfall regions as well as low rainfall regions. We take the example of the upper catchment area of Cauvery basin in peninsular India and one of the catchments of Sabarmati River basin in North Gujarat of western India.

In Palanpur area of Banaskantha district in north Gujarat, which has semi arid to arid climatic conditions, the rainfall records show a variation from a lowest of 56 mm in 1987 to 1584mm in 1907. The runoff estimated on the basis of regression equation developed for a sub-basin, named, Hathmati of Sabarmati basin in north Gujarat, which is physiographically quite similar to Palanpur area of Banaskantha, shows that the runoff can vary from a lowest of 0.6mm to 541 mm. But the occurrence of actual runoff could be different from this based on how other variables that are not considered in the regression viz., the intensity and pattern (over space and time) of rainfall, influence the runoff intensity. Thus the lowest runoff is close to $1/1000^{th}$ of the highest runoff. Though what can occurs at the sub-basin level may not be representative of that in small upper catchments, the difference cannot be drastic. Even for a humid, high rainfall region of Wayanad district in Kerala, the runoff estimated for a small catchment of Karappuzha on the basis of the rainfall-runoff relationship developed for Kabani sub-basin (catchment area of 7040 sq. km) of Cauvery river basin, to which the area falls, and the observed rainfall of the area, range from 528mm in the lowest rainfall year (2002) to 1458 mm in the highest rainfall year (1994) in a 31-year period from 1973-2003.

When there is a high inter-annual variability in the runoff a catchment generates, a major planning question which arises is "for what capacity the water harvesting system should be designed". When scarcity is acute, highest consideration is given to capturing all the water that is available. If all the runoff which occurs in a high rainfall year is to be captured, then the cost of building the storage system would be many hundred times more than what is required to capture the one which occurs during the lowest rainfall. But, the system would receive water to fill only a small fraction of its storage capacity in the rest of the years. This could make it cost-ineffective. The issue of variability is applicable to the design of large head works as well. But, in large systems, the water in excess of the storage capacity could be diverted for irrigation and other uses to areas which face water shortages during the same season, thereby increasing the effective storage.

In order to illustrate this point, we use the data generated from Ghelo river basin in Saurashtra. The basin has a total catchment area of 59. 20 sq. km. It had a medium irrigation reservoir with a storage capacity of 5.68 MCM and has been functional since 1966. On the basis of inflow data of the reservoir for the period 1969-95 showed that the total runoff generated in the basin varied from zero in the year corresponding to a rainfall of 39 mm to a maximum of 17.78 MCM in the year corresponding to a rainfall of 1270 mm. Today, the total capacity of water harvesting systems built in the upstream of Ghelo reservoir is 0.15 MCM. During the period from 1969 to 2005, the reservoir showed overflow for 13 years with a total quantum of 60.936 MCM. If one million cubic metres of runoff had to be captured in addition to the 5.89 MCM that would be captured by the medium irrigation reservoir, it would cost around 0.09 X/m^3 of water, while capturing 3 MCM would cost 0.11 X/m^3 of water. If the maximum runoff observed in the basin, i.e., 17.785 MCM has to be captured, the total volume of water captured would be only 60.91 MCM, in which case the unit cost of water harvesting would be around 0.21 X/m^3 of water. Here, "X" is the cost of storage structures for creating an effective storage space of one MCM. Here, again, we are not considering the incremental financial cost of the special structures for capturing high magnitudes of runoff, which cause flash flood.

3.6 Maximizing Local Benefits Vs Optimum Benefits for Basin Communities

Generally, in any river basin, the upper catchments are rich in terms of their ability to contribute to the basin yields. This is mainly because of the unique physiographical features, and partly because of the climatic conditions—such as steep slopes, high rainfall in the mountains, and high humidity—, which provide favourable environment for runoff generation. The upper catchments also provide good source of base flows due to forest cover which causes favourable conditions for water storage and infiltration. On the demand side, these regions generally are less endowed in terms of availability of arable land. Over and above, the demand rates for irrigation are generally low. On the other hand, the lower catchments are generally characterized by lower rainfalls and higher levels of aridity (rainfall deficit to meet ET demands) and better access to arable land, increasing the aggregate demand for irrigation.

There are numerous examples for this. A few to cite are: the upper catchment of Cauvery basin in the south, Narmada basins in central India, Sabarmati basin in western India, tributaries of Indus in the north western India, Krishna basin in Central India and Mahanadi basin in eastern India. Some parts of Kabani sub-basin of Cauvery river basin have cold and semi humid climate, and parts of this sub-basin receives the second highest rainfall in India after Chirapunji with the mean annual rainfalls crossing 4000 mm. Irrigation demands in these regions are low owing to high precipitation and low reference evapo-transpiration, and low per capita availability of arable land. On the other hand, the lower parts of Cauvery in Tamil Nadu are hit by scarcity of water for irrigation owing to lower rainfalls and high evapo-transpiration.

We have defined the agricultural water demand as a function of per capita net sown area and the ratio of ET_0 (reference evapo-transpiration) and rainfall; and water availability as a function of rainfall. It is assumed that: higher the ET_0/R ratio, higher would be the irrigation requirement for a unit of land; higher the per capita (rural population) net sown area, higher would be the aggregate demand for irrigation per capita. Table 6 shows the estimated values of two selected agricultural water demand variables, viz., ET_0/R and per capita arable land; and one water availability variable, i.e., rainfall. It also shows that the irrigation demand is much higher in the lower catchment areas, and availability higher in upper catchments in all these six important basins.

Major water resource/irrigation projects undertaken in the past tap stream flows generated from the upper catchments, but cater to either the lower parts of these basins or other less water endowed regions outside these basins (Verghese, 2001 and 2002). Bakhra reservoir and Nangal diversion projects located in the high rainfall Shivalik hills of Himachal Pradesh essentially cater to the ravenous low rainfall and drought prone regions of Punjab and scanty rainfall regions of Rajasthan (Verghese, 2002); the

Sardar Sarovar dam harnesses water from ample rainfall areas in Narmada valley and takes it to the drought-prone areas of north Gujarat and Saurashtra which are characterized by low and erratic rainfall (Verghese, 2001). Similarly, the large reservoir projects in Cauvery transfer water to the drought-prone regions in Tamil Nadu and Karnataka. As such the water demand for irrigation is extremely low in the upper catchments.

More over, as irrigation water use efficiency and water productivity are likely to be high in areas with variability in rainfall and high drought- proneness (Rockström, 2002), with transfer of water from the well-endowed regions to the poorly-endowed regions, the economic value of water in agriculture increases. The recent research done in water-scarce and land-rich western Punjab and water-rich and land-scarce eastern Uttar Pradesh showed that the value of water realized from irrigation is much higher in Punjab than in eastern UP. The economic value of water was Rs. 14.85/m^3 in western Punjab, where as it was Rs. 11/m^3 in eastern Uttar Pradesh. Due to scarcity of water, the farmers in Punjab make better economic use of water by choosing cropping systems that are economically more efficient and doing agronomic practices to obtain higher yields, higher physical productivity and economic efficiency (Kumar et al., 2008).

But, often water harvesting initiatives, especially those by NGOs, are driven by considerations other than economic efficiency, most important of which are social equity and environmental justice. Impounding water in the upper catchments might serve social objectives of meeting drinking water requirements.

As evident from the above illustrations, there is a clear trade off between meeting economic efficiency objectives, and these developmental goals. Therefore, any water resource intervention in the upper catchment areas which reduce the downstream uses should be done with due consideration to the net change in "gross value product" of water in the basin due to the interventions. The "gross value product" can be defined as the sum total of the incremental value product from the economic uses, environmental services and social uses the basin's water

Table 6. Comparison of Agricultural Water Demand Variables in Upper and Lower Catchment Districts of Selected Indian River Basins

Name of Basin	*Name of Upper Catchment District (UCD)*	*Name of Lower Catchment District (LCD)*	*Mean annual rainfall (mm) in*		*Mean Annual Potential Evapo-transpiration (mm) in*		ET_0/R		*Per Capita Net Sown Area (Ha)*	
			UCD	*LCD*	*UCD*	*LCD*	*UCD*	*LCD*	*UCD*	*LCD*
Sabarmati	Dungarpur	Ahmedabad	643.7	821.0	1263.0	1788.8	1.96	2.18	0.14	0.47
Indus	Shimla	Ludhiana	1597.0	525.0	986.60	1698.6	0.62	3.24	0.14	0.25
Narmada	Shahdol	Jhabua	1352.0	792.04	1639.0	2127.0	1.21	2.69	0.35	0.35
Cauvery	Wayanad	Nagapattianan	3283.0	1337.0	1586.9	1852.5	0.48	1.39	0.18	0.13
Krishna	Raigarh	Guntur		1029.0		1785.9		1.74	0.13	0.22
Mahanadi	Raipur	Puri	1388.0	1440.0	1667.0	1667.0	1.20	1.16	0.18	0.06

UCD: Upper catchment district; LCD: Lower Catchment District.

Source: authors' own estimates based on Agricultural Statistics of India and FAO data on precipitation (R) and reference evapo-transpiration (PET).

resources meet. The amount of water to be captured upstream through RWH interventions should also be optimized to derive maximum regional social equity, environmental value and overall output from the economic uses of water. In basins where the available water resources are already committed (closed basins), the challenge is bigger as maximizing the gross value product might mean reallocating some water from one low valued use to a high valued use.

4. Major Findings

Following are the major findings emerging from an extensive review of the research on water harvesting in India, and a macro analysis of the critical issues in rainwater harvesting from the point of view of hydrological opportunities, economic viability and socioeconomic impacts when scale considerations are involved.

- Macro level hydrological analysis shows that rainwater harvesting solutions offers extremely limited potential in terms of its ability to reduce the demand-supply imbalances and provide reliable supplies in water scarce regions. The reason being: (a) significant part of these regions (states 1 and 2) are characterized by low mean annual rainfalls, high inter-annual variability in rainfall, with high potential evaporation and larger share of evaporation occurring during rainy season, reducing the runoff potential and increasing the occurrence of hydrological stresses; and (b) another significant part is characterized by medium rainfalls, with medium inter-annual variability, but "medium to high evaporation", making surface storage difficult.
- A large part of the water-scarce regions, which fall under the "medium rainfall-medium to high evaporation" regime are underlain by hard rock formations such as basalt, crystalline rocks and other consolidated formations such as sandstones. The percolation tanks, the most preferred recharge structures, are likely to have low efficiency in these hard rock areas and also areas having silty-clay and clayey soils. In high rainfall, and medium evaporation regions which experience high

reliability in rainfall such as parts of Orissa and western Ghat, the overall potential and reliability of water supplies from RWHS would be high.

- Inefficient recharging in hard rocks is due to lack of integration of groundwater and surface water use. In these regions, planning of recharge schemes should consider surface water impoundment of all the available excess flows, than direct recharge of runoff. This should be followed by water use programming to create underground storage for incoming surface flows. The data on water level fluctuations collected from Ghelo river basin in Saurashtra show that wells in the vicinity of check dams start overflowing during the monsoon due to lack of storage capacity in the shallow aquifer which gets recharged.
- Many naturally water-scarce regions have water demands which far exceed the supplies, with vulnerability to hydrological stresses, that they would require exogenous water.
- Rigorous analysis of the data available from pilot experiments done by CGWB on the cost of water harvesting/recharge structures shows that they are prohibitively expensive in terms of cost per unit volume of water, and are economically unviable if the newly created water is diverted for irrigating crops.
- Scale considerations are extremely important in evaluating the cost and economics of water harvesting/ groundwater recharge structures because of the integration of catchments at the level of river basins. The economics of water harvesting cannot be performed for structures based on their individual benefits and costs, when the amount of surplus water available in a basin is limited; but on the basis of incremental benefits. In addition to the direct economic costs and benefits, there are also negative externalities induced by water harvesting on the society due to social and environmental effects. Higher the degree of basin

development, higher will be the marginal social cost and lower would be the marginal social benefit.

- The basins which experience high inter-annual variability in the stream flows are many and cover significant areas in India. In such basins, the trade off between hydrological impacts of water harvesting and economic benefits is likely to be large. With increasing storage capacity of RWH systems, the economic viability becomes poorer as the average cost of water harvesting per unit volume of water increases. The historical data on reservoir inflow obtained for Ghelo river catchment illustrate this.
- In "closed basins", there is apparent trade off between local benefits and downstream benefits. U/S diversions reduce the prospects of storage and diversions systems d/s. Examples of closed basins are river basins in north Gujarat, Saurashtra, Kachchh, western Rajasthan and basins in Peninsular India, such as Cauvery, Pennar and Vaigai. Narmada is another basin which in immediate future would join this category of river basins. The detailed hydrological data collected from Ghelo river basin in Saurashtra also illustrate this.
- In many important basins, there is an apparent trade off between maximizing overall benefits for basin communities in terms of enhancing the gross value product of water, and maximizing the local benefits of water harvesting. This is owing to the fact that in these basins, water from well-endowed regions with low water demands is being diverted to poorly-endowed regions having high water demands, enhancing its social and economic value.

5. Conclusions

In the most water-scarce regions of India, RWH offers limited potential. In many other regions, which have medium rainfalls, but experience "medium to high evaporation", the poor groundwater potential of hard rock which underlie these regions pose a constraint for recharging. This was illustrated by water level fluctuation data in wells of Ghelo river basin in Saurashtra.

Economic evaluation of water harvesting systems poses several complexities due to the problems in quantifying the hydrological impacts, and the various benefits. Economics of water harvesting cannot be worked out for structures on the basis of individual benefits, but on the basis of incremental benefit. In many water-scarce basins, there is a strong trade off between maximizing the hydrological benefits from RWH and making them cost effective. In many water-scarce basins, RWH interventions lead to distribution of hydrological benefits, rather than augmentation. This was also illustrated by historical flow series data from Ghelo river basin. There is an optimum level of water harvesting which a basin can undergo which can help optimize the gross value product of water vis-à-vis economic, social and environmental outputs basin-wide.

References

Agarwal, Anil and Sunita Narain (1997) *Dying Wisdom: Rise and Fall of Traditional Water Harvesting Systems*, Centre for Science and Environment, New Delhi.

Athawale, R. N. (2003) *Water Harvesting and Sustainable Supply in India*, published for Environment and Development Series, Centre for Environment Education, Rawat Publications, Jaipur and New Delhi.

Bachelor, Charles, Ashok Singh, MS Rama Mohan Rao and Johan Butterworth (2002) Mitigating the Potential Unintended Impacts of Water Harvesting, paper presented at the IWRA International Regional Symposium 'Water for Human Survival', 26-29 November, 2002, Hotel Taj Palace, New Delhi.

Badiger, S, R. Sakthivadivel, N. Aloysius and H. Sally (2002) Preliminary Assessment of a Traditional Approach to Rainwater Harvesting and Artificial Recharging of Groundwater in Alwar District, Rajasthan, paper presented at the annual partners' meet of IWMI-Tata Water Policy Research Programme, Anand, February 19-20.

Down to Earth (2004) Water Woes in Wet Kerala, Cover Story, *Down to Earth*, May 31, pp. 26-33.

Frederick, K. D. (1993) *Balancing Water Demand with Supplies: The Role of Management in a World of Increasing Scarcity*, Technical Paper 189, Washington D. C: World Bank.

Garg, S. K. (1987) *Hydrology and Water Resources Engineering*, Khanna Publishers, Delhi, pp. 110-181.

Government of Gujarat (1994) Integrated Plan of Sabarmati River Basin, Draft Report prepared by Gujarat State Water Resources Planning Group, Gandhinagar, Gujarat.

Government of India (1999) Integrated Water Resource Development: A Plan for Development, Report of the National Commission for Integrated Water Resources Development Vol. I, Ministry of Water Resources, Government of India, New Delhi.

Government of India (2007) Report of the Expert Group on "Groundwater Management and Ownership," Planning Commission, *Yojana Bhawan*, New Delhi.

Government of Madhya Pradesh (1972) *Master Plan for Development of Water Resources of The Narmada in Madhya Pradesh*, Volume –II, Statements, Government of Madhya Pradesh.

Government of Rajasthan (1992) Effect of Rainfall and Potential Evapo transpiration on Groundwater Levels of Rajasthan, Groundwater Department, Jodhpur.

Gupta, R. K. (2000) Regional Water Transfer and Human Rights: Some Reflections on Sardar Sarovar Project, *ASIAN Journal* (Formerly Journal of Transportation and Infrastructure, 7 (4) pp: 112-127.

Hira, G. S. and K. L. Khera (2000) Water Resource Management in Punjab under Rice Wheat Production System, Department of Soils, Punjab Agricultural University, Ludhiana.

Hurd, Brian, Neil Leary, Russell Jones and Joel Smith (1999) Relative Regional Vulnerability of Water Resources to Climate Change, *Journal of the American Water Resources Association*, 35 (6): 1399-1419.

Kumar, M. Dinesh (1997) Water Use Study for Coastal Saurashtra and Kachchh, report submitted to the Water Resources Development and Management (WARDEMA) Project, Rajkot, VIKSAT, Ahmedabad.

Kumar, M. Dinesh (2000a) Dug-well Recharging in Saurashtra: Are the Impacts and Benefits Over-stretched? *Journal of Indian Water Resources Society*, July.

Kumar, M. Dinesh (2000b) Institutions for Efficient and Equitable Use of Groundwater: Irrigation Management Institutions and Water Markets in Gujarat, Western India. *Asia-Pacific Journal of Rural Development*, Vol. X (1), July.

Kumar, M. Dinesh (2002a) Integrated Water Management in the face of Growing Demand and threatened Resource Base in North Gujarat: Constraints and Opportunities: A Pilot Project to protect North Gujarat's Groundwater Ecology and Agriculture Economy, paper presented at the annual partners' meet of the IWMI-Tata Water Policy Research Programme, Anand, February 19-20.

Kumar, M. Dinesh (2002b) *Reconciling Water Use and Environment: Water Resource Management in Gujarat, Resource, Problems, Issues, Strategies and Framework for Action*, report submitted to Gujarat Ecology Commission for the Hydrological Regime Subcomponent of the State Environmental Action Programme supported by the World Bank.

Kumar, M. Dinesh (2003) Food Security and Sustainable Agriculture in India: The Water Management Challenge, Working Paper 60, International Water Management Institute, Colombo, Sri Lanka.

Kumar, M. Dinesh (2004) Roof Water Harvesting for Domestic Water Security: Who Gains and Who Loses? *Water International*, 39 (1): 43-53.

Kumar, M. D. Shashikant Chopde, Srinivas Mudrakartha and Anjal Prakash (1999) "Addressing Water Scarcity: Local Strategies for Water Supply and Conservation Management in Sabarmati Basin, Gujarat," in M. Moench, E. Caspari and A. Dixit (eds.) Rethinking the Mosaic: Investigations into Local Water Management. Kathmandu and Boulder: Nepal Water Conservation Foundation and Institute for Social and Environmental Transition.

Kumar, M. Dinesh, Vishwa Ballabh and Jayesh Talati (2000) Augmenting or Dividing: Surface water Management in the Water Scarce River Basin of Sabarmati, IRMA Working Paper 147, Institute of Rural Management, Anand.

Kumar, M. Dinesh, Vijay Kumar Malla and Sushanta Kumar Tripathy (2008) Economic value of water in agriculture: comparative analysis of a water-scarce and a water-rich region in India, *Water International*, 33 (2): 214-230.

Kumar, M. Dinesh, Shantanu Ghosh, Ankit Patel, O. P. Singh and R. Ravindranath (2006) Rainwater Harvesting in India: Critical Issues for Basin Planning and Research, *Land Use and Water Resources Research*, 6 (1): 1-17.

Lalljee, B. and S. Facknath (1999) Water Harvesting and Alternative Sources of Water for Agriculture, PROSI Magazine, September 1999.-N 368-Agriculture.

Llamas, M. Ramon (2000), La Inserción De Las Aguas Subterráneas En Los Sistemas De Gestión Integrada, Paper presented at *II Congresso Ibérico Sobre Planeamento E Gestão De Água*, 9-12 November 2000, Oporto.

Mayya, S. G. (2005) Water harvesting and groundwater recharge in the west coast of India-the Myth and the Truth, paper presented at the 4th Annual Partners' Meet, IWMI-Tata Water Policy Research Program, Anand, 24-26 February, 2005.

Moench, Marcus and M. Dinesh Kumar (1993) Local Water Management Initiatives: NGO Activities in Gujarat, VIKSAT-Pacific Institute Monograph, VIKSAT, Ahmedabad.

Molle, Francois, Alireza Mamanpoush and Mokhtar Miranzadeh (2004) *Robbing Yadullah's Water to Irrigate Saeid's Garden Hydrology and Water Rights in a Village of Central Iran*, Research Report 80, International Water Management Institute, Colombo, Sri Lanka.

Muralidharan, D. and R. N. Athawale (1998) Artificial Recharge in India, base paper prepared for Rajiv Gandhi National Drinking Water Mission, Ministry of Rural Areas and Development, National Geophysical Research Institute.

National Geo-physical Research Institute (2000) Geo-hydrological Investigations in M. C. Tanda Watershed, Anantapur District for Formulation of Suitable Artificial Recharge Strategies, interim report, September.

Oweis, T. A. Hachum and J. Kijne (1999) Water Harvesting and Supplementary Irrigation for Improved Water Use Efficiency in Dry Areas. SWIM Paper, Colombo, Sri Lanka.

Pandey, D. Narayan, Anil K. Gupta and David M. Anderson (2003) Rainwater harvesting as an adaptation to climate change, Review Article, *Current Science*, 85 (1), 10 July.

Patel, A. S. (2002) Impact of Groundwater Recharge Activities in Saurashtra, paper presented at the annual partners' meet of the IWMI-Tata Water Policy Research Programme, Anand, February 19-20.

Perry, Chris J. (2001) World Commission on Dams: Implications for Food and Irrigation, *Irrigation and Drainage*, 50: 101-107.

Phadtare, P.N. (1988) Artificial recharge of groundwater, paper submitted in the meeting of the working group on Water Harvesting, NCL, Pune, August 5, 1988.

Phansalkar, Sanjiv and Shilp Verma (2004) "Improved Water Control as a Strategy for Improving Tribal Livelihoods," Review of Agriculture, *Economic and Political Weekly*, XXXIX (12).

Pisharoty, P. R. (1990) Characteristics of Indian Rainfall, Monograph, Physical Research Laboratories, Ahmedabad.

Prinz, D. (2002) The Role of Water Harvesting in Alleviating Water Scarcity in Arid Areas, Keynote Lecture, Proceedings, International Conference on Water Resources Management in Arid Regions. 23-27 March, 2002, Kuwait Institute for Scientific Research, Kuwait (Vol. III. 107-122).

Rangachari, R., Nirmal Sengupta, Ramaswamy R. Iyer, Pranab Banergy, and Shekhar Singh (2000) Large Dams: India's Experience, Final Report, prepared for the World Commission on Dams, Cape Town, South Africa, Secretariat of World Commission on Dams.

Rockström, J., Jennie Barron and Patrick Fox (2003) Water productivity in rain-fed agriculture: Challenges and opportunities for smallholder farmers in drought-prone tropical ecosystems. In Jacob Kijne and others (Eds.) *Water Productivity in Agriculture: Limits and Opportunities for Improvement*, Comprehensive Assessment of Water Management in Agriculture. UK: CABI Publishing in Association with International Water Management Institute.

Sahuquillo, Andres (1985) Groundwater in Water Resource Planning: Conjunctive Use, *Water International,* 10 (1985) 57-63.

Sakthivadivel, R. Nihal Fernando and Jeffrey Brewer (1997) *Rehabilitation Planning for Small Tanks in Cascades: A Methodology Based on Rapid Assessment*, Research Report 13, International Irrigation Management Institute, Colombo, Sri Lanka.

Seckler, David J. (1996) *The New Era of Water Resources Management: From Dry to Wet Water Savings*, Research Report # 1, International Irrigation Management Institute, Colombo, Sri Lanka.

Shah, Tushaar (2001) Wells and Welfare in Ganga Basin: Public Policy and Private Initiative in Eastern Uttar Pradesh, India, Research Report 54, International Water Management Institute, Colombo, Sri Lanka

Shah, Tushaar (2002) Decentralized Water Harvesting and Groundwater Recharge: Can these Save Saurashtra and Kachchh from Desiccation, paper presented at the annual partners' meet of the IWMI-Tata Water Policy Research Programme, Anand, February 19-20.

Sharma, Abhishek (2002) Does Water Harvesting Help in Water-Scarce Regions? A Case Study of Two Villages in Alwar, Rajasthan, paper presented at the annual partners' meet of the IWMI-Tata Water Policy Research Programme, Anand, February 19-20.

Verghese, B. G. (2001) Sardar Sarovar Project Revalidated by Supreme Court, *International Journal of Water Resources Development*, Vol. 17 (1), 79-88.

Varghese, B. G. (2002) Water and Energy for Future India, paper presented at the International Regional Symposium on Water for Human Survival, 26-29, November, 2002, Hotel Taj Residency, New Delhi.

Zhu, Zhongping, Mark Giordano, Ximing Cai and David Molden (2004) Yellow River Basin Water Accounting, International Water Management Institute, Colombo, Sri Lanka.

Footnotes

1. The regression equation for Kabani estimated by National Water Development Board based on observed flows was R = 0.6363 N-233.7 where N is the rainfall (mm) and R the runoff (mm).

2. For a basin, if only a small fraction of the drainage area is under cultivation, then effective renewable water availability per unit of cultivated land would be more, and vice versa.

3. Many parts of Kachchh, which records one of the lowest mean annual rainfalls (350 mm) experienced floods during 1992 and 2003 with many WH structures overflowing. Flash flood occurs even in some of the semi arid and water scarce basins such as Sabarmati and Banas (Kumar, 2002b).

4. The specific yield can be estimated as the ratio of the rise in water level (m) and the cumulative rainfall (m) that is responsible for the water level fluctuation, if we consider the lateral flows in groundwater as negligible and assume that pumping from the observation wells during the time of recharge is zero. The rise in water level is between 10.5 and 12 m and the rainfall is 0.2 m.

4

Using Power Tariff as a Tool to Manage Groundwater in Over-exploited Areas

ABSTRACT

In this chapter, we analyze the potential impacts of energy pricing on efficiency, equity and sustainability in groundwater use. The analysis uses empirical data on water productivity in agriculture for crops, dairying and farms for north Gujarat, east UP and south Bihar. For north Gujarat, the analysis uses data from well owners who pay flat rate tariff, and well owners who pay pro rata tariff. For eastern UP and south Bihar, the analysis uses data from well owners and water buyers from diesel and electric well commands. The analysis also compares data from diesel well owners and electric well owners in south Bihar. The findings show that in water scarce regions, it would be possible for farmers to maintain net farm surpluses at higher energy tariff by improving productivity of water use. The empirical evidence further reinforces that the arguments against pro rata pricing are flawed. Raising power tariff in the farm sector to achieve efficiency, equity and sustainability in groundwater use is socially and economically viable.

Keywords: *Physical water productivity, water productivity in economic terms, effective water use, effective water productivity, farm level water productivity*

1. Introduction

In arid and semi arid regions of India, groundwater withdrawal for crop production exceeds the average annual recharge (Kumar, 2007). Uncontrolled withdrawal of groundwater for crop production, which is supported by subsidized electricity in the farm sector, leads to fast decline in water level in many parts of the country.

As irrigation is the main user of groundwater in India, raising water productivity in the ground water irrigated areas is essential for reducing groundwater draft (Amarasinghe *et al.*, 2005; Kumar, 2005; Kumar, 2007). Many Indian states are contemplating re-introduction of electricity metering in the farm sector, to manage groundwater demand. The basic premise is that at higher power tariff, with induced marginal cost of electricity and water, the farmers will improve water use efficiency (Kumar and Singh, 2001; Kumar, 2005) and enhanced water productivity. Such proposals face fierce resistance from farmers' lobby. Further, political parties and scholars alike argue that it will lead to a collapse of farmers in many water-scarce regions due to reduced net farm returns, making electricity metering in farm sector socially and economically unviable.

In 2001-02, agriculture accounted for almost 29 per cent of the total power consumption in India (GOI, 2002). Electricity to the farm sector in India is subsidised under both flat rate and pro-rata tariff systems. The subsidy in terms of sale to agricultural consumers is estimated to have increased from Rs. 15586 crore in 1996-97 to Rs. 30462 crore in 2000-01. This is because of increasing use of electricity for groundwater pumping, which in turn increases groundwater draft[1]. In most of the states, farmers pay electricity charges based on connected load and not on the basis of units of power consumed. Some of the Indian states are providing electricity to farm sector free of cost. Due to poor financial condition of the State Electricity Boards, they fail to supply good quality power to the agriculture sector. Pricing of electricity, in which the charge paid by farmers does not reflect actual consumption creates incentive for inefficient and unsustainable use of both power and groundwater (Kumar, 2005; Kumar and Singh, 2001).

While metering appears to be a solution to the problem, researchers question its viability on two grounds: 1] transaction cost of metering is very high, which increases the cost of supply of electricity, thereby reducing net social welfare (Shah *et al.*, 2004); and 2] tariff levels at which electricity and water demand curve becomes elastic to price changes would be so high that it becomes socio-economically viable (Saleth, 1997); and 3] political opposition to metering is so high that governments shy away from the option.

A recent research by Kumar (2005) questions the validity of the first two arguments. Empirical evidence shows that with higher tariffs, the farmers use water more efficiently (by providing lower dosages to the crop), increase gross water productivity (Rs/m^3); and secure higher returns per unit of water used. They are motivated to allocate more water for less water-consuming water efficient crops, provided they receive high quality, sustained water supply.

Figure 1: Geographical Coverage of Study

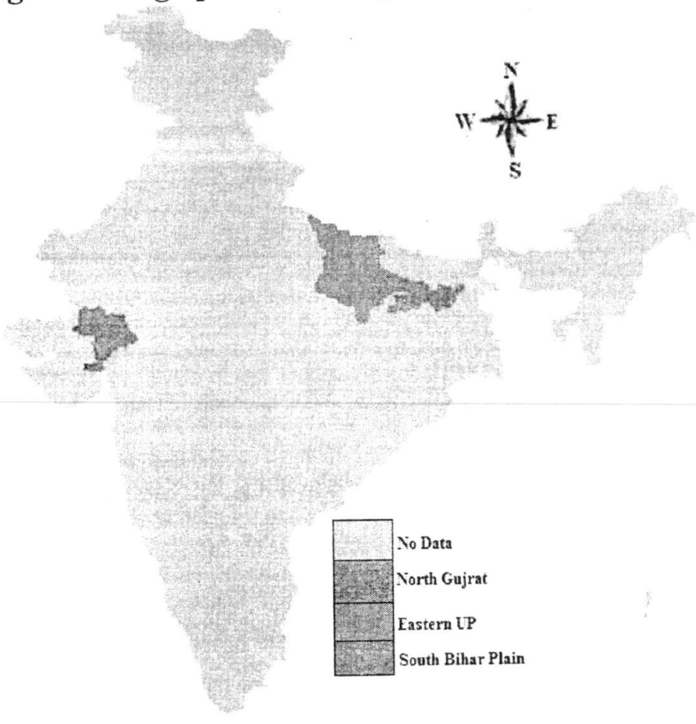

Some scholars cite positive impact of flat rate pricing of electricity on access and equity of groundwater (for instance,

Shah, 1993). They argue that with competitive water markets, water prices are kept low with the result that a major share of the electricity subsidy benefits are transferred to water buyers. However, the zero marginal cost of production of water from wells does not seem to influence the prices at which water is traded, in favour of buyers of water for irrigation. A recent research shows that flat rate pricing increases the monopoly power of large well owners (Kumar, Singh and Singh, 2001). Also, flat rate pricing leads to inequitable distribution of power subsidy benefits among well owners (Kumar and Singh, 2001; Howe sand Murugai, 2003). Kumar (2007), on the basis of evidence from Mussafarpur in Bihar argued that the monopoly power enjoyed by water sellers cannot be reduced by pricing policies, but by improving the transferability of groundwater.

As a way to cope with the increasing financial burden due to revenue losses through subsidies and growing power deficits, the State Electricity Boards in many agriculturally prosperous states have introduced heavy cuts in power supply hours to the farm sector (GOI, 2002)[2]. They assume that this would reduce the energy use and groundwater draft for agriculture. There is no evidence to support this logic. The electricity boards have not analyzed the impact of such cuts on equity in access and efficiency in use of groundwater. On the contrary, with reduction in hours of power supply, the quality of irrigation can be adversely affected[3]. The economic prospects of irrigated farming are more elastic to quality of irrigation water rather than its cost (Kumar and Patel, 1995; Kumar and Singh, 2001). The rich well owners always find ways to overcome the crisis of power cuts. This can further increase their monopoly in water trading.

Nevertheless, the recent past has seen some positive developments in some states. Since 2001, the government of Gujarat had only provided metered connections for agriculture. Nearly 12,000 farmers are already having metered power connections in north Gujarat alone. Here, farmers pay Rs. 0.7/ KWhr for electricity consumed. In Orissa, which is agriculturally one of the most backward states, electricity supply to farmers is through villages electricity co-operatives, known as *Vidyut Sanghs*, which does metering and billing. The agency does metering at the feeder level, and charges to the co-operatives.

Studies on the impact of such policy interventions in promoting efficiency, access equity and sustainability in resource use are lacking.

3. Objectives and Hypothesis

The overall objective of the study is to analyze the socio-economic viability of pro rata pricing of electricity in agriculture. Specific objectives are: 1] to study the impact of change in mode of electricity pricing on efficiency and sustainability of groundwater use by well owners; 2] to analyze the overall impact of electricity pricing on the farming system of well owners, including the economic prospects of farming; and, 3] to analyze the impact of change in mode of electricity pricing on the functioning of water markets.

The major hypothesis tested in this study is that with mounting cost of energy used for groundwater pumping, farmer would use energy and groundwater water more efficiently; shift their cropping system towards water efficient and high valued crops, take higher farming risks, thereby overcoming the potential negative impacts.

4. Approach and Methodology

4.1 Study Area

North Gujarat, which is a water scarce region and the eastern plain regions of Uttar Pradesh and Bihar, which are water rich regions constitute the geographical area for the present study.

The semi arid north Gujarat region receives a mean annual rainfall of 735 mm. Grey brown, coastal alluvium types of soils are found in this regions The mean annual precipitation in the eastern plain region of Uttar Pradesh is about 1025 mm and the region's climate varies from dry sub-humid to moist sub-humid. The soil type in this sub-zone is light alluvial and calcareous clay.

The Patna district falls under the south Bihar plains; receives a mean annual rainfall of 1103mm and climate condition of region varies from dry to moist sub-humid. The soil types found in the region are old alluvium sandy loam to clayey and the larger areas under the *Tal* and *Diara*.

4.2. Sampling Procedure and Data Collection

Primary and secondary data relating to crop and livestock production was obtained. The primary data included: quantum of crop inputs and outputs and their prices; cropping pattern; electricity prices; diesel consumption and price; well command area; number of water buyers and sellers; quantum of livestock inputs (dry and green fodder, feed, drinking water) and outputs, and unit price of inputs and outputs.

The districts of Mirzapur and Varanasi were selected from Bihar and UP for the study. Five contiguous villages were selected for primary survey to draw the required sample for diesel and electric well owners, and water buyers. The sample size was 60 electric pump owners, 60 diesel pump owners, 60 water buyers from electric pumps and 60 water buyers from diesel pumps.

Two talukas - Palanpur and Vadgam of Banaskantha district were selected from north Gujarat. Samples of 120 farmers who have metered electricity connection were obtained from 29 villages for data collection. Of this, 60 electric pump owners who paid power tariff on the basis of the connected load, and remaining 60 electric pump owners paid power tariff on the basis of actual consumption of electricity.

In south Bihar, Patna, Maner and Danapur development blocks were selected for primary survey. From each block, one village was selected. Thus, the two villages selected were Baluan and Hathiyakand. The sample farmers of the Baluan village were dependent on diesel pumps whereas in Hathiyakand, farmers are dependent on electric pumps. From Baluan village, 60 diesel pump owners and 60 water-purchasing counterparts were selected. Likewise, from Hathiyakand, 60 electric pump owners and their water purchasing counterparts were selected. The detail of sample size is given in Table 1.

4.3. Methodology

Analysing the efficiency and sustainability impacts of change in mode of pricing

There are very few locations in India where farmers pay for electricity based on consumption. Gujarat is one such state.

Table 1. Sampling Procedure and Sample Size

Name of the Regions	*Name of the district*	*Types of Energy Tariff*				*Diesel pump*		*Total sample size*
		Flat Rate		*Unit Pricing*		*Well owner*	*Water buyers*	
		Well owner	*Water buyers*	*Well owner*	*Water buyers*			
Water Scarce								
North Gujarat	Banaskantha	60	-	60	-	-	-	120
Water Rich								
Eastern UP	Varanasi and Mirzapur	60	60	-	-	60	60	240
South Bihar	Patna	60	60	-	-	60	60	240
Total		**180**	**120**	**60**	**-**	**120**	**120**	**600**

Therefore, to analyze the potential impacts of introducing pro-rata pricing of electricity in farm sector, with marginal cost of using groundwater, the farmers who are using diesel pumps for well irrigation and water buyers are used as proxy for pro-rata tariff.

The price of electricity used for pumping groundwater influences water productivity in many different ways (Kumar, 2005). The efficiency impacts change in mode of pricing by comparing water productivity of crops in physical terms. We can examine the impact of change in mode of pricing on economic viability of farming by comparing the overall water productivity of crops, livestock and farming system under the two conditions. The sustainability impacts of price changes can be analyzed by looking at the changes in groundwater withdrawal by well owning farmers.

In the study, we only consider the applied (pumped) water for estimation of water productivity at the field and farming system level, and not the depleted water that takes into account the contribution of rainfall to total water input to the crop and return flows into groundwater. This does not disturb the inferences drawn from the study due to three reasons: i] we are concerned with the changes in water productivity in the same field or farm, which means that the level of use of rainfall by the crop does not change. If rainfall use increases, it will not change the recharge to groundwater.

As discussed in detail in Chapter 6 of this book on micro irrigation, return flows would be insignificant in semi arid north Gujarat due to deep water table conditions. However, return flows from irrigation can be quite significant in both UP and Bihar plains due to alluvial geology and sub-humid climatic conditions. The farmers in this region would be concerned with the total amount of water applied rather than the actual amount of water depleted. The reason is that applied water would determine the amount of energy required to pump groundwater, which is scarce in the regions. The farmers in these two regions will not be concerned with reducing the depleted water per se, as it is in abundance.

(B) Estimating Water Productivity of Farming System

The physical water productivity for a given crop (kg/m^3) will be estimated using data on crop yield and the estimated volume of water applied for all sample farmers growing that crop. The combined physical and economic water productivity in Rs/m^3 is estimated using data on net returns from crop production in Rs/ha and estimated volume of water in cubic meter. To estimate the net income from a particular crop, the data on inputs for each crop was obtained by primary survey of farmers. This included cost of seed, labour, fertilizer, pesticides and insecticides, irrigation, ploughing, harvesting and threshing.

The physical productivity of water in milk production for livestock (litres/m^3) can be defined as:

$$WP_{Milk} = \frac{Q_{MP}}{\Delta_{Milk}} \qquad ...(1)$$

Where, Q_{MP} is the average daily milk output by one unit of livestock category over the entire live cycle (litres/animal/day). Δ_{Milk} is the total volume of water used per animal per day, including the water embedded in feed and fodder inputs, used in dairying for an animal in a day, worked out for the entire animal life cycle (m^3/animal/day). It is estimated as:

$$\Delta_{Milk} = \frac{Q_{cf}}{WP_{cf}} + \frac{Q_{df}}{WP_{df}} + \frac{Q_{gf}}{WP_{gf}} + \Delta_{DW} \qquad ...(2)$$

(Singh, 2004; Kumar, 2007)

Where, Q_{cf}, Q_{df} and Q_{gf} are the average quantities of cattle feed, dry fodder and green fodder used for feeding a livestock unit per day (kg/animal/day); WP_{cf}, WP_{df} and WP_{gf} and are the physical productivities (kg/m^3) of cattle feed, dry fodder and green fodder, respectively; Δ_{DW} is the daily drinking water consumption by livestock (m^3/day). It is the average volume of water required by a dairy animal per day over its entire life cycle, including the water embedded in feed and fodder.

Q_{cf}, Q_{gf}, Q_{df} and Δ_{DW} for a given category of livestock would be estimated for the entire life cycle of the animal from the following: i] weighted average of the average daily figures of these inputs for each season for animals in different stages of the life cycle, viz., calving, lactation stage, dry stage; and ii] the time period in each stage of animal life cycle for that category of life stock.

Since all the farmers in the sample may not have animals that represent all the different stages of the life cycle in a particular category of livestock at a given point of time, the average values of inputs are worked out as value of above mentioned variables for the sample farmers. Likewise, the average values of physical productivity of water in green fodder and dry fodder are used for estimation. Q_{MP} (lit/animal/day) is estimated from: i] the weighted average of average daily figures of milk yield for different seasons; and ii] the ratio of time period in lactation and the average life span of the animal in that category.

WP_{gf} and WP_{df} is estimated by taking their respective quantities and the volume of water required for growing that crop. In the case of by-products of crops used as fodder, the water used for growing that crop is allocated as the main product and by product in proportion to the market prices of the respective (Singh, 2004).

The net return of milk production, NR_{milk} (Rs/animal/day) is estimated using values of Q_{MP}, the price of milk (Rs/litre) and the cost of production of the average amount of cattle inputs required in a day (Rs/animal/day) estimated for the entire animal life cycle as proposed by Singh (2004) and Kumar (2007). It is important to mention here that with import of green or dry fodder in a farm, the cost of fodder input could also go up. This in turn would affect net water productivity in dairying WP_{milk} (Rs/m^3). It can be estimated as:

$$WP_{dairy} = \frac{NR_{milk}}{\Delta_{milk}} \quad (3)$$

(Singh, 2004; Kumar, 2007)

In the case of purchase of inputs market price is used. If the inputs are from the farmers' own fields, the actual cost of production is estimated. If farmer uses crop by-products for dairying, the total cost of production of the given crop is allocated among the main product and by-product on the basis of the potential revenues that can be earned from their sale. The quantity of inputs (feed and dry and green fodder) and milk outputs are worked out for the entire animal life cycle and not on the basis of the actual use of inputs and milk yield at the point under consideration.

The total volume of water used for milk production annually by one unit of livestock V_{dairy} (m^3/animal/annum) is estimated by dividing the total annual milk production by one unit of livestock (Q_{AMP}) by the physical productivity of water in milk production (WP_{dairy}).

The water productivity of the farm WP_{farm} (Rs/m^3), including crops and dairy is estimated as:

$$WP_{form} = \frac{\sum_{i=1}^{m} WP_{cropi} V_{crop,i} + \sum_{j=1}^{n} WP_{dairy} V_{dairy,j} N_j}{\sum_{i=1}^{m} V_{crop,i} + \sum_{j=1}^{n} V_{dairy,j}} \quad ...(4)$$

Here, $WP_{crop,i}$ is the water productivity of main product of crop i; $V_{crop,i}$ is the total volume of water used for crop i; $WP_{dairy,j}$ is water productivity in dairy production for livestock type j; and $V_{dairy,\ j}$ is the volume of water used for dairy production per animal for livestock category j, N_j is the total number of livestock in category j.

(C) Impacts of Different Modes of Energy Pricing on Equity in Access to Groundwater

The equity impact of different modes of energy pricing on groundwater use is analyzed by comparing the water charges (Rs/m^3) paid by the water buyers under the flat rate and unit pricing of electricity against the cost (Rs/m^3) farmers have to incur for access to groundwater if he decides to have his own well under both situations i.e., flat rate and unit pricing. For this, data was collected on: (i) water charges paid by water buyers under both the tariff regimes; (ii) cost of installation of bore/tube well; (iii) energy charges under flat and unit pricing paid by farmers annually; (iv) the land holding size; and, (v) well repair and maintenance cost.

5. Results and Discussion

5.1 Distribution of Land Holdings

The average size of land holding of different categories of farmers in the study area is provided in Table 2. In north Gujarat, the average size of land holding is higher for tube well owner who are paying power tariff on connected load basis (3.79 ha) as compared to their counterparts having metered connection (3.28 ha). About 90 per cent of the area is under irrigated crop production and remaining 10 per cent area is cultivated under rain-fed condition.

In Eastern UP, the average size of land holding is larger for diesel well commands as compared to electric well commands. Differences are significant between well owners and water buyers. Diesel pump owners have average land holding size of 1.35 ha while their water buyers have landholding size of 0.94 ha. The average size of land holding for electric pump owner is 1.30 ha, whereas their water buyers have an average land holding size of 0.56 ha.

In south Bihar like eastern UP, the average size of land holdings for both well owners and water buyers in the diesel pump commands is higher than that of their counterparts in electric pump commands. The well owners in electric well commands have larger sized holdings (0.73 ha) as compared to their water buyers (0.53 ha). In diesel pump commands, the differences are larger. The average size of land holding of well owner here is 1.26 ha, whereas for water buyers it is 0.57 ha.

Hence, the average size of land holding in water abundant eastern Uttar Pradesh and south Bihar plains is much smaller when compared to water scarce north Gujarat. This is one of the important factors for utilizing available water resources. In case of water abundant region, the limited land availability should motivate farmers to maximize returns per unit of land. Against this, in water scarce region, water availability is a limiting factor for maximizing returns from crop production, and hence generally, they would be motivated to maximize the returns from every unit of water (Kumar *et al.*, 2008). However, lack of resources for investing in wells and energizing devices is a limiting factor for many farmers in south Bihar and eastern UP to access the water.

5.2. Cost of Groundwater Irrigation

The cost of groundwater irrigation was estimated for well owners by taking into account the following: 1] cost of well construction and pump set installation; 2] cost of obtaining power connection; 3] cost of operational and maintenance of the well and the pump set; 4] life of the well and the pump set; 5] the average hours of groundwater pumping per year; and 6] discharge of the pump set. In the case of electric wells with metered connections, the hourly operation cost is worked out using the energy charges per kwhr of use. Similarly, in the case of diesel wells, the operation cost was worked out using the price of one litre of diesel and the amount of diesel consumption per hour of running. The cost of irrigation was finally worked out per cubic metre of water using well output data. In the case of wells with flat rate electricity connection, the implicit cost per hour of irrigation is worked out using the annualized cost, and the number of hours of irrigation per annum.

Based on the figures of well discharge, cost estimates were worked out for western UP, northern Gujarat and south Bihar and are presented in the Table below.

Area	*Water source*	*Average (Rs/m^3)*	*Range (rs/m^3)*
Western UP	Electric Pump owner	0.18	0.10 – 0.30
	Electric pump buyers	0.65	0.52 – 0.84
	Diesel pump owners	1.38	0.99 – 2.04
	Diesel pump buyers	2.81	2.07 – 3.63
North Gujarat	Metered connections	1.07	0.14 – 3.91
	Non metered connections	1.60	0.19 – 4.27
South Bihar	Electric Pump owner	0.77	0.17 – 3.39
	Electric pump buyers	0.70	0.31 – 0.92
	Diesel pump owners	1.87	1.51 – 2.95
	Diesel pump buyers	2.15	1.84 – 2.42

Source: author's own estimates.

Table 3. Cropping Pattern of Well Owner and Water Buyers under Different Energy Regime, Eastern Uttar Pradesh

Name of the Crops	Electric Pump				Diesel Pump			
	Owner		Water Buyers		Owner		Water Buyers	
	Area (Ha)	% to GCA	Area (Ha)	% to GCA	Area (Ha)	% to GCA	Area (Ha)	% to GCA
Kharif Season								
1. Paddy	0.71	11.51	0.36	14.81	1.55	26.18	0.91	22.14
2. Bajra	0.32	5.15	0.14	5.85	0.23	3.85	0.13	3.25
3. Maize	0.24	3.97	0.12	4.78	0.23	3.81	-	-
4. Lady's Finger	0.32	5.18	0.23	9.53	-		-	
5. Other Vegetables	0.32	5.30	0.17	7.08	0.14	2.41	0.34	8.35
6. Arhar	-		-	-	-	-	0.30	7.42
7. Black gram	0.27	4.39	0.11	4.68	-	-	0.11	2.78
8. Green gram	0.37	6.06	-	-	-	-	0.11	2.78
9. Sesamum	0.08	1.30	0.06	2.34	0.23	3.85	0.11	2.78
10. Groundnut	0.33	5.34	-	-	-	-	-	-
11. Sugarcane	0.11	1.77	0.06	2.34	0.16	2.68	-	-
12. Chary (Green fodder)	0.16	2.60	0.08	3.20	0.11	1.89	0.10	2.38

Source: Author's own estimate based on primary data.

Rabi Season								
1. Wheat	0.67	10.94	0.29	12.00	1.27	21.48	0.83	20.29
2. Barley	0.23	3.73	0.08	3.28	-	-	0.09	2.23
3. Pea	0.23	3.80	0.13	5.47	0.34	5.73	0.17	4.08
4. Gram	0.17	2.85	0.04	1.46	0.42	7.02	0.20	4.84
5. Mustard	0.70	10.06	0.53	4.45	0.27	4.55	0.14	3.50
6. Linseed	0.06	0.93	-	-	0.34	5.78	0.10	2.50
7. Potato	0.50	8.15	0.29	11.94	0.37	6.24	0.23	5.57
8. Barseem (Green fodder)	0.07	1.14	0.05	1.89	0.06	1.05	0.07	1.64
Summer Season								
1. Sunflower	0.10	1.58	-	-	-	-	-	-
2. Vegetables	0.11	1.86	-	-	0.11	1.93	-	-
3. MP chary (Green fodder)	0.15	2.38	0.12	4.89	0.09	1.55	0.14	3.48
Gross Cropped Area (GCA)	**6.13**	**100.00**	**2.44**	**100.0**	**5.92**	**100.00**	**4.10**	**100.0**

Source: Author's own estimate based on primary data.

The unit rates charged by diesel pump owners for irrigation services are much higher than that of electric pump owners.

5.3 Cropping Pattern in Eastern UP

The cropping pattern of well owners and water buyers under different modes of energy pricing i.e., connected load (electric well) and unit consumption (diesel well) in eastern UP is presented in Table 3. The crops grown in the study villages are food-grains, pulses, oilseeds, vegetables, cash crops and fodder crops. Paddy and wheat are the dominant crops. During the kharif season, well owners and water buyers under both energy regimes allocate larger portion their land holding under paddy.

In diesel well commands, pump owners allocate about 26% of the gross cropped area under paddy cultivation, whereas in the case of water buyers, it is only 22%. In electric well commands, pump owners allocate 11.51% to paddy and water buyers allocate about 14.8% to paddy. Electric pump owners also grow groundnut. Water buyers in both electric and diesel well commands allocate larger portion of the gross cropped area under green fodder and other vegetables during kharif season as compared to pump owners. Water buyers in diesel well commands grow *Arhar.* Water buyers in electric well commands grow lady's finger.

Major crops grown during winter season are wheat and barley, potato, pea, gram, mustard, linseed and barseem. In electric well commands, the area allocated under wheat, potato, pea, barseem is lower for pump owners whereas gram, mustard, linseed and barley area allocation is higher for water buyers.

In diesel well commands, pump owners allocate larger share of their cropped area under winter crops as compared to water buyers. Such sharp difference is not seen in case of electric well commands. During the summer season, major cops grown in electric pump commands are green fodder, sunflower and vegetables. While all these crops are grown by the electric pump owners, only green fodder is grown by water buyers. In diesel well commands, crops grown during summer season are green fodder and vegetables. Both diesel well owners and water buyers here allocate some area under green fodder.

5.4 Cropping Pattern in North Gujarat

In the case of north Gujarat, major crops grown by the tube well owners under both tariff regimes are green fodder (fodder bajra and alfalfa), food grain crops (jowar and bajra), pulses (black gram and green gram), groundnut and cash crops (cluster bean, cotton and castor). The farmers of this region allocate small area under green fodder throughout the year. Table 4 gives the cropping pattern of well owners in north Gujarat.

During kharif, tube well owners under pro-rata tariff regime allocate slightly larger percentage of the cropped area under cotton, castor and fodder bajra. During winter, tube well owners under flat rate tariff regime are allocating more area under green fodder, wheat and mustard. The tube well owners under pro rata tariff regime allocate slightly larger area under cumin, which is a high valued and sensitive cash crop. The major crops grown during summer season are green fodder and bajra. The area allocated by flat and unit pricing tariff tube wells owners under the bajra crop is about 10% of the gross cropped area.

5.5 Cropping pattern in South Bihar

Cropping pattern of well owners and water buyers under different energy regimes and area allocated by the farmers under different crops in south Bihar are presented in Table 5. In the region, very high monsoon rain results in submergence of most of the cultivated land during kharif season. During this season, farmers grow two crops viz., paddy and green fodder, with larger area under paddy. Out of the gross cropped area, nearly 38% is under paddy and less than 3% is under green fodder. During winter, farmers grow wheat, gram, mustard, barseem (fodder), vegetables (potato, radish and carrot) and coriander. Largest area is under wheat. During summer, farmers grow onion, maize and green fodder.

There is very little difference in kharif cropping pattern found between well owners and water buyers in electric well commands or diesel well commands. During winter, water buyers in electric well commands cultivate gram and carrot. Diesel pump owners and water buyers in both diesel and electric well commands allocate larger area for potato. During summer, only diesel pump owners and water buyers in their commands

Table 4. Cropping Pattern of Well Owner under Different Energy Pricing Regime, North Gujarat

Season	*Name of the Crops*	*Electric Pump Owner – Flat Rate*		*Electric Pump Owner – Unit Pricing*	
		Area (Ha)	*% to GCA*	*Area (Ha)*	*% to GCA*
Kharif	1. Fodder Bajra	0.26	1.58	0.39	2.91
	2. Alfalfa (Green Fodder)	0.36	2.23	0.41	3.05
	3. Jowar	1.07	6.58	1.01	7.52
	4. Bajra	0.98	6.03	0.89	6.63
	5. Black gram	0.81	5.00	0.53	3.90
	6. Green gram	0.76	4.69	0.87	6.47
	7. Groundnut	0.95	5.82	0.51	3.81
	8. Cluster bean	0.85	5.24	1.06	7.87
	9. Cotton	0.63	3.87	0.61	4.52
	10. Castor	1.17	7.17	1.10	8.17
Rabi	1. Alfalfa (Green Fodder)	0.33	2.01	0.28	2.10
	2. Chekudi (Green Fodder)	1.33	8.15	0.23	1.69
	3. Wheat	1.27	7.82	0.96	7.14
	4. Barley	0.23	1.41	0.63	4.66
	5. Rajgaro	0.91	5.62	0.73	5.39
	6. Mustard	1.14	7.00	0.75	5.53
	7. Cumin	0.90	5.50	0.81	6.04
Summer	1. Alfalfa	0.38	2.35	-	-
	2. Fodder Bajra	0.25	1.55	0.41	3.01
	3. Bajra	1.69	10.37	1.29	9.58
	Gross Cropped Area (GCA)	**16.27**	**100.00**	**13.49**	**100.00**

Source: Author's own estimate based on primary data.

Table 5. Cropping Pattern of Well Owner and Water Buyer in Diesel and Electric Well Commands, South Bihar Plain

Name of the Crops	*Electric Pump*				*Diesel Pump*			
	Owner		*Water Buyers*		*Owner*		*Water Buyers*	
	Area (Ha)	*% to GCA*	*Area (Ha)*	*% to GCA*	*Area (Ha)*	*% to GCA*	*Area (Ha)*	*% to GCA*
Kharif Season								
1. Paddy	0.751	38.97	0.467	38.42	1.083	37.68	0.541	38.0[illegible]
2. Masureya (Green fodder)	0.028	1.47	0.016	1.34	0.077	2.69	0.026	1.8[illegible]
3. Maize (Green fodder)	0.004	0.22	0.002	0.17	-	-	-	
Rabi Season								
1. Wheat	0.474	24.63	0.351	28.88	0.625	21.74	0.315	22.1[illegible]
2. Potato	0.134	6.98	0.120	9.86	0.343	11.94	0.145	10.1[illegible]
3. Barseem (Green fodder)	0.042	2.18	0.024	1.97	0.066	2.31	0.029	2.0[illegible]
4. Mustard	0.059	3.05	-	-	0.207	7.21	0.077	5.3[illegible]
5. Gram	-	-	0.011	0.89	-	-	-	
6. Radish	0.025	1.32	0.023	1.85	-	-	-	
7. Carrot	-	-	0.002	0.17	-	-	-	
8. Coriander	-	-	-	-	0.019	0.65	-	
Summer Season								
1. Onion	0.353	18.32	0.170	14.03	0.356	12.38	0.218	15.3[illegible]
2. Maize	0.055	2.87	0.029	2.42	0.093	3.25	0.068	4.7[illegible]
3. NP Chary (Green fodder)	-	-	-	-	0.005	0.16	0.003	0.2[illegible]
Gross Cropped Area (GCA)	**1.93**	**100.0**	**1.22**	**100.0**	**2.88**	**100.0**	**1.42**	**100.[illegible]**

Source: Author's own estimate based on primary data.

Table 6. Water Use, and Water Productivity in Physical and Economic Terms under Electric Pumps, Eastern Uttar Pradesh

Name of the Crops	Electric Pump – Owner				Electric pump – water buyer			
	Depth of irrigation water use (cm)	Water productivity (Kg/m^3)		Net water productivity (Rs/m^3)	Depth of irrigation water use (cm)	Water productivity (Kg/m^3)		Net water productivity (Rs/m^3)
		Main Product	By-product			Main Product	By-product	
Kharif Season								
1. Paddy	7.1	1.9	8.47	3.4	3.61	2.3	10.59	3.6
2. Chary (GF)	1.6	14.3	-	-	0.78	26.2	-	-
3. Vegetable	3.3	6.0	-	26.3	1.73	10.7	-	26.6
4. Lady's Finger	3.2	2.3	-	10.8	2.33	3.9	-	21.2
5. Maize	2.4	2.9	19.4	9.4	1.17	5.7	18.79	18.8
6. Sesamum	0.8	1.2	-	14.2	0.57	1.3	-	9.6
7. Sugarcane	1.1	12.4	-	6.7	0.57	10.6	-	8.1
8. Bajra	3.2	1.5	10.2	4.5	1.43	4.1	30.83	10.5
9. Black gram	2.7	1.9	-	39.1	1.14	2.4	-	46.3
10. Groundnut	3.3	2.6	-	31.7	-	-	-	-
11. Green gram	3.7	2.0	-	46.2	-	-	-	-

Rabi Season								
1. Wheat	6.7	2.4	11.3	7.8	2.93	2.6	12.36	7.
2. Potato	5.0	5.7	-	8.6	2.91	6.0		9.
3. Pea	2.3	1.9	-	13.5	1.33	2.1		15.
4. Barseem	0.7	12.6	-	-	0.46	12.3		
5. Gram	1.8	1.8	-	27.03	0.36	1.6		31.
6. Mustard	1.6	1.4	-	10.8	1.20	1.4		11.
7. Linseed	0.6	0.9	-	4.4	-	-	-	
8. Barley	2.3	3.4	16.0	9.1	0.80	4.3	14.57	14.
Summer Season								
1. MP chary	1.5	11.1	-	-	1.19	10.8	-	
2. Sunflower	1.0	1.0	-	3.40	-	-	-	
3. Vegetables	1.1	2.4	-	15.15	-	-	-	

GF: Green folder.
Source: Author's own estimate based on primary data.

cultivate green fodder. In general, electric pump owners allocate larger area under different crops as compared to electric pump water buyers. There is a similar trend in case of diesel pump command areas.

6. Results and Discussion

6.1 Irrigation Water Application and Crop Water Productivity

In this section, we present the estimates of irrigation water application, physical water productivity (kg/m^3) of main and by-products and net water productivity in economic terms (Rs/m^3) of different crops grown by electric/diesel pump owners and water buyers in their commands. Higher physical productivity of water use for a given crop indicates more efficient use of irrigation water through on farm water management or better farm management through better agronomic input.

Eastern UP: Electric Pumps

Table 6 presents the estimates of irrigation water dosage productivity of water in physical (kg/m^3) and economic terms (Rs. m^3) under electric pump ownership and irrigation water purchase for villages in eastern UP. In case of electric pump owner, total amount of irrigation water applied for crop production is higher as compared to irrigation water buyers. For most of the crops, both physical and economic productivity of water are higher for water buyers than their water-selling counterparts.

Eastern UP: Diesel well Commands

Similar values for diesel pump owners and water buyers are presented in Table 7 (annexure). The cropping pattern of pump owners and water buyers is almost the same, except that water buyers do not grow sugarcane and maize. To economize on irrigation water, water buyers cultivate water efficient crops such as arhar, black gram and green gram during kharif season. The cropping pattern during winter is same for diesel pump owner and water buyers. During summer season, only pump owners grow vegetables.

Table 7 shows that the water buyers in diesel well commands apply less amount of water to their crops as compared to their

Table 7. Water Use, and Water Productivity in Physical and Economic Terms under Diesel Well Command, Eastern Uttar Pradesh

Name of the Crops	*Diesel Pump – Owner*				*Diesel pump – water buyer*			
	Depth of irrigation water use (cm)	*Physical water productivity (Kg/m³)*		*Net water productivity (Rs/m³)*	*Depth of irrigation water use (mm)*	*Water productivity (Kg/m³)*		*Net water productivity (Rs/m³)*
		Main Product	*By-product*			*Main Product*	*By-product*	
Kharif Season								
1. Paddy	15.53	1.86	8.50	2.62	9.09	2.39	8.49	2.92
2. Chary (GF)	1.12	18.44	-	-	0.98	29.74	-	-
3. Vegetables	1.43	0.77	-	0.37	3.43	1.94	-	25.26
4. Arhar	-		-	-	3.05	3.54	-	46.49
5. Maize	2.26	2.56	20.05	13.20	-	-	-	-
6. Sesamum	2.29	0.89	-	17.39	1.14	0.88	-	17.72
7. Sugarcane	1.59	10.13	-	2.50	-	-	-	-
8. Bajra	2.29	3.43	15.54	7.47	1.33	4.41	22.24	17.83
9. Black gram	-	-	-	-	1.14	1.30	-	28.69
10. Green gram	-	-	-	-	1.14	1.73	-	59.98

Rabi Season								
1. Wheat	12.74	2.57	13.34	6.22	8.33	3.50	14.40	7.80
2. Potato	3.70	7.23	-	17.87	2.29	7.40	-	-
3. Pea	3.40	1.56	-	12.19	1.67	1.74	-	12.36
4. Barseem (GF)	0.62	15.97	-	-	0.67	14.57	-	-
5. Gram	4.16	1.58	-	15.33	1.99	1.82	-	17.78
6. Mustard	2.70	1.56	-	10.87	1.44	1.15	-	11.99
7. Linseed	3.43	1.36	-	13.70	1.03	1.53	-	16.77
8. Barley	-	-	-	-	0.91	5.61	14.90	14.90
Summer Season								
1. MP Chary (GF)	0.92	10.68	-		1.43	11.77	-	-
2. Vegetable	1.14	2.41	-	17.49	-	-	-	-

GF: Green fodder

Source: Author's own estimate based on primary data.

Table 8. Water, Use and Water Productivity in Physical and Economic Terms under Flat and Unit Energy Pricing Regime, North Gujarat

Name of the Crops	*Electric Pump Owner – Flat Rate*				*Electric Pump Owner – Unit Pricing*			
	Depth of irrigation (cm)	*Physical water productivity (Kg/m³)*		*Net water productivity (Rs/m³)*	*Depth of irrigation (cm)*	*Water productivity (Kg/m³)*		*Net water productivity (Rs/m³)*
		Main Product	*By-product*			*Main Product*	*By-product*	
Kharif Season								
1. Rajka Bajra	2.57	8.24	-	-	3.93	10.83	-	-
2. Alfalfa (GF)	3.63	5.42	-	-	4.11	5.64	-	-
3. Jowar	10.71	2.76	4.06	8.27	10.14	2.26	1.51	6.62
4. Bajra	9.81	1.00	3.48	5.13	8.94	1.45	2.14	6.39
5. Black gram	8.13	1.07	-	15.14	5.26	1.50	-	16.75
6. Green gram	7.62	0.91	-	10.85	8.73	0.98	-	11.20
7. Groundnut	9.47	0.58	-	3.58	5.14	0.56	-	4.68
8. Cluster	8.52	1.02	-	9.09	10.62	1.11	-	9.37
9. Cotton	6.29	0.41	-	5.34	6.10	1.15	-	19.28
10. Castor	11.66	0.59	-	5.06	11.02	0.62	-	6.52

Rabi Season								
1. Alfalfa (GF)	3.27	3.65	-	-	2.83	5.71	-	-
2. Chekudi (GF)	13.26	2.96	-	-	2.29	5.45	-	-
3. Wheat	12.72	0.82	2.64	4.64	9.63	0.91	2.08	5.17
4. Barley	2.29	0.47	9.33	0.70	6.29	1.11	2.89	6.17
5. Rajgaro	9.14	0.56	-	4.11	7.27	0.89	-	8.50
6. Mustard	11.38	2.86	-	22.25	7.46	2.10	-	23.50
7. Cumin	8.95	0.82	-	36.71	8.14	0.99	-	47.71
Summer Season								
1. Alfalfa (GF)	3.82	2.30	-	-	-	-	-	-
2. Rajka Bajra	2.53	3.27	-	-	4.06	8.15	-	-
3. Bajra	16.87	1.95	2.36	6.43	12.92	1.94	3.02	7.31

GF: Green Fodder.

Source: Author's own estimate based on primary data.

water selling counterparts. Further, the physical productivity of water (kg/m^3) and water productivity in economic terms (Rs/m^3) is higher for water buyers as compared to diesel pump owners for all the crops.

North Gujarat: Flat and Unit Energy Pricing Regimes

Table 8 (annexure) presents similar data for different energy pricing regimes. Electric pump owners pay marginal cost for electricity and therefore maintain higher water productivity in both physical and economic terms for all the crops.

The mean values of irrigation water dosage and water productivity in physical and economic terms for both pump owners and water buyers in electric pump command area in south Bihar plain for all crops are presented in Table 9 (annexure). Water buyers apply less water to their crops, and maintain higher physical water productivity values for many crops in comparison to electric well owners. However, they maintain lower water productivity in economic terms for most of the crops, except radish and onion. This could be due to the higher cost of irrigation water, which eventually reduces the values of numerator of water productivity. Table 10 presents figures of water use and water productivity of diesel well commands of south Bihar plains - both in physical and economic terms.

Diesel pump owners and water buyers grow almost similar crops. For all crops except onion and summer green fodder, water buyers in diesel well commands secure higher physical water productivity as compared to pump owners. Again, for all crops except onion, the water buyers secure higher water productivity in economic terms as compared to pump owners.

Consolidated picture of net water productivity in economic terms for different geographical segments of the study area and for different energy regimes is given in Table 13. The trends are as follows: (A) The net water productivity of water buyers from electric pumps is more both in east UP and south Bihar; (B) Net water productivity of electric pump owners under flat rate provision is comparatively less than that under unit price tariff; (C) Water productivity of electric pump owners in economic terms is less than that of diesel pump owners; and, (D) Economic

Table 9. Water, Use and Water Productivity in Physical and Economic Terms under Electric Well Command, South Bihar Plain

Name of the Crops	*Electric Pump – Owner*				*Electric Pump – Water Buyer*			
	Depth of irrigation water use (cm)	*Physical water productivity (kg/m³)*		*Net water productivity (Rs/m³)*	*Depth of irrigation water use (cm)*	*Water productivity (kg/m³)*		*Net water productivity (Rs/m³)*
		Main Product	*By-product*			*Main Product*	*By-product*	
Kharif Season								
1. Paddy	7.51	2.5	12.90	6.35	4.67	2.69	12.60	8.4
2. Masureya	0.40	11.7	-	-	0.35	10.15	-	-
3. Maize (GF)	2.50	20.5	-	-	1.25	27.34	-	-
Rabi Season								
1. Wheat	4.82	1.8	8.87	5.56	3.51	1.76	7.43	5.8
2. Potato	1.92	13.1	-	43.16	2.00	11.74	-	41.8
3. Barseem	0.56	10.4	-	-	0.40	11.91	-	-
4. Mustard	2.67	1.8	-	20.16	-	-	-	-
5. Gram	-	-	-	-	0.93	0.66	-	9.2
6. Radish	1.27	10.0	-	13.92	0.96	9.59	-	18.5
Summer Season								
1. Onion	4.60	4.4	-	18.48	2.18	5.40	-	23.2
2. Maize	2.07	5.9	-	21.66	1.76	6.86	-	19.1

GF: Green Fodder
Source: Author's own estimate based on primary data.

water productivity of water buyers from electric pumps is less than those buying water from diesel pump sets.

6.2. Livestock Water Productivity

1. Feed and Fodder Use

Farmers of eastern UP keep buffalos, crossbred cows and indigenous cows. Most of the farmers in the region keep a combination of livestock i.e., buffalo with indigenous cow or buffalo with crossbred cow. The reason behind this is that while buffalo milk fetches higher price, cow milk is used for domestic consumption. Green fodder includes chary, barseem and MP chary. *Bhusa* (which is a concentrate of barley flour and mustard cake) is used as dry fodder. In general, farmers feed larger quantity of green fodder for milking animals.

Weighted average of feed and fodder input to livestock worked out for the entire animal lifecycle by farmers for west UP are presented in Table 11.

Table 11. Average Feed and Fodder Used Based on Lifecycle of Animal in eastern UP

	Feed and Fodder Use (kg/day/animal)					
	Electric Pump–Owner			*Electric Pump–Water Purchaser*		
	Buffalo	*Cross-bred Cow*	*Indi-genous Cow*	*Buffalo*	*Cross-bred Cow*	*Indi-genous Cow*
Total Green Fodder	14.09	14.88	13.61	13.77	19.49	14.81
Total dry fodder	10.11	12.07	9.58	8.89	12.73	9.29
Total Concentrates	1.19	1.53	1.13	1.01	1.78	1.17

Source: Author's own estimate based on primary data.

Similar estimates for livestock inputs for farmers in diesel well command in eastern UP were carried out. In case of pump owners, the average amount of feed and fodder fed to livestock were about 36, 43.35 and 31.71 kg/day/animal for buffalo, crossbred cow and indigenous cow, respectively. The corresponding numbers for water buyers were 37.5, 38.06 and 33.72 kg/day/per animal, respectively.

In north Gujarat, estimates of average feed and fodder input were made separately for farmers with metered and non-metered power connections. Farmers with metered power connection on average fed 13.68, 15.77 and 9.39 kg/day/animal of green fodder and 14.96, 16.32 and 12.13 kg/day/animal dry fodder to buffalo, crossbred cow and indigenous cow respectively. Quantity estimates were greater for farmers with non metered connections at 19.56, 23.18, and 9.25 kg/day/animal green fodder and 21.78, 25.64 and 20.95 kg/day/animal dry fodder to buffalo, crossbred cow and indigenous cow, respectively.

Similar estimates are available separately for farmers in the electric well commands and diesel well commands for south Bihar. The average amount of feed and fodder supplied by pump owner farmers in electric well commands to buffalo, crossbred cow and indigenous cow are 24.07, 24.75 and 16.09 kg/day/animal, respectively. The corresponding figures for water buyer-farmers in electric well commands are 21.92, 33.37 and 19.81 kg/day/animal, respectively. In case of diesel well commands, the average feed and fodder fed by diesel pump owner to buffalo, crossbred cow and indigenous cow are 35.34, 25.82 and 21.05 kg/day/animal, respectively. The corresponding figures for water buyers are 26.31, 27.56 and 29 kg/day/animal, respectively.

In general, in eastern UP and south Bihar, water buyers (in both diesel and electric well commands) and farmers with non metered connections fed more input to their cattle.

2. Average Milk Production

The estimates of average milk production from dairy animals for electric well owners, worked out for the entire animal life cycle, are 2.91, 4.64 and 1.81 litres/day/animal for buffalo, crossbred cow and indigenous cow, respectively. This is higher than that for water buyers, in whose case the figures are 2.64, 4.08 and 1.89 litres/day/animal. The corresponding estimates for farmers in the diesel well commands are; for well owners, 2.08, 4.01 and 1.95 litres and for water buyers, the values are 2.23, 3.23 and 2.01, for buffalo, crossbred cow and indigenous cow, respectively.

The estimates of average daily milk production in north Gujarat region are as follows. In case of farmers who have metered electricity connections, the average milk production from buffalo, crossbred cow and indigenous cow are 5.14, 7.5 and 1.91 litres/animal/, respectively. Same estimates for non metered connections are higher at 6.96, 9.32 and 6.43 litres. Such higher yields in the case of farmers with flat rate connections are due to the higher amount of feed and fodder that they are providing to dairy animals.

The estimates of average milk production for different dairy animals in electric well commands in South Bihar are as follows. For pump owners, the average milk production figures from buffalo, crossbred cow and indigenous cow are 2.0, 2.36 and 0.79litres/day/animal, respectively. In the case of water buyers, they are 1.86, 2.97 and 0.88 litres/day/animal. The figures for farmers of diesel well commands are 1.69, 3.53 and 0.96 litre/day/animal respectively, whereas, in case of water buyers, the corresponding values are 1.68, 2.30 and 1.18 litre/day/animal.

3. Water Use for Milk Production

The estimates of the volume of water used for milk production and gross water productivity in milk production in economic terms for buffalo, crossbred and indigenous cows for the sample farmers in the electric well commands in Eastern UP are presented in Table 12. Dairy farmers, who own pump-sets, use larger quantity of water for producing green and dry fodder, in comparison to water buyers. However, the amount of water embedded in the concentrate used for dairy production is higher for water buyers. The net result is that the gross water productivity for milk production is higher for electric pump owner as compared to irrigation water buyers.

For diesel well commands, the estimates of volume of water used for milk production by water sellers are 3.02 m^3, 3.48 m^3 and 2.68 m^3/day/animal for buffalo, crossbred cow and indigenous cow respectively, whereas in case of irrigation water buyers, the corresponding figures are 3.00 m^3, 3.21 m^3 and 2.64 m^3/day/animal. The physical productivity of water for milk production are 0.69, 1.15 and 0.73 litre/m^3, respectively for pump owner and 0.75, 1.00 and 0.76 litre/m^3 for water buyers. The average values of gross water productivity in milk production in economic terms from buffalo, crossbred cow and indigenous

Table 12. Water Use for Milk Production in Electric Pump Command Area, Eastern Uttar Pradesh (m^3/day)

Types of Feed & Fodder	*Electric Pump – Owner*			*Electric Pump – Water Purchaser*		
	Buffalo	*Crossbred Cow*	*Indigenous Cow*	*Buffalo*	*Crossbred Cow*	*Indigenous Cow*
Green Fodder	1.11	1.17	1.08	0.96	1.36	1.03
Dry Fodder	0.89	1.07	0.85	0.72	1.03	0.75
Concentrates	0.61	0.77	0.57	0.49	0.94	0.58
Drinking Water (m^3)	0.018	0.019	0.013	0.018	0.019	0.013
Total Water Use (m^3)	2.63	3.02	2.50	2.19	3.35	2.38
Milk Production (Lt)	2.91	4.64	1.81	2.64	4.08	1.89
Milk WP (Lt/m^3)	1.11	1.54	0.72	1.20	1.22	0.79
Gross WP (Rs/m^3)	11.95	15.52	6.72	12.97	12.31	7.35

Source: Author's own estimates based on primary data.

cow are Rs. 11.03/m^3, 16.13/m^3 and 5.45/m^3 respectively for pump owner and Rs 11.93/m^3, 14.06/m^3 and 11.38/m^3 for water buyers.

For north Gujarat farmers, the estimates of embedded water used for milk production and the water productivity in physical and economic terms are as follows. In the case of farmers who have flat rate connections, average volume of water used for milk production from buffalo, crossbred cow and indigenous cow/ day/animal are 9.77 m^3, 10.43 m^3 and 8.39 m^3, respectively. The corresponding average values of physical productivity of water in milk production (lt/m^3) are 0.53, 0.72 and 0.23, respectively and of gross water productivity in economic terms (Rs/m^3) are is 8.48, 10.43 and 2.96, respectively. In the case of well owner having metered connections, the average values of total volume of water used for milk production are 14.63 m^3, 17.39 m^3 and 10.90m^3/day/animal for buffalo, crossbred cow and indigenous cow, respectively. The corresponding values of physical water productivity for milk production (lt/m^3) are 0.48 litres, 0.54 and 0.59, respectively and of gross water productivity in economic terms (Rs/m^3) are 7.39, 6.47 and 8.85, respectively for buffalo, cross bred cows and indigenous cows respectively.

The estimates of embedded water used in milk production in electric well commands for south Bihar plains are as follows. The electric pump owners use an average of 3.96 m^3, 4.92 m^3 and 2.81 m^3 of water per animal per day for buffalo, crossbred cow and indigenous cow, respectively. The corresponding figures for water buyers in their commands are 4.09 m^3, 5.36 m^3 and 3.37 m^3, respectively. The physical productivity of water used in milk production (lit/m^3) from buffalo, crossbred cow, and indigenous cow in the case of water buyers are 0.45, 0.48 and 0.28. The corresponding values of gross water productivity in economic terms (Rs/m^3) are 7.01, 6.66 and 3.95, respectively.

The estimates available for farmers in diesel well commands are as follows. The diesel pump owners use an average of 4.88, 3.93 and 2.73 m^3 of water/animal/day for buffalo, crossbred cow and indigenous cow, respectively. For water buyers, the corresponding figures are 3.62, 3.18 and 3.04, respectively. The physical productivity of water for milk production (lit/m^3) in case of pump owners for buffalo, cross bred cow and indigenous cow are 0.35, 0.90 and 0.50, respectively. The corresponding figures for water buyers are 0.46, 0.72 and 0.39, respectively. The average values of water productivity in milk production in economic terms (Rs/m^3) are 4.85, 10.60 and 7.00 respectively for buffalo, cross bred crow and indigenous cow. The corresponding figures for water buyers are 6.50, 8.52 and 5.45, respectively.

4. Net Water Productivity in Economic Terms

The net water productivity in economic terms for dairy production was estimated by considering the cost of milk production, which includes the cost of production of dry fodder, green fodder, cattle feed and other expenses for maintaining dairy animals in the water productivity analysis. The total cost of green fodder, dry fodder and concentrate, the income from milk and cow dung and total and effective water use for dairy production were estimated. Based on these data, both the net water productivity and effective net water productivity in economic terms were estimated for all the three locations (i.e., for well owners, and water buyers in electric and diesel well commands in eastern UP and south Bihar and electric well owners with and without metered connections in north Gujarat).

The results for farmers in electric commands in Eastern UP are presented in Table 14.

Table 14 shows that well owners secure higher net water productivity in milk production than water buyers for all types of livestock. Analysis of similar estimates for diesel well commands in eastern UP shows the following. The values of net water productivity in economic terms for the pump owners are 1.74, 6.89 and 0.46 for buffalo, cross bred cow and indigenous cows, respectively. The corresponding values for water buyers are 0.43, 1.8 and -1.72. Comparing electric and diesel well commands, it appears that pump owners in electric well commands secure highest effective net water productivity in economic terms, followed by water buyers in their command, diesel pump owners and lowest for buyers of water from diesel pump owners.

In north Gujarat, the average values of effective net water productivity in economic terms for milk production from buffalo,

Table 14. Water Productivity in Economic Terms in Milk Production, Electric Pump, Eastern Uttar Pradesh

Types of Feed & Fodder	*Electric Pump – Owner*			*Electric Pump – Water Purchaser*		
	Buffal o	*CB Cow*	*Indigenous Cow*	*Buffalo*	*CB Cow*	*Indigenous Cow*
1. Green fodder (Rs)	3.29	3.50	3.29	4.52	6.4	4.9
2. Dry fodder (Rs)	3.03	3.62	3.03	2.67	3.82	2.79
3. Concentrates (Rs)	6.51	8.39	6.51	5.54	9.58	6.38
4. Total expenditure (Rs/day)	12.84	15.52	12.84	12.73	19.80	14.03
5. Milk production (Lt)	2.91	4.64	1.81	2.64	4.50	1.89
6. Gross income from milk (Rs)	31.39	46.86	16.83	28.44	45.48	17.51
7. Income from dung (Rs/day)	0.50	0.50	0.50	0.5	0.5	0.5
8. Gross income (Rs/day)	31.89	47.36	17.33	28.94	45.98	18.01
9. Net income (Rs/day)	19.05	31.84	4.50	16.21	26.18	3.98
10 Net water productivity (Rs/m^3)	7.25	10.55	1.80	7.39	7.82	1.67

Source: Author's own estimate based on primary data.

crossbred cow and indigenous cow under flat energy pricing regime are Rs 3.73/m^3, Rs 5.88/m^3 and Rs -1.85/m^3, respectively. In case of farmers under pro rata pricing regime, the values are Rs 3.31/m^3, Rs 2.29/m^3 and Rs 3.37/m^3, respectively. It is clear that over all effective net water productivity is higher under pro rata pricing regime.

In south Bihar, the estimates of average effective net water productivity in milk production for electric well commands for electric pump well owner are Rs 2.18/m^3, 1.96/m^3 and -1.0/m^3 and for water buyers are the values are Rs 1.65/m^3, 3.89/m^3 and -0.64/m^3 for buffalo, crossbred cow and indigenous cow respectively. For diesel well commands, pump owner's effective net water productivity in economic terms (Rs/m^3) are -0.47, 5.68 and -250; and for water buyers are 0.07, 2.09 and -1.26, for buffalo, cross bred cow and indigenous cow, respectively.

6.3 Farm Level Water Productivity

Using more water means paying more for the pump rental services. Farmers should try and economize on the use of water, though it is not a scarce resource in eastern UP and south Bihar. Farms are the unit for many investment decisions by farmers in agriculture including water allocation decisions. They try to optimize water allocation over the entire farm, rather than individual crops, to maximize their returns. Hence, the impact of power pricing on the efficiency with which water is used by farmers should be analyzed by looking at the water productivity for the entire farming system.

Our analysis clearly shows that the farm level water productivity is much higher for water buyers in diesel well commands in eastern UP and south Bihar. In electric well commands also, the differences exist in favour of water buyers in spite of very low marginal cost of using water (Rs.0.65/m^3). The farm level water productivity is much higher for farmers who are confronted with marginal cost of electricity in north Gujarat as compared to those who pay for electricity based on connected load. The water productivity improvement in highest in eastern UP in the diesel well commands, where the water buyers' marginal cost of using irrigation service is Rs. 2.81/m^3. Water productivity difference is also quite substantial in north

Table 15. Farming System Level Water Productivity in Agriculture under Different Pricing Regimes (Rs/m³)

Name of the Regions	*Name of the district*	*Electric Well Command*		*Diesel Well Command*	
		Flat Rate	*Unit Pricing*	*Well owner*	*Water buyers*
North Gujarat	Banaskantha	6.20	7.90	NA	NA
		Well Owner	Water Buyer	Well Owner	Water Buyer
Eastern UP	Varanasi and Mirzapur	10.95	11.18	8.67	12.89
South Bihar Plains	Patna	9.28	10.13	11.97	12.43

Gujarat between farmers with flat rate connection and those with metered connections.

Further, comparison between electric well owners and diesel well owners in both the locations substantiates the earlier point that positive marginal cost promotes efficient use of water at the farm level.

6.4. Equity in Access to Groundwater

As discussed in the methodology, the impacts of energy pricing on access equity in groundwater can be examined by studying how the increase in cost of production of groundwater influences the price at which water is traded. This can be studied by analyzing the changes in monopoly price ratios[4] for water traded in the market with change in mode of pricing. In the case of north Gujarat, we had a real life situation of farmers shifting from flat rate system to the pro rata system of electricity consumption. However, these farmers are not into water trading. Hence, the water markets in electric and diesel well commands of eastern UP and south Bihar were compared vis-à-vis the monopoly price ratios and the volume of water traded.

Through this analysis, we would test one dominant hypothesis by Shah (1993) that under flat rate system of pricing, well owners would have a strong incentive to pump out more water and as a result, the price at which water is traded in the market would come down, and come close to the cost of production of water. Kumar (2007) had challenged this hypothesis arguing that it is rather the number of potential sellers against the number of potential buyers citing evidences from Mussafarpur in Bihar.

Table 16 shows that in eastern UP, the MPR (monopoly price ratio) was higher in the case of electric well commands than that in diesel pump well commands. While the price charged by electric pump owners was 3.6 times more than their cost of pumping, the price charged by diesel pump owners is only 1.8 times higher than their cost of pumping. In south Bihar, the trend is just the opposite. The average price charged by electric well owners is lower than the implicit cost of pumping water

Table 16. Selling Price of Well Water and the Monopoly Price Ratio under different Pricing Regimes

Name of the Regions	*Name of the district*	*Selling Price of Water and Monopoly Price Ratio in*			
		Electric Well Command		*Diesel Well Command*	
		Selling Price	*MPR*	*Selling Price*	*MPR*
North Gujarat	Banaskantha				
Eastern UP	Varanasi and Mirzapur	0.65	3.50	2.81	1.85
South Bihar Plains	Patna	0.70	0.90	2.15	1.15

(Rs.0.70/m^3 against Rs. 0.77/m^3). Whereas the average price charged by diesel well owners (Rs. 2.15/m^3) is higher than the cost they incur for pumping groundwater (Rs.1.87/m^3).

These are based on average figures of cost and price. A look at the cost and price figures for individual wells brings out a different picture. A few farmers have very high implicit cost of pumping groundwater, higher than the selling price. The reason is that the capital cost of the well and the pump set constitutes a major chunk of the cost, and the unit cost becomes high only because the wells run for fewer hours[5]. But, the monopoly price charged by many other farmers is higher under flat rate system for electric wells, as compared to those for diesel wells. These are farmers who have larger holdings due to which the pumping becomes very low.

Another interesting phenomenon found in both electric and diesel well commands is that the selling price of water is more or less same across the farmers, though the unit cost of pumping water varies across farmers. The selling price is decided by the market conditions irrespective of the cost farmers incur for pumping water (Kumar *et al.*, 2001). Fewer numbers of potential sellers against a large number of potential buyers would increase the monopoly power of well owners. This is due to the poor transferability of water. Perhaps this is what is happening in the village with electric pumps in eastern UP. On the other hand, presence of large number of sellers against a few buyers would reduce the monopoly power of well owners. They would be forced to sell water at prices conditioned by the market (Kumar, 2007). Perhaps this is what is happening in the village with electric pumps in south Bihar.

In nutshell, the mode of pricing of electricity does not influence the monopoly prices being charged by well owners in the market. On the other hand, the flat rate pricing puts large well owners in a very advantageous position as they could bring down their implicit unit cost of pumping groundwater.

6.5. Groundwater Pumping by Farmers

Often the distinction between efficiency and sustainability is not made (Moench and Kumar, 1993). Pricing would introduce

Table 17. Average Hours of Groundwater Use by Farmers under Different pricing Regimes

Name of the Regions	*Name of the district*	*Groundwater Pumpage by Electric Pump Owners*		*Diesel pump*	
		Unit Pricing	*Flat Rate*	*Well owner*	*Water buyers*
North Gujarat	*Banaskantha*	*303.88*	*443.88*	*NA*	*NA*
		Groundwater Use in Electric Well Command by		Groundwater Use in Diesel Well Command by	
		Well Owner	Water Buyer	Well Owners	Water Buyers
Eastern UP	Varanasi and Mirzapur	175.38	183.93	222.23	148.00
South Bihar	Patna	329.97	249. 74	231.11	197.91

efficiency, but may not ensure sustainability of resource use (Kumar, 2005). The total amount of groundwater pumpage per unit of cultivated area is determined by the cropping pattern and the cropping intensity. Increased allocation of cultivable area under highly water intensive crops would increase the demand for irrigation water by a farmer. Hence, total pumpage per unit cultivated area could be a good indicator of the sustainability impacts of change in mode of pricing on groundwater. However, farmers with very small land holding size are more likely to intensify cropping, which would increase the total pumpage. This would mean larger hours of pumpage per ha of cultivable area as value of numerator would increase and that of denominator would reduce.

But, the results from three locations show that the pumpage of groundwater per unit area of cultivated land is lower for water buyers, in spite of them having lower sized holdings. The data for north Gujarat shows that in spite of having smaller sized land holdings (2.95 ha against 3.45 ha), the pump owners having metered connections use much less water per unit of land as compared to their counterparts having flat rate connections (303.88 hours per year against 443.88 per year). The difference in aggregate pumping is much higher between farmers with meters and those without meters. Such a high reduction is water usage per unit of cultivated land, which is disproportionately higher than the reduction in net return per unit of land, is made possible through high improvements in water productivity in economic terms.

But, in spite of slight reduction in pumping, the net return from unit of land is higher for water buyers in eastern UP and South Bihar plains. This is achieved through high enhancement in water productivity through selection of crops that are less water consuming and high valued.

8. Important Findings

1. Farmers who have metered power connection not only incur marginal cost of using well water, but also pay higher price for every unit of irrigation water (Rs/m^3) as compared to their counterparts having flat rate connections. Similarly, farmers who are buyers of water from electric pump owners and diesel

Table 18. Net Income from Crop and Milk Production, three Locations

Type of Well Command	*Type of farmer*	*Gross cropped area (Ha)*	*Net income from crops (Rs)*	*Net income from dairying (Rs/day)*	*Total Farm level Income (Rs)*	*Farm level net income (Rs/Ha)*
Electric Well	Well owner	5.29	124587.3	7152.3	131739.6	24880
	Water buyer	2.21	54637.6	6165.0	60802.6	27570
Diesel Well	Well owner	5.66	74764.5	7429.5	82193.9	14528
	Water buyer	3.79	62323.1	6260.6	68583.7	18075
Electric Well	Flat Rate	13.35	369119.7	30048.0	768287.4	57531
	Metered	11.77	311806.9	45636.0	669250.2	56882
Electric Well	Well owner	3.14	120477	10292.6	130769.5	210345
	Water buyer	1.70	61517.7	8130.9	76023.9	190031
Diesel Well	Well owner	2.49	140105.0	9958.1	150063.6	191387
	Water buyer	1.60	71810.0	12232.2	84042.5	197895

Authors' own estimate based on primary data.

well owners in eastern UP and south Bihar also incur positive marginal cost of using irrigation water pay higher unit costs of irrigation water compared to water selling counterparts.

2. The water buyers (in eastern UP and south Bihar) and farmers who have metered electricity connections allocate some amount of land for highly water-efficient crops, which are also less water consuming.

3. When confronted with positive marginal cost of irrigation water, farmers are encouraged to use water more efficiently. This is implied by the fact that water buyers in diesel and electric well commands, and the farmers who have meter connections secure higher water productivity in physical terms (kg/m^3) for most crops as compared to water selling well owners.

4. When confronted with positive marginal cost of irrigation water, farmers would be encouraged to improve economic efficiency of water use. This is implied by the fact that water buyers in diesel and electric well commands, and farmers who have metered connections secured higher WP in economic terms for many crops as compared to water selling well owners.

5. When confronted with positive marginal cost of irrigation water, farmers are encouraged to use water more efficiently over the entire farm from economic point of view. When confronted with higher cost of irrigation water, the farmers venture into adopting farming system and optimizing use of inputs to secure higher returns from every unit of water to offset the increase in costs of irrigation. This is supported by the evidence that water buyers in diesel and electric well commands, and the farmers who have metered connections secure higher water productivity at the farm level as compared to water selling well owners. The diesel well owners also secure higher water productivity at the farm level as compared to electric well owners, as shown by data from south Bihar.

6. Higher net water productivity in economic terms (Rs/m^3) which farmers obtain even at high cost of irrigation water is indicative of the fact that it is possible to keep irrigation costs high enough to induce improved efficiency in water use in both physical and economic terms without compromising on farming prospects.

7. The monopoly price charged by well owners is not a function of the mode of energy pricing. The farmers who are confronted with zero marginal cost of using energy charge even higher monopoly rates for water as compared to diesel well owners. On the other hand, the flat rate pricing puts large well owners in a very advantageous position as they could bring down their implicit unit cost of pumping groundwater. Therefore, pro rata pricing of electricity would promote equity in groundwater use, if many farmers from within the same area have access to electricity connections.

8. The water buyers in diesel and electric well commands are using much less water for every unit of net cultivated area as compared to the farmers who are well owners. In addition, the farmers who are using metered power connections are using less amount of water per unit of cultivated land. Such reduction in groundwater pumping, with a disproportionately lower reduction in net return from unit of land in the case of farmers with metered connections in north Gujarat, and no reduction in net returns in the case of eastern UP and south Bihar plains, is possible through water productivity improvement in economic terms. This indicates that introducing marginal cost for water and electricity not only promotes efficient use of water, as manifested by higher farm-level water productivity, but also more sustainable use of water.

9. Conclusions

Our analysis shows that introducing marginal cost for electricity motivates farmers to use water more efficiently at the field level from physical, agronomic and economic point of view through careful use of irrigation water, use of better agronomic inputs and optimizing costly inputs. Also, it would motivate farmers to use water more efficiently at the farm level through careful use of irrigation water in crops; better agronomic inputs; optimizing costly inputs for crops; careful selection of crops and cropping patterns, and livestock composition that give higher return from every unit of water and low water consuming crops. It also shows that higher cost of irrigation water affected by higher energy cost will not lead to lower net return from every unit of water used as the farmers modify farming system itself in response to increase in energy cost.

The analysis also shows that changing the power tariff structure from flat rate to pro-rata would not have any adverse effects on equity of access in groundwater in terms of increasing the monopoly power of well owners. This is because the monopoly prices are largely governed by the number of potential water sellers against the number of potential buyers of water in an area. In addition, pro rata pricing has significant impact in reducing groundwater pumpage from every unit of irrigated land, which is disproportionately higher than the reduction in net return from unit of land. This shows positive impact on sustainability of groundwater use.

The empirical evidences further reinforce the fact that the arguments against pricing are flawed. One argument against price change is the higher marginal cost of supplying electricity under metered system, could reduce the net social welfare as a result of reduction in: 1] demand for electricity and groundwater; and 2] net surpluses individual farmers could generate from cropping. The second argument is that for power tariff levels to be in the responsive region of power demand curve, prices are often so high that it may become socially unviable.

It is understood that the aggregate demand for electricity and groundwater in irrigation is a function of the demand rates (electricity and water requirements per unit of land), and the total area under irrigation. The empirical analyses from all locations show that the demand for water/energy per unit of land was lower for water buyers due to increase in unit price of water/energy. However, the net income surpluses from every unit of water/energy used increased. Also, the net aggregate return was higher in Bihar and Uttar Pradesh. Overall, the net returns per unit of land were marginally lower for farmers who paid on pro rata basis in north Gujarat.

But this is not a concern, as in water-scarce regions like north Gujarat farmers would not have constraint of land in maximizing returns. With higher water productivity (Rs/m^3), they would be able to maintain the same level of net farm return as in the past with much less amount of water. This is more so because there is no need for regulating power supply under metered system of pricing, whereas it is compulsory under flat rate system of pricing to control the revenue losses to the electricity boards. Now, if one considers the positive externalities on the society due to energy and water saving resulting from their efficient use, the net social welfare would be even more.

10. Directions for Policy

The evidence provided in the paper corroborates with the earlier evidence provided by Kumar (2005) to the effect that raising pro-rata power tariff to levels that induce improvement in productivity of energy and water use would not have any adverse impacts on the economic viability of farming. This means that introducing high power tariff in the farm sector would be socio-economically viable. But, the proposals for metering electricity in the farm sector, and metering electricity and introducing pro rata pricing get rejected on flimsy grounds. One of them is that farmers are rural vote banks, and that raising power tariff is highly unpopular as it would make farming less attractive. It is to an extent true that merely raising power tariff would only lead to increasing the cost of irrigation in areas where power supply is of very poor quality. Another argument against metering and pro rata pricing is the transaction cost of metering large number of wells in remote rural areas.

But, one important factor that is missed out in the entire discussion on raising power tariff is the improved quality of power supply possible under metered tariff. Under flat rate tariff, it is important to regulate the power supply to reduce the negative effects on welfare such as excessive pumping and misuse of groundwater and electricity (Shah, 1993) and inequity in distribution of subsidy benefits and greater revenue losses to the electricity board. This affects the quality of irrigation. But, as Kumar (2005) notes, this is not necessary under pro rata pricing. Improving the quality of power supply would change the energy-irrigation nexus as we have seen in the analysis presented in this paper and also earlier analysis by Kumar (2005).

Hence, these are rather excuses used by officials and other functionaries of electricity departments to cover up the revenue losses due to poor operational efficiencies, resulting from transmission losses, and distribution losses which include thefts. Also, unmetered connections attract more bribe, as detecting power theft is much more difficult under flat rate system. A recent survey in north Gujarat showed that farmers are resorting to under-reporting of connected load, after the implementation of the much-publicized *Jyotigram Yojna*[6] in villages, which made direct power theft from feeder line difficult. Obviously, detecting thefts like this would require field visits by the vigilance team, and checking the connected load. Hence, the flat rate system is patronized by a section of the engineering staff of electricity boards. As a result, the state governments find it rather convenient to continue with such policies. Such degenerative policies act as a major constraint to improving water productivity in agriculture. But, it is important to recognize the fact that resistance to metering is not from the farming lobby, but from the bureaucracy itself.

References

Central Ground Water Board (1998) *Groundwater Problems of Mehsana District*, report, Central Ground Water Board, West-Central region, Ahmedabad.

Government of India (1999) Government of India (1999) Integrated Water Resource Development: A Plan for Development, Report of the National Commission for Integrated Water Resources Development Vol. I, Ministry of Water Resources, Government of India, New Delhi.

Government of India (2002) Annual Report on the Working of State Electricity Boards and Electricity Department – 2001-02, Planning Commission (Power and Energy Division), Government of India, May, 2002. Visit us at: http://planningcommission.nic.in/

Howes, S and R. Murugai (2003) Incidence of Agricultural Power Subsidies: An Estimate, *Economic and Political Weekly*, April 19.

Kumar, M. Dinesh (2005) Impact of Electricity Prices and Volumetric Water Allocation on Groundwater Demand Management: Analysis from Western India, *Energy Policy*, 33 (1): 39-51

Kumar, M. Dinesh (2007) *Groundwater Management in India: Physical, Institutional and Policy Alternatives*, New Delhi: Sage Publications.

Kumar, M. Dinesh and O.P. Singh (2001) Market Instruments for Demand Management in the Face of Scarcity and Overuse of Water in Gujarat. *Water Policy*, 3 (5): 387-403.

Kumar, M. Dinesh, OP Singh and Katar Singh (2001) Groundwater Development and Its Socio-economic and Ecological Consequences in Sabarmati River Basin", Monograph-2, Anand: INREM Foundation.

Kumar, M. Dinesh and P. J. Patel (1995) Depleting buffer and farmers' response: study of villages in Kheralu, Mehsana, Gujarat. In: Moench, M. (Ed.), Electricity Prices: A Tool for Groundwater Management in India?. VIKSAT-Natural Heritage Institute, Ahmedabad.

Kumar, M. Dinesh, O.P. Singh, Madar Samad, Chaitali Purohit and Malkit Singh Didyala (2008) Water Productivity of Irrigated Agriculture in India: Potential Areas for Improvement, proceedings of the 7th Annual Partners Meet, IWMI-Tata Water Policy Research Program "Managing Water in the Face of Growing Scarcity, Inequity and Diminishing Returns: Exploring Fresh Approaches," ICRISAT Campus, Patancheru, 2-4 April, 2008.

Moench, M., ed. (1995) *Electricity Pricing: A Tool for Groundwater Management in India?* Ahmedabad: VIKSAT-Natural Heritage Institute.

Saleth, R. Maria (1997) Power Tariff Policy for Groundwater Regulation: Efficiency, Equity and Sustainability. *Artha Vijnana*, XXXIX (3): 312-322.

Shah, Tushaar (1993) *Water Markets and Irrigation Development: Political Economy and Practical Policy*. Bombay: Oxford University Press, 1993.

Shah, Tushaar, Christopher Scott, Avinash Kishore and Abhishek Sharma (2004) *Energy Irrigation Nexus in South Asia: Improving Groundwater Conservation and Power Sector Viability*, IWMI Research Report # 70, Colombo, Sri Lanka.

Singh, O. P. (2004), Water Productivity of Milk Production in North Gujarat, Western India, Proceedings of the *2nd Asia Pacific Association of Hydrology and Water Resources (APHW) Conference*, Vol. 1: 442-449.

Footnotes

1. Due to subsidised power supply to agriculture sector, the annual losses to State Electricity Board are estimated to be Rs. 26000 crore and it is growing with a compound growth rate of 26 per cent per annum.

2. In the hard rock areas of Gujarat, farmers are unable to run their pump for 6-8 hours continuously due to lack of water availability in the wells and higher rate of drawdown, resulting farmers are forced to run tube wells only for a 2-3 hours at a time and stop pump for 3-4 hours to accumulate water in the well.

3. Due to interruptions in power supply accompanied by poor quality of power, farmers do not have absolute control over irrigation water. Under this situation, they show increasing tendency to over irrigate the crops when electricity is available. Water delivery often does not coincide with the critical stages of watering of crops. The result is that they are getting less output per unit of irrigation water.

4. It is the ratio of the price of water and its actual cost of production incurred by the well owner.

5. Such an approach to working out the unit cost, in which the capital cost is considered along with O & M, is valid only in long term marginal cost calculations. But, in reality the farmers do not consider this cost in their decision making framework is for short time duration. Therefore, the real marginal cost of pumping is very low, which means the MPR is high.

6. It involved separation of feeder line for agriculture and domestic power supply.

5

When do Micro-Irrigation Technologies Become the Best Bet Technologies?

ABSTRACT

The ultimate objective of this research is to find out under what conditions micro irrigation system offer the best bet technology, and what benefits it can yield. The research aims at determining the potential benefits from the use of MI systems in India. This is done through assessing: (a) the conditions that are favourable for MI system adoption; (b) the field level and aggregate level impacts of the systems on water use; and (c) the yield and economic benefits from adoption. The research also aims at assessing the potential future coverage of MI systems in India, and the potential reduction in aggregate water requirement in crop production.

The findings with regard to constraints in MI system adoption are: (i) lack of independent source of water and pressurizing device for many farmers; (ii) poor quality of groundwater in many semi arid and arid regions; (iii) the mismatch between water delivery schedules and irrigation schedules required in MI systems in surface irrigation systems; (iv) cropping systems that dominate field crops in semi arid regions; (v) dominance of small and marginal farmers, and small plot sizes; (vi) low opportunity costs of pumping groundwater due to lack of well-defined water rights; (vii) negative technical externalities in groundwater use; (viii) poor extension services; and (viii) poor administration of subsidies.

The other findings are: (1) the extent of real water-saving and water productivity gains at the field level from adoption of MI systems varies across crops, climate, geo-hydrology and type of MI devices used; (2) the potential benefits of MI systems in terms of real field level water saving are likely to be realized in semi arid and arid areas with deep water table conditions, for widely spaced row crops; (3) the economics of pressurized MI systems depend on the capital cost of the system, size of the plot, type of crop irrigated, extent of water and energy saving and the market value of the produce; (4) being capital intensive, the economic viability of MI systems is sound for high valued cash crops and orchards, especially in areas where groundwater availability is extremely limited; and (5) in many areas, due to flat rate system of pricing and heavy subsidy in electricity, zero opportunity cost of using groundwater, energy and water saving does not result in cost saving and improved economic returns from MI.

The future potential of MI systems to improve basin water productivity is primarily constrained by the physical characteristics of the basins vis-à-vis the opportunities they offer for real water-saving at the field level and basin water productivity improvements, and area under crops that are conducive to MI in those basins. Preliminary analysis shows a very modest potential of MI systems to the tune of 5.6 m. ha, with the impact of drip systems in reducing aggregate water requirement for crop production to the tune of 44.46 BCM.

1. Introduction

Demand management becomes the key to the overall strategy for managing scarce water resources (Molden *et al.*, 2001). Since agriculture is the major competitive user of diverted water in India (GOI, 1999), demand management in agriculture in water-scarce and water-stressed regions would be central to reducing the aggregate demand for water to match with the available future supplies, thereby reducing the extent of water stress that the country is likely to face (Kumar, 2003a and Kumar 2003b). Improving water productivity in agriculture is important in the overall framework for managing agricultural water demand, thereby increasing the ability of agencies and other interested parties to transfer the water thus "saved" to economically more efficient or other high priority domestic and industrial use sectors (Barker *et al.*, 2003; Kijne *et al.*, 2003).

Three dimensions of water productivity include: physical productivity, expressed in kg per unit of water consumed; combined physical and economic productivity expressed in terms of net return per unit of water consumed, and economic productivity expressed in terms of net income returns from a given amount of water consumed against the opportunity cost of using the same amount of water (Kijne *et al.*, 2003). The discussion in the present paper would be largely on the first parameter, i.e., physical productivity. There are two major ways of improving the physical productivity of water used in irrigated agriculture. *First*: the water consumption or depletion for producing a certain quantum of biomass for the same amount of land is reduced. *Second*: the yield generated for a particular crop is enhanced without changing the amount of water consumed or depleted per unit of land. Often these two improvements can happen together with an intervention either on the agronomic side or on the water control side.

There are several conceptual level issues in defining the term "water saving" and irrigation efficiency. This is because with changing contexts and interests, the "unit of analysis" changes from field to farm to irrigation systems to river basins. With the concepts of "dry" and "wet" water saving", which capture the phenomena such as "return flows from field" and "depleted water", becoming dominant in irrigation science literature in the last one decade, the old concepts of "water saving" and irrigation efficiencies have become obsolete. The real water saving or the "wet water" saving in irrigated production at the field level can come only from reduction in depleted water and not the water applied (Molden *et al.*, 2001). But, there are methodological and logical issues involved in estimating the depletion fraction of the water effectively applied to the crop. These are due to the complex considerations, including agronomic, hydrologic, geo-hydrological and geo-chemical, in determining the "depletion" fraction. Nevertheless, for the limited purpose of analysis, throughout this paper, "water saving" refers to "wet" water saving.

Water productivity is an important driver in projecting future water demands (Amarasinghe *et al.*, 2005; Kijne *et al.*, 2003).

Efficient irrigation technologies help establish greater control over water delivery (water control) to the crop roots, reduce the non-beneficial evaporation from field and non-recoverable percolation[1], and return flows into "sinks" and often increases the beneficial ET, though the first component could be very low for field crops. Water productivity improves with reduction in depleted fraction and yield enhancement. Since at the theoretical level, water productivity improvements in irrigated agriculture can result in saving of water used for crop production, any technological interventions which improve the crop yields are also, in effect, water saving technologies. Hence, water saving technologies in agriculture can be broadly classified into three: water saving crop technologies; water saving and yield enhancing irrigation technologies; and, yield improving crop technologies.

There are several technologies and practices for water-saving in irrigation. They include: (1) broad beds or small border irrigation; (2) improved furrow irrigation (surge, cutback, proper management) (3) laser leveling of fields; (4) plastic mulches and tunnels; (5) improved soil moisture retention sub-surface barriers; (6) alternative wetting and drying for rice; (7) system of rice intensification; (8) direct seeding of rice; (9) aerobic rice; (10) on-farm storage; and, (11) allowing better control and timing of surface irrigation (micro-irrigation, sprinklers and their variants). But, only micro irrigation technologies, which are based on plastics, are dealt with in this report.

India stands 27th in terms of the scale of adoption of water-saving and yield enhancing micro irrigation devices (Source: www.oznet.ksu.edu/sdi/News/Whatisnew.htm). There are several constraints to adoption of MI devices. These are physical, socio-economic, financial, institutional—pricing, subsidies, extension service—and policy-related related in nature (Narayanamoorthy, 1997; Kumar, 2002a). Nevertheless, a systematic attempt to find out the conditions under which MI systems become a best bet technology, and assess the magnitude of reduction in water requirement possible through them is hardly ever made. Such efforts are crucial from the point of view of assessing our ability to address future water scarcity problems at the regional and national level.

The ultimate objective of this research is to find out under what conditions micro irrigation system offer the best bet. It aims at determining the potential benefits from the use of MI systems. This includes assessing: (a) the conditions that are suitable or unsuitable for MI systems; (b) the field level and aggregate level impacts of the systems on water use; and (c)165 the yield and economic benefits due to adoption of MI system. The research also aims at assessing the potential future coverage of MI systems in India, and the reduction in aggregate water requirement in crop production possible with that.

This chapter first provides an over-view of the benefits of "MI technologies. It then covers the present spread of MI systems in India. It deals with the potential physical and economic impacts of MI systems in India. This is based on analysis of: (i) physical, socio-economic and institutional constraints for its adoption in the country; (ii) field level water saving, and impacts on drivers of water demand; (iii) and cost-benefit analysis of MI systems for different crops under different socio-economic conditions, and policy environments. A macro level analysis of the potential future impact of drip systems on agricultural water requirements in India is provided. This is done by: (a) assessing the actual cropped areas that can be brought under drip systems in the basins which would benefit from them in terms of water productivity improvements; and b] potential future reduction in water requirement of selected crops through drips. The fifth section deals with the impact of existing water and energy related policies in India, and discussions on institutional and policy alternatives for spreading MI system adoption.

2. Available Water-saving and Yield Improving Irrigation Technologies in Indian Agriculture and their Potentials

Water-saving and yield enhancing irrigation devices which are in use in India and the crops for which they can be used are given in Table 1. While listing these devices, we have considered their technical feasibility for the crop in question and their actual preference by farmers, and are not based on their analysis of the social costs and benefits of using them. Synthesizing the information provided in the last column, it is clear that highest growth in water productivity would be possible with green house, which reduces the consumptive use of water and enhances the yield substantially.

Table 1. Nature of Water Saving for Different Crops under Different Types of Efficient Irrigation Devices

Sr. No.	*Name of water-saving and yield enhancing micro irrigation technology*	*Names of crops for which the technology can be used ideally*	*Nature of Saving in Applied Water*
1.	Pressurized drip systems (inline and on-line drippers, drip tape)	All fruit crops; cotton; castor; fennel; maize; coconut; arecanut; chilly; cauliflower; cabbage; ladies finger; tomatoes; egg plant; gourds; mulberry; sugarcane; water melon[2]; flowers	1. Reduces non-beneficial evaporation (E) from the area not covered by canopy 2. Reduces deep percolation 3. Water saving also comes from reduction in evaporation from fallow after harvest 4. Extent of water saving higher during initial stages of plant growth 5. Significant yield and quality improvement.
2.	Overhead (movable) sprinklers (including rain guns)	Wheat; pearl millet; sorghum; cumin; mustard; cow pea; chick pea, grasslands and pastures, tea estates	1. Reduces the losses in conveyance 2. Improves the distribution efficiency slightly3. Reduces deep percolation 3. Yield growth marginal
3.	Micro sprinklers	Potato; ground nut; alfalfa; garlic and onion, herbs and ornamentals	1. Reduces the seepage and evaporation losses in conveyance. 2.

		Reduces deep percolation over furrow irrigation and small border irrigation 3. Yield growth and quality improvement significant.
4. Plastic mulching	Potato; ground nut; cotton; castor; fennel; brinjal; chilly; cauliflower; cabbage; ladies finger; flowers; maize	1. Completely checks the evaporation component of ET 2. Stops non-beneficial evaporation (E), kills weeds and pests 3. Extent of water saving higher over drip irrigation 4. Faster germination and significant yield growth.
5. Green houses	All vegetables, high valued fruits such as strawberry; and exotic flowers, nurseries, vegetative propagation	1. Controls the ambient temperature and humidity, 2. Checks the wind, thereby reducing transpirative demand of plant. 3. The water-saving is highest as compared to other technologies 4. Substantial yield growth, quality improvement and nutrient savings.
6. Micro tube drips	All horticultural and plantation crops	1. Reduces non-beneficial evaporation 2. Distribution uniformity is poor and depends on number of micro tubes on a lateral.

3. Contribution of Micro-irrigation Technologies in Indian Agriculture

3.1 Present Spread of Micro-irrigation Technologies in Indian Agriculture

There were no systematic attempts in the past to assess the spread for water-saving irrigation technologies in India. The most recent data shows that nearly 1.3 m ha of irrigated land is under drip irrigation (see Narayanamoorthy, 2004b).

Researchers cited high initial cost (including mis-targetted subsidies), clogging of drippers and cracking of pipes, lack of adequate technical inputs, damages done by rodents; high cost of spare components; and insufficient extension education effort as the major problems in the slow rate of adoption of drips. The National Committee on Irrigation and Drainage also added factors such as salinity hazards to the list of problems (GOI, 1994). Difficulty in inter-cultivation was found as another reason for non-adoption by Shiyani and others (1999), where as Palanisamy and others (2002) cited joint ownership of wells as additional reason for non-adoption based on their study in Coimbatore (Tamil Nadu). However, some of the problems listed above such as clogging, lack of adequate technical inputs and high cost of spare components, to a limited extent, are being bypassed with the introduction of low cost micro irrigation systems in India, pioneered by International Development Enterprises.

The recent data released by the Task Force on Micro Irrigation in India shows that during the past four years, peninsular India had recorded highest growth in adoption of drip systems. Maharashtra ranks first, followed by Andhra Pradesh and Karnataka. Table 2 presents the data of adoption of drip irrigation systems under various programmes, viz., macro management plan; technology mission on horticulture; cotton development programme and oil palm development programme. The major crops for which drip systems are currently adopted are: cotton, sugarcane; banana, orange, grapes, pomegranate, lemon, citrus, mangoes, flowers, and coconut.

Though exact state-wise data on the spread of sprinkler systems are not available, it has been found that sprinkler systems are in vogue in regions where conditions are unfavourable for traditional method of irrigation such as loose sandy soils and highly undulating fields. These are well-irrigated areas. Farmers in other well-irrigated areas have also procured the system under government subsidy programme, but were found to be using the HDPE pipes for water conveyance in the field except during droughts when they are used for providing supplementary irrigation to kharif crops.

Table 2. Rate of Adoption of MI Systems during 2001-05 under various programmes

Sr. No.	*Name of State*	*Area Under Micro Irrigation Systems in the year (ha)*				
		2001-02	*2002-03*	*2003-04*	*2004-05*	*Total*
1.	Andhra Pradesh	9117	4227	12	4200	17556
2.	Arunachal Pradesh	110	100	248	500	958
3.	Assam	22	16	17	350	405
4.	Bihar	500	141	0	0	641
5.	Chhattisgarh	444	227	0	100	771
6.	Goa	70	48	0	305	423
7.	Gujarat	2130	2109	1035	3650	8924
8.	Haryana	226	0	236	230	692
9.	Himachal Pradesh	111	85	0	0	196
10.	Jammu and Kashmir	0	5	30	0	35
11.	Jharkhand	179	0	0	0	179
12.	Karnataka	9480	397	2635	4219	16731
13.	Kerala	939	457	180	489	2065
14.	Madhya Pradesh	1190	1007	200	375	2772
15.	Maharashtra	14391	6875	248	844	22358
16.	Manipur	10	20	25	100	155
17.	Meghalaya	28	0	55	60	143
18.	Mizoram	0	50	20	450	520
19.	Nagaland	60	55	100	50	265
20.	Orissa	250	0	285	650	1185
21.	Punjab	0	80	0	0	80
22.	Rajasthan	1400	1000	1700	1200	5300

Sr. No.	Name of State	Area Under Micro Irrigation Systems in the year (ha)				
		2001-02	2002-03	2003-04	2004-05	Total
23.	Sikkim	30	30	0	50	110
24.	Tamil Nadu	814	635	25	1986	3460
25.	Tripura	118	0	278	300	696
26	Uttar Pradesh	454	264	0	235	953
27	Uttaranchal	100	100	0	0	200
28	West Bengal	0	0	0	99	99
	Total	42173	17928	7329	20442	87872

Source: Task Force on Micro Irrigation, Ministry of Agriculture, Government of India

In India, sprinkler systems are mainly used for field crops such as wheat, sorghum, pearl millet, groundnut and mustard. But the use of sprinklers is often limited to certain part of the crop season when farmers face severe shortage of water in their wells. Normally, this is just before the onset of monsoon when the farmers have to do sowing of these crops, or when there is a long dry spell during the monsoon season. Sprinkler for groundnut is common in Saurashtra in Gujarat; sprinkler for mustard is common in Khargaon district of Madhya Pradesh and Ganga Nagar district of Rajasthan. In the high ranges of Kerala and Tamil Nadu, sprinklers are used for irrigating tea and coffee plantations. However, recently, farmers have started using micro sprinklers and mini micro sprinklers for potato, groundnut and alfalfa.

3.2 Potential Contribution of Micro-irrigation Technologies in India

3.2.1 Physical impact of micro-irrigation technologies on water demand for crop production

Analyzing the potential impact of MI systems on the aggregate demand for water in crop production involves three important considerations. The first concerns the extent of coverage that can be achieved in MI system adoption at the country level. The second concerns the extent of real water saving possible with MI system adoption at the field level. The third concerns what farmers do with the water saved through MI systems, and the changes in the cropping systems associated with adoption. But, most of the past research on physical impacts of MI systems had dealt with the issue of changes in irrigation water use, crop growth and crop yield.

There is limited analysis available on the potential coverage of MI systems in India, and the water saving possible at the aggregate level. But, these analyses suffer from severe limitations. *First:* the analyses of potential coverage of MI systems are based on simplistic considerations of the area under crops that are amenable to MI systems, and do not take into account the range of physical, socio-economic and institutional factors that induce severe constraints to adoption of these technologies. *Second*: they do not distinguish between saving in applied water and real water saving, while the real water saving that can be achieved through MI adoption could be much lower than the saving in applied water. *Third*: there is an inherent assumption that area under irrigation remains the same, and therefore the saved water would be available for reallocation. But, in reality, it may not be so. With introduction of MI systems, farmers might change the very cropping system itself, including expansion in irrigated area. Therefore, all these assumptions result in over-estimation of the potential coverage of MI systems and the extent of water-saving possible with MI adoption. These complex questions are being addressed in the subsequent sections of this paper.

(A) Physical constraints and opportunities for adoption of MI Systems

Determining the potential coverage that can be achieved in MI system adoption require a systematic identification of the conditions that are favourable or un-favourable for adoption and a geographical assessment of areas where such conditions exist. Such conditions can be physical, socio-economic or institutional. These physical, socio-economic and institutional constrains in the adoption of MI systems are discussed below.

If we do not consider the difficult options of shifting to less water intensive crops and crops having higher water productivity, there are two major pre-requisites for reducing the overall demand for water in agriculture in the region. They are: (i) reducing the non-beneficial evapo-transpiration from crop land; and (ii) maintaining the area under irrigation. The second issue is not being dealt with here. The time-tested and widely available technology for increasing water productivity is pressurized irrigation systems such as sprinklers and drips (or trickle irrigation). However, their adoption is very low in India. This includes even areas where the capital investment for creating irrigation source is very high such as Kolar district in Karnataka, Coimbatore district in Tamil Nadu and alluvial north and central Gujarat. While, there are several constraints at the field level, which limit the adoption of this technology by the farmers, some of the very critical ones that are physical in nature are analyzed here.

First of all, MI systems need reliable daily water supply. But, nearly 41.24% of the net irrigated area in the country gets their supplies from surface sources such as canals and tanks (source: GOI, 2002). Drips and sprinklers are not conducive to flow irrigation due to two reasons. First is the mismatch between water delivery schedules followed in canal irrigation and that to be followed when MI systems are to be used. Normally, in surface command areas in India, farmers get their turn once in 10-15 days at flow rates ranging from 0.5 to 1 cusec. But, for drips and sprinklers to give their best, water should be applied to the crop either daily or once in two days with lower flow rates equal to the evapo-transpiration. This means, intermediate storage systems would be essential for farmers to use water from surface schemes for running MIs. Storage systems are also required as settling tanks for cleaning large amounts of silt contents in the canal water supplies. Second, there is a need for pumps for lifting water from the storages and running the MI systems. These two investments would reduce the economic viability of MI.

Therefore, in the current situation adoption of MI would be largely limited to areas irrigated by wells. Having said that, an increasingly large number of farmers in groundwater irrigated areas manage their supplies from water purchase. This also includes areas where groundwater over-draft is not a concern like Bihar and western Orissa, and where economic access to water is a problem. It is difficult for these farmers to adopt any MI devices.

Need for pressuring devices limits the adoption of MI systems. In groundwater over-exploited areas such as north and central Gujarat, Coimbatore district in Tamil Nadu and Kolar district of Karnataka, ownership of wells mostly does not remain with individual farmers but with groups. Also, a large number of farmers have to depend on water purchase. They get water through underground pipelines at almost negligible water pressure (head). In order to use the conventional sprinkler and drip systems, high operating pressure (1.0-1.2 kg/cm^2) is required. Unless the systems are directly connected to the tube well, the required amount of "head" to run the sprinkler and drip system cannot be developed. The need for a booster pump and the high cost of energy required for pressurizing the system to run the sprinklers and drips reduce the economic viability. But, there are new MI technologies, which require very low operating head such as sub-surface irrigation systems and the micro-tube drips. The farmers who are either water buyers or share wells can store the water in small tanks, lift it to small heights to generate the required head for running the sub-surface drip system or micro tube systems.

Another important constraint is the poor quality of groundwater. Due to the high TDS level of the pumped groundwater (the TDS levels are as high as 2000 ppm (parts per million) in many parts of India where groundwater is still being used for irrigation), the conventional drippers that are exposed to sunlight get choked up due to salt deposition in the dripper perforations. The saline groundwater areas include south western Punjab, north and central Gujarat, parts of Rajasthan, and many parts of Haryana. This needs regular cleaning using mild acids like the hydrochloric acid. This is a major maintenance work, and farmers are not willing to bear the burden of carrying out this regular maintenance. However, in limited cases, rich farmers in South West Punjab use large surface tanks for storing canal water when it is available, and blend it with brackish groundwater, and use for irrigating *kinnow* (a kind of citrus) orchards. These farmers can also use this water for drip irrigation to prevent problems of clogging.

In addition to areas irrigated by groundwater, there are hilly areas of the western and eastern Ghat regions, north-western Himalayas (Himachal Pradesh, J & K and Uttaranchal) and states in north-eastern hill region, where surface streams in steep slopes could be tapped for irrigating horticulture/ plantation crops. Such practices are very common in the upper catchment areas of many river basins of Kerala, which are hilly. Farmers tap the water from the streams using hose pipes and connect them to sprinkler systems. The high pressure required to run the sprinkler system is obtained by virtue of the elevation difference, which is in the order of 30-40 metres. Such systems are used to irrigate banana, vegetables and other cash crops such as vanilla. With the creation of an intermediate storage, drips could be run for irrigating crops such as coconut, aracnut and other fruit crops during the months of February to June.

Geological setting has a strong influence on MI adoption in well-irrigated areas. In hard rock areas, farmers will have strong incentive to go for MI systems. The reason is dug wells and bore wells in hard rock areas of Maharashtra, Madhya Pradesh, Tamil Nadu, Karnataka and Andhra Pradesh have very poor yield and well owners leave a part of their land fallow due to shortage of water. In most of these areas, farmers will have to discontinue pumping after 2-3 hours for the wells to recuperate. When pressurized irrigation systems are used, the rate at which water will be pumped will reduce. This will also give enough opportunity time for wells to recuperate. Since, pump will eventually run for more number of hours, the same quantity of water could be pumped out, and the command area can be expanded. This factor provides a great economic incentive for farmers to go for water-saving micro irrigation systems.

(B) Socio-economic and institutional constraints for MI adoption

Another major constraint in adoption of conventional MI technologies is the predominant cropping pattern in the water-scarce regions. MI systems are best adaptable for horticultural crops from an economic point of view (Dhawan, 2000). The

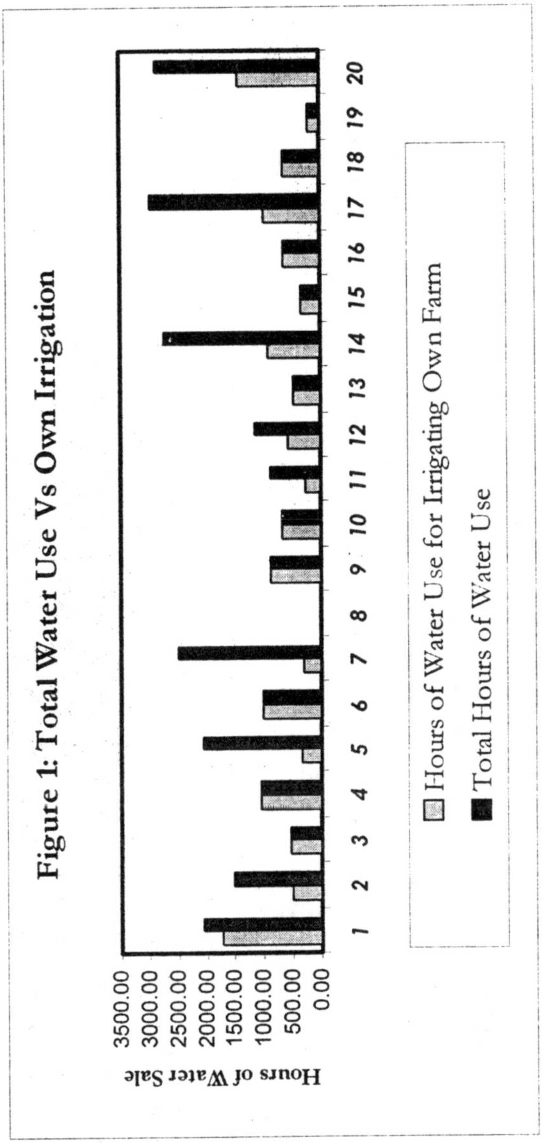

Figure 1: Total Water Use Vs Own Irrigation

analyses presented in Table 10 also substantiate this point. This is because the additional investment for drips has to be offset mainly by the better yield and returns farmers get as the saving in input costs are not very significant (Kumar, 2007). But, percentage area under horticultural crops is very low in these regions, except Maharashtra[3]. Though the low cost drip irrigation systems appear to be a solution, they have low physical efficiency when used for crops in which the plant spacing is small (chilly, vegetables, groundnut and potato) (Source: IWMI research in Banaskantha). In such situations, they also score low on the economic viability front. The low cost systems can be used for some of the row crops such as castor, cotton and fennel, which are very common. However, to use the system for these crops, it is very important that the farmers maintain a fixed spacing between different rows and different plants. So far as maintaining the spacing between rows is concerned, farmers pay sufficient attention. But, spacing between plants is not maintained. Due to this un-even (un-favourable) field conditions, designing and installing drippers becomes extremely difficult. Therefore, for adoption of these water saving technologies, the farmers' agricultural practices need major changes.

Further, there are crops such as paddy for which neither drips nor sprinkler irrigation systems are feasible. Paddy is an important crop in many arid and semi arid regions where water levels are falling. Certain studies at ICAR (Patna) have developed Low-Energy Water Application (LEWA) systems which apply regulated water supplies to paddy and have demonstrated potential to save water. But the technology is still in its infancy and requires large scale testing before field scale adoption. Adopting suitable cropping patterns that would increase the adoptability of water saving technologies is one strategy. But, as mentioned in the beginning of the section, "crop shift" is a harder option for farmers.

The socio-economic viability of crop shifts increases with the size of the operational holding of farmers. Given the fact that small and marginal farmers account for large percentage of the operational holders in India, the adoptability of horticultural crops by farmers in these regions cannot be expected to be high. This is because these crops need at least 3-4 years to start yielding returns, (except for pomegranate, papaya). It will be extremely difficult for these farmers to block their parcel of land for investments that do not give any returns in the immediate future, say after a season or so. Market is another constraint. Large-scale shift to fruit crops can lead to sharp decline in the market price of these fruits. Labour absorption is another major issue when traditional crops such as paddy, which are labour-intensive, get replaced by orchards. Orchards require less labour, it is also seasonal, and the chances for mechanization are higher.

Plot size also influences farmers' choices. Conventional MI systems will be physically and economically less feasible for smaller plots due to the fixed overhead costs of energy, and the various components of these irrigation systems such as filters, overhead tanks (Kumar, 2003).

The following equation calculates the pressure "head" required to pump water for running pressurized irrigation systems.

$$P_{req} = \frac{(P_2 + P_L)}{(w + Z)}$$

Where is the residual pressure required at the well outlet. P_2 is the pressure required at the sprinkler nozzle or dripper and P_L is the pressure loss during conveyance of water from the tube well to the sprinklers or the drips. Z is the difference in elevation. If the sprinkler/drip systems are located at a higher elevation than the pump outlet, then 'Z' will be negative. The equation shows that the additional energy required for running the system will reduce with every additional sprinkler, the reason being that only the pressure loss increases with increase in number of sprinklers/drip irrigated area. However, organizations like International Development Enterprises (IDE) have developed and promoted MI systems for very smallholder farmers/ plots which use small storage cisterns for providing the required pressure.

Poor rural infrastructure, that mainly concern power connections to agro wells and quality of power supply, is another major constraint for adoption of MI systems. Difficulty in obtaining power connections for farm wells, and poor quality of power supply forces farmers to use diesel pump sets for irrigating their crops. Use of diesel pump increases the cost of abstraction of well water. Regions such as Bihar, eastern UP and Orissa are examples. Here, many cash-starved farmers do not own wells, and depend on water purchased from well owners for irrigation. Drips and sprinklers are energy intensive systems, and installing such systems would mean extra capital investments for installing higher capacity pump sets as well as recurring expenses for buying diesel. These factors act as deterrents for adopting MI systems.

The current water pricing and energy pricing policies that exist in most states[4] also reduce the economic incentives for MI adoption. Due to these policies, the water-saving and energy-saving benefits from the use of MI systems do not get converted into private benefits.

Un-scientific water delivery schedules followed in surface irrigation systems, and power supply restrictions for farm sector also induce constraints for MI adoption. It is common in surface irrigation systems that while plenty of water is released for the crops for certain part of the season, in the last leg of the crop season the crops are subject to moisture stress. Poor reliability of water delivery services or lack of adherence to a standard delivery schedules and poor control over volumetric supplies force farmers to adopt crops that are less sensitive to water stress such as paddy and sugarcane and resort to flood irrigation. Regulated power supply in agriculture is also reducing the economic incentive for adoption of MI systems that are energy-intensive. Many states including Punjab, Madhya Pradesh, Tamil Nadu, Gujarat and Karnataka had consistently reduced the duration of power supply to farm sector, due to growing power crisis. In future, this would emerge as a major impediment for large-scale MI adoption.

Poor extension services offered by concerned agencies pose another major constraint. It is not common for the extension wings of Agricultural Universities to set up demonstration of new technologies in farmers' fields. This is applicable to companies which manufacture and sell MI devices. Because of this, there is very little knowledge about MI technologies among the farmers in water-scarce regions. The existing knowledge is filled more with misconceptions. Many farmers believe that MI systems have severe limitations vis-à-vis crops for which they could be used. Another misconception is that coverage of sprinklers being circular leaves a lot of dry spots in the irrigated fields. This belief has mainly come from the experience of farmers who have used the system with improper designs.

The administration of subsidies in MI devices also works against the interest of promotion of MI systems. Since in many states, the governments continue to pay the subsidy directly to the manufacturers, many farmers purchased MI systems just to avail of the subsidy benefits, and do not maintain them. The suppliers do not to offer any after-sales services to the farmers and hence are not interested in ensuring quality control. The systems being supplied are often of sub-standard quality. Over and above, as the amount funds available for subsidies are limited, the smartest of farmers take the benefit. On the other hand, the government officials, who come and inspect the systems installed, only check the amount of materials supplied, and work out the subsidy that has to be paid to the irrigation company. Since the manufacturers had the hassle of doing the entire documentation for obtaining the subsidy, they keep the price (without subsidy) high enough to recover their interests on capital and transaction costs.

The present institutional framework governing the use of groundwater, which puts no limit on the amount of water farmers can pump from aquifer, does not provide clear economic incentives to use water efficiently. This is particularly so for well owners, who have good sources of water supply. Examples are the Indo-Gangetic alluvium and alluvial areas of Gujarat. Though it is the opportunity cost of using water, which influences farmers' decision-making framework, such opportunity costs are not felt clearly. This is in spite of the prevalence of water markets[5] in these regions. The reason is that the demand for water from the water buyers and for ones own irrigation use, is much less than the number of hours for which the farmers could run their pumps[6] (see Figure 1). In such cases, the direct additional financial returns farmer gets by introducing MI systems are from the increased crop yield. This will not happen unless the farmer adopts new agronomic practices.

Due to this reason, the well owners would rather pump for extra hours to sell water to the needy farmers than trying to use water more efficiently by making substantial capital investments. The reason being that the economic efficiency of water use for the irrigated crops grown in the area even with the current inefficient practices is much higher than the price at which water is traded (Kumar and Singh, 2001).

Presence of negative externalities in groundwater pumping poses an important constraint for those who like to adopt MI systems. Well interference is very common in hard rock areas. Under such conditions, pumping by one farmer will have effect on the prospects of pumping by another farmer. Due to this reason, the efforts to cut down pumping rates by a farmer may not result in increased future availability of groundwater for him/her. The efforts to save water from the system by an individual farmer might mean increased availability of groundwater for pumping by his/her neighbouring farmers. Hence, under such situations, the farmers do not have any incentive to invest in MI systems. The technical externality becomes negative externality for well irrigators in the absence of well-defined water rights in groundwater.

(C) Real Water Saving and Water Productivity Impacts of MI Systems in the Field

The real water saving impact of MI systems at the field level depends on the improvements in water use efficiency. All the available data on the efficiency impact of micro irrigation systems are on application[7] efficiency. The classical definition of irrigation efficiency is the ratio of amount of water consumed by the crop to the amount of water applied. But in estimating water-saving, what matters is the amount of depleted water, rather than the amount of water applied. The depleted water includes moisture evaporation from the exposed soil and non-recoverable deep percolation. It would be less than the applied water so long as the un-consumed water is not lost in natural sinks like saline aquifer or swamps (Allen *et al.*, 1998). This means, the application of the concept of irrigation efficiencies are no longer useful in analyzing the performance of irrigation systems, with greater understanding of agro-hydrology and appreciation of deep percolation from irrigated fields[8] as a component of the available water resources (Keller *et al.*, 1996), except in situations where the groundwater is saline or deep or the unconsumed water goes into swamps.

Water use efficiency improvements through MI adoption, and therefore the field level water-saving impacts, depend on three major factors: (1) the geo-hydrological environment, including the depth to groundwater table and the nature of aquifer, whether freshwater or saline; (2) the type of crops; and (3) the agro-climate.

In regions where water table is deep and showing declining trends, MI adoption can lead to real water saving at field level. The reason is deep percolation that occurs under traditional method of irrigation, does not reach the groundwater table. This can be explained in the following way. The reason is that the depth of groundwater table is in the range of 20 m to 135 m. The 20-135 m thick vadose zone holds the vertically moving water as hygroscopic water and capillary water. Some of the water from the soil profile within or below the root zone, having higher levels of moisture, also can move up due to differential hydraulic gradients (Ahmed *et al.*, 2004). All this water would eventually get evaporated from the crop land after the harvest if the fallow period is significant depending, on the climate. The depth of soil below the surface from which evaporation could take place can be up to 2-3 metres in semi arid and arid regions (Todd, 1997). Some water in the deep vadoze zone would get sucked away by the deep-rooted trees around the farms during the non-rainy season.

Since, under MI system, water is applied daily in small quantities to meet the daily crop water requirements, deep percolation is prevented. Such regions include alluvial tracts of north and central Gujarat, central Punjab, hard rock areas of northern Karnataka, Tamil Nadu, Andhra Pradesh, Maharashtra, Madhya Pradesh and many parts of Rajasthan. Though deep percolation could be quite significant in paddy irrigation, so far no water-saving irrigation devices are being tried in paddy, though many water saving practices have evolved over time in paddy irrigation.

Nevertheless, in areas where groundwater levels are still within 20 metres below ground level, the saving in applied water achieved through MI devices would mostly result in saving in pumping cost, but no real saving in water from the system. The reason is that a good share of the excess water used in irrigation under the traditional irrigation practices finally goes back to the groundwater system through return flows. It is important to note that the areas having high water table conditions coincide with areas with low level of aridity or mostly sub-humid or humid climate where evaporation losses from soil would be low even in summer months.

The real water saving that can be achieved through MI system would be high under semi arid and arid climatic conditions. This is because the non-beneficial depletion of moisture from the exposed soil could be high under such situation due to high temperature, wind speed and low humidity. Such losses would be significant during initial stages of crop growth when canopy cover is small[9].

For instance, direct dry seeded rice in wet season and direct wet seeded rice in dry season were found to be effective ways of saving water in rice irrigation over transplanted rice (Tabbal *et al.*, 2002). Similarly, large amount of research in India has demonstrated the benefits of applying irrigation after 2-3 days of disappearance of applied and ponded water. Field studies conducted on System of Rice Intensification (SRI) also showed significant reduction in applied water use owing to reduction in the duration for which the field remains under submerged conditions (Satyanarayana, 2004; Tiyagarajan, 2005). Majority of this reduction could have possibly come from reduction in deep percolation of water from the paddy field. However, the area under SRI, aerobic rice and other methods of improved irrigation is still very small in India.

The real water saving would be more for row crops, including orchards, cotton, fennel, castor, and many vegetables, where the spacing between plants is large. The reason is the area exposed to solar radiation and wind between plants would be large, and as a result the non-beneficial evaporation would be a major component of the total water depleted, under traditional method of irrigation. With drip irrigation, water could be directly applied to plants, preventing this loss. Such row crops are widely grown with drips and sprinklers in arid and semi arid regions of India. Examples are mulberry in Karnataka; cotton, sugarcane, banana, groundnut, coconut and vegetables in Tamil Nadu; chilly and mangoes in Andhra Pradesh; orange, banana, pomegranate, mangoes, grapes, flowers, sugarcane and vegetables in Maharashtra; cotton, mustard, rapeseed and wheat in Madhya Pradesh; oil seed crops such as cotton, groundnut, castor, mustard and fennel, and wheat, potato and alfalfa in Gujarat; mustard and chilly in Rajasthan; and wheat and potato in Punjab. Hence, the reduction in non-beneficial evaporation from soils and non-recoverable deep percolation, and hence actual water saving through micro irrigation could be in the range of 10-25 per cent depending on the type of crops and the natural environment (soils, climate and geo-hydrology).

There are no scientific data available in India on the actual impact of MI systems on water use efficiency, which estimates the depleted water against the water consumed by the crop, or which takes into account the amount of water available for reuse from the total water applied. The extent of which would be determined by the climate (arid, semi arid or sub-humid or humid), depth to groundwater table and groundwater quality, and the amount of water available for deep percolation.

There is effectively no research in India quantifying the real water saving and water productivity impacts of water saving irrigation technologies on various crops, at the field level. An extensive review of literature shows that all the data on water-saving are based on applied water, and within that more reliable ones are on experimental farms, for limited number of crops and system types and for a few locations. Data on water-saving, yield rise and water use efficiency improvements with drip irrigation over flood irrigation in several crops, which were compiled from experimental data from different research stations across India, in Narayanamoorthy (2004) are presented in Table 3. The reduction in water consumption varies from a mere 12 per cent for ash gourd and bottle gourd to 81 per cent for lemon.

As seen from the data, some of the figures on water saving are quite high. But, it is important to remember here that the condition of flood irrigation system chosen for comparison influences the findings on water saving and yield improvements in DMI (drip method of irrigation). Poorly managed flood irrigation systems used for comparison could significantly affect the result in favour of DMI. However, to obtain high efficiencies, surface methods (furrow, border, and basin) are generally demanding of operating skills and require a high degree of flexibility in water supply. In contrast, much of the complexity of drip and sprinkler irrigation systems is in their design rather than their operation, and they can more easily be operated (but are not always) with low losses. Generally, the natural environment imposes constraints on realistically achievable efficiency levels (Carter *et al.*, 1999)[10], and therefore in what environments the comparisons are made is also important. But, it is a truism that with the same technology, and with the same crop, the water saving and yield impacts of these irrigation technologies would depend on the agro climate.

One major limitation of the database is that they are generated for a single location. Another limitation is that it compares DMI with one traditional method only. But, the extent of field level water saving through DMI would be heavily influenced by the conventional irrigation method practiced for that crop in the region under consideration, and the precision irrigation followed in drip irrigation. Flooding in large basins is just one of the many traditional irrigation methods used by Indian farmers. Its use is generally limited to canal irrigated

Table 3. Saving in Applied Water and Productivity Gains through Drip Irrigation

Name of the crops	*Water consumption (or application?) (mm / ha)*		*Yield (Ton / ha)*		*Water saving over FMI (%)*	*Yield increase over FMI (%)*	*Water consumption per ton of yield (mm/ton)*	
Vegetables	FMI	DMI	FMI	DMI			FMI	DMI
Ash gourd	840	740	10.84	12.03	12	12	77.49	61.51
Bottle gourd	840	740	38.01	55.79	12	47	22.09	13.26
Brinjal	900	420	28.00	32.00	53	14	32.14	13.13
Beet root	857	177	4.57	4.89	79	7	187.53	36.20
Sweet potato	631	252	4.24	5.89	61	40	148.82	42.78
Potato	200	200	23.57	34.42	Nil	46	8.49	5.81
Lady's finger	535	86	10.00	11.31	84	13	53.50	7.60
Onion	602	451	9.30	12.20	25	31	64.73	36.97
Radish	464	108	1.05	1.19	77	13	441.90	90.76
Tomato	498	107	6.18	8.87	79	43	80.58	12.06
Chilly	1097	417	4.23	6.09	62	44	259.34	68.47
Ridge gourd	420	172	17.13	20.00	59	17	24.52	8.60
Cabbage	660	267	19.58	20.00	60	2	33.71	13.35
Cauliflower	389	255	8.33	11.59	34	39	46.67	22.00

Name of the crops	*Water consumption (or application?) (mm/ha)*		*Yield (Ton/ha)*		*Water saving over FMI (%)*	*Yield increase over FMI (%)*	*Water consumption per ton of yield (mm/ton)*	
Fruit Crops								
Papaya	2285	734	13.00	23.00	68	77	175.77	31.91
Banana	1760	970	57.50	87.50	45	52	30.61	11.09
Grapes	532	278	26.40	32.50	48	23	20.15	8.55
Lemon	42	8	1.88	2.52	81	35	22.34	3.17
Watermelon	800	800	29.47	88.23	Nil	179	27.15	9.07
Sweet Lime*	1660	640	100.0	150.00	61	50	16.60	4.27
Pomegranate*	1440	785	55.00	109.00	45	98	26.18	7.20
Other Crops								
Sugarcane	2150	940	128.00	170.00	65	33	16.79	5.53
Cotton	856	302	2.60	3.26	60	25	329.23	92.64
Groundnut	500	300	1.71	2.84	40	66	292.40	105.63

*: Yield in 1000 numbers;

Source: INCID (1994) and NCPA (1990) as cited in Narayanamoorthy (2004): pp 122

Note: FMI and DMI refer to flood method of irrigation and Drip Method of Irrigation, respectively.

fields, and fields irrigated by wells in canal command areas due to high flow rates from canals. The well irrigators generally use other methods viz., small border irrigation, trench irrigation and furrow irrigation. On-farm efficiencies are much higher under furrow, trench and small border irrigation as compared to flooding. Another limitation is that data obtained from experimental farms are for ideal conditions, and using such data can lead to over-estimation of field level water saving and water use efficiency impacts of DMI. The reason is it is difficult to simulate the ideal conditional of experimental farms in farmers' fields.

The rest of the data on field level water savings and yield improvements through MI systems are from socio-economic studies based on respondent surveys involving adopters and non-adopters. The results from such studies are summarized in Table 4. The data on water saving are arrived at using figures of total applied water. The available data from the experimental farms do not enable analysis of reduction in depleted water under various treatments. Based on the earlier discussions, it is reasonable to assume that for traditional methods of irrigation, the "applied water" would be very close to the depleted water for row crops, under semi arid and arid climatic conditions, there are no hard empirical data obtained from experiments to prove this. Here, one unknown parameter is deep percolation.

While MI systems are expected to have likely impact on deep percolation from the fields, such deep percolation can be treated as loss into the sink because of the following reasons: (1) drip irrigation is normally used in well-irrigated fields; (2) the amount of water percolating in non-paddy irrigated fields would normally be low (source: based on Ahmed *et al.*, 2004;) especially for well irrigation, as the dosage per watering is generally low ; (3) depth of vadoze zone in which the percolating water could be held as hygroscopic water or capillary water would be high in arid and semi arid areas which depend on groundwater; and, (4) part of the water going into the vadoze zone can get lost in soil evaporation during fallow period (based on Todd, 1997). Hence, applied water saving which the available literature refer to can be treated as real water saving.

Table 4. Results available from past studies on water saving and yield impacts of drip irrigation

Name of researchers	*Location*	*Nature of study*	*Results on*	
			Saving in Applied Water	*Crop Yield*
Jadhav *et al.* (1990)	Haryana	Socio-economic	31 per cent saving in water use in tomato	Yield increase by 50 %
Hapase *et al.* (1992)	Maharashtra	Socio-economic	50-55 per cent saving in water in sugarcane crop	Yield increase in the range of 12-37%
Muralidharan and others (1994)	Kolar, Karnataka	Socio-economic	Water-saving benefits highlighted, not quantified	
Narayanamoorthy (1996)	Nashik, Maharashtra	Socio-economic (respondent survey)	41 per cent water saving for banana and 59 per cent for grapes	Productivity higher under DMI for both crops
Reddy and Thimmegowda (1997)	Bangalore, Agricultural University Research Station	Experimental farm measurements	Water-saving benefits not quantified	Seed cotton yield increased by 13% under drip tap; 16% under emitter drip Ratoon yield by 3% under drip tape; and 6% under emitter drip
Dahake and others (1998)	Akola district of Maharashtra (Orange)	Socio-economic survey	Uniform distribution and conservation of water in orchards	

R. L. Shiyani and others (1999)	Four districts of Saurashtra in Gujarat viz., Junagadh, Rajkot, Amreli and Bhavnagar (Cotton)	Socio-economic survey	Water saving not quantified; but estimated reduction in irrigation cost as varying from 25% to 51%; increase in irrigation cost in Bhavnagar	Yield enhancement in cotton in all districts, averaging 22%
Palanisamy and others (2002)	Coimbatore (Coconut)	Socio-economic survey	50 % water saving in coconut	20-30 per cent increase in coconut yield
Kumar and other (2004)	Banaskantha, Gujarat (Alfalfa)	Techno-economic evaluation of drips in demo farms of alfalfa	Reduction in water application in the range of 7-43 per cent	Yield increase in the range of 5-10 per cent
Kumar, Singh, Singh and Shiyani (2004)	Four districts in Gujarat (several crops)	Socio-economic survey	Extent of water saving varies from crop to crop and from system to system	Yield increase in all crops; but variation in yield benefits across crops
Waykar and others (2003)	Ahmednagar district of Maharashtra (Sugarcane)	Socio-economic survey	Data on water-saving not available	Higher yield of sugarcane (up to 27%) for adopters of drip systems.

Source: Synthesis of various studies by the authors.

But, these studies are not complete in themselves, as they cover only a few crops, and a few MI devices. Also, these studies have serious limitations. First, they are mostly based on data obtained from respondent surveys, which capture relative benefits of the technology from the farmers' perspective. Second, they are also likely to be influenced by respondents' bias. In order to understand the extent to which the water productivity of crops could be enhanced through MI technologies, it is crucial to get realistic data on potential changes in irrigation water use and crop yield, the two determinants of water productivity, with different technologies.

Field experiments were conducted in Banaskantha district of Gujarat with different MI devices on various crops to analyze the impact of the technology on irrigation water use, crop yield and water productivity. Banaskantha district falls in semi arid to arid climatic conditions. The mean annual rainfall for the location (Palanpur) was 682mm (source: authors' own analysis based on data provided by Gujarat Agriculture University, Anand). The annual reference evapo-transpiration (ET_0) for the nearest location (Radhanpur) was estimated to be 1750mm. Thirty two per cent (32%) of this evapo-transpirative demand is during the four months of July-October when the region receives monsoon rains (source: Indian Meteorological Department, Ahmedabad as cited in Figure 6 of Kumar, 2002b: page 17). The soil type in the area varies from sandy to sandy loam and loamy sand.

The crops covered are: alfalfa, castor, groundnut and potato. The technologies used are: inline drip system for alfalfa; micro tube drip with and without plastic and organic mulching, and flooding with and without plastic/organic mulching; micro tubes and inline drippers in groundnut; and inline drippers and micro tubes in potato. The results from these experiments are presented in Table 6-8.

The treatments used for alfalfa are: different spacing of drippers without changing the water delivery through drippers (30 cm*40 cm in F1 to 50 cm*40 cm in F4); maintaining the same spacing of drippers (30 cm*30 cm) with different intensities of daily irrigation (G1 to G4); maintaining same spacing of drippers with different intensities of irrigation, and with watering on alternate days; small level border irrigation with different intensities and with various irrigation schedules (from an average of 7-8 days in winter to 5 days in summer to an average of 6 days in winter to 4 days in summer). FYM was applied in all the plots in equal dozes, and no chemical fertilizers were used. The volume of water applied in the field was measured using water meters each time when irrigation is done, and output is weighted each time harvest/cutting is done.

The results are presented in Figure 2. It shows that the yield is highest for plot with a dripper spacing of 30 cm* 40 cm (11.36 kg/m^2) of green matter, followed by one with a spacing of 35 cm*40 cm (10.71 kg/m^2). But, water productivity was highest (7.8 kg/m^3 of water) for the plot which recorded second highest yield (F_2). Therefore, the highest yield corresponds to a depth of application of 1.6 m, while highest water productivity corresponds to a depth of 1.37 m. With flood irrigation, the yield values were highest for treatment I_5 in which the amount of water applied was 4.3 m. Though these are very high figures for small border irrigation, it can be attributed to sandy soils. Here, I1 is a case of over-irrigation with very heavy doses of irrigation (139 mm) and can be discarded. The figures are relevant in the sense that even with such high dozes of irrigation no field run off was generated, meaning there are chances for farmers to actually apply such high doses in sandy soils under well irrigation.

The yield figure almost touched that obtained with daily irrigation through drips (F_1 and F_2). But, the amount of water applied was far higher than that under F type treatments—almost 3 times in most cases. The water productivity values were in the range of 1.47 kg/m^3 and 2.79 kg/m^3, which were only 20 to 30 per cent of that obtained with drip irrigation under F_2 treatment. The results show that with drip irrigation, the water productivity could be enhanced significantly in alfalfa without compromising on the yield. As regards economic viability, even if we compare the drip irrigated plots with some of the best plots under flood irrigation, the reduction in water use is very substantial, with modest improvements in yield. Therefore,

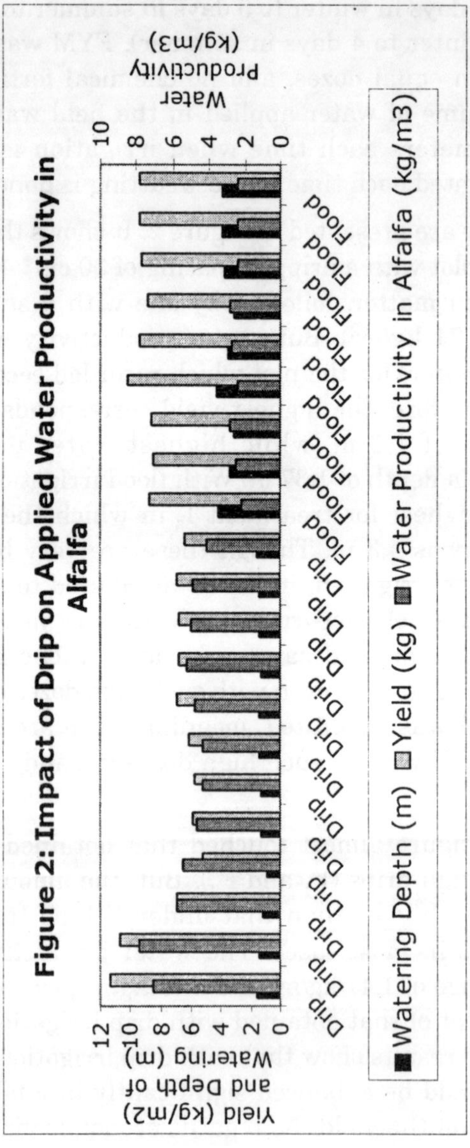

Figure 2: Impact of Drip on Applied Water Productivity in Alfalfa

when water availability becomes a constraint, drip for alfalfa would be economically viable under a lateral spacing of 30cm*40 cm. This is because, one of the earlier analysis with similar type of drip system on alfalfa showed that even with 10% increase in yield, and 45% reduction in water use, drips could be economically viable, when the social benefits of water saving are taken into account. Here, in this case, reduction in water use is much higher when F1 and F2 are compared with any of the flood-irrigation plots. Increase in yield is 10% when F2 is compared against the best flood irrigated plot, and much higher than 10% when compared against other flood-irrigated plots.

The results (I_1 to I_{10}) also show that there are significant variations in water productivity levels of alfalfa under flood irrigation with changing irrigation intensity. Highest yield was obtained under second highest level of water application (4.33m over the full crop year). Highest water productivity (2.79 kg/m^3) was obtained with the lowest level of irrigation (3.15 m). The lowest water productivity (1.47 kg/m^3) was obtained under highest level of irrigation (6.0 m).

Experiments carried out with micro tube drips with plastic and organic mulching and micro tubes with broad furrows as the control in Manka village of Vadgam in Banaskantha. There were four treatments followed. In the first three treatments, watering was done daily with daily irrigation water requirement estimated roughly on basis of the crop water requirement (K_c* ET_0), and daily dosage was adjusted on the basis of the field observations of soil moisture conditions. In the fourth case, the irrigation water dosage was determined by making provision for evaporative losses from the exposed soil in the crop land and deep percolation losses. The scheduling was same as that practiced in the area for castor for traditional method. While a total of 96 watering were done with C_1, C_2 and C_3, irrigation was applied nine times under C_4. The results showed that water application rate was lowest when micro tube drips were used with plastic mulching (treatment C_1), followed by micro tube with organic mulch (treatment C_2). The water application rate was highest for broad furrow treatment (C_4). The yield was highest for C_1, followed by C_4. The water productivity was

Table 6. Impact of Drip Irrigation on Applied Water, Yield and Applied Water Productivity in Castor in Manka

Plot No.	*Method of Irrigation*	*Agronomic Practices*	*Plot Size (M^2)*	*No. of Watering*	*Water Application Rate (mm / irrigation)*	*Per Sq. Meter Area*		
						Water use (m^3)	*Production (Kg)*	*Water Productivity (kg/m^3)*
C - 1	Micro-tube	P M	1110	96	2.09	0.201	0.135	0.67
C - 2	Micro-tube	O M	1110	96	2.35	0.225	0.099	0.44
C - 3	Micro-tube		1110	96	3.14	0.302	0.113	0.37
C - 4	Flooding		1110	9	40.64	0.366	0.126	0. 34

PM = Plastic Mulching; OM = Organic Mulching

Source: Authors' own analysis

highest for C_1, and second highest for C_2. The difference in water productivity was in the order of 100 per cent between first and the last treatment.

Experiments conducted on groundwater with inline drip systems and micro tube drips showed highest level of reduction in applied water use in the case of inline drippers when compared against border irrigation. The treatment included daily application of water to the plot through inline drippers and micro tube drips. The fertilizer doses were same in all the plots which were of the same size. The reduction in water dosage was nearly 18 cm, while the yield was higher by 0.013 kg/m^2, with a net effect on water productivity in the order of 0.18 kg/m^3 of water (see Table 8). The micro tube irrigated plot though gave same yield as that of furrow irrigated plot the applied water was less with micro tube. The study shows that the inline drippers are physically more efficient than furrow method and inline drip irrigation.

Another interesting experiment was done with different types of MI devices to understand the physical productivity of applied irrigation water in potato. In this experiment, five different types of MI devices were used, viz., inline drippers; easy drips (or drip systems with flexible laterals having a thickness ranging from 125 microns to 500 microns and have perforations instead of drippers to emit water); micro tube drips; micro sprinklers; and mini sprinklers. The results are presented in Table 9. It can be seen that the yield and physical productivity of water is highest for field irrigated with micro sprinklers, followed by mini sprinklers. This is in spite of the fact that the water dosage was more than double in the case of treatments P4 and P5.

On the basis of the values of irrigation dosage and the corresponding yield and water productivity values under different treatments, one could infer that water dosage was much lower than required in the case of inline drip, easy drip and micro tube drip irrigated plots, resulting in water stress and significant yield losses. Also, another inference is that in all the treatments, water dosage was in the ascending part of the yield and water productivity response curves for irrigation water

Table 7: Impact of Drip Irrigation on Applied Water, Yield and Applied Water Productivity in Groundnut (Kumbhasan)

Plot No.	*Method of Irrigation*	*Plot Size (M^2)*	*No. of Watering*	*Water Application Rate (mm / irrigation)*	*Per Sq. Meter Area*		
					Water use (m^3)	*Production (Kg)*	*Water Productivity (kg/m^3)*
G - 1	Inline Drip	192	49	6.54	0.320	0.130	0.41
G - 2	Micro-tube	192	49	7.05	0.345	0.117	0.34
G - 3	Furrows	192	8	62.85	0.503	0.117	0.23

Source: Authors' own analysis.

Table 8. Impact of Drip Irrigation on Applied Water, Yield and Applied Water Productivity in Potato (Manka)

Plot No.	*Method of Irrigation*	*Plot Size (M^2)*	*WST (cm)*	*No. of Watering*	*Water Application Rate (mm / irrigation)*	*Per Sq. Meter Area*		
						Water use (m^3)	*Production (Kg)*	*Water Productivity (kg / m^3)*
P - 1	Inline drip	304	52.5 x 30	56	7.50	0.420	0.375	0.893
P - 2	Easy drip	304	52.5 x 30	56	7.50	0.420	0.411	0.979
P - 3	Micro-tube drip	304	52.5 x 30	56	7.50	0.420	0.148	0.352
P - 4	Micro-Sprinkler	304	310 x 290	59	15.96	0.942	1.316	1.397
P - 5	Mini-Sprinkler	304	730 x 720	59	15.96	0.942	0.905	0.961

Source: Authors' own analysis.

application, which also means that with higher dosage of irrigation, the chances for getting higher yield are higher. It can be seen that with micro tubes, though the amount of water applied was same as that with inline drips (P1), the yield (0.148 kg/m^2) was much lower than that with P1. This could be due to poor distribution efficiency obtained with micro tubes.

(D) Potential aggregate impact of MI systems on water use for crop production

There is debate about the extent of water saving at system and basin level due to the widespread adoption of MI systems. This concerns the real water savings at the first place, and the use of saved water. We have addressed the first question in the earlier section. As regards the second question, many scholars believe that the aggregate impact of drips on water use would be similar to what it makes on water use in unit area of land. While several others believe that with reduction in water applied per unit area of land, the farmers would divert the saved water for expanding the area under irrigation, subject to favourable conditions with respect to water and equipment availability, and power supplies for pumping water (Kumar, 2002)[11], and therefore the net effect of adoption of micro irrigation systems such as drips and sprinklers on water use could be nil or insignificant at the system level. At the same time, there are others who believe that with adoption of WSTs, there is a greater threat of depletion of water resources, as in the long run, the return flows from irrigated fields would decline, while area under irrigation would increase under WSTs.

These arguments have, however, missed certain critical variables that influence farmers' decision making with regard to area to be put under irrigated production, and the aggregate water used for irrigation. They are: groundwater availability vis-à-vis power supply availability; crops chosen; and amount of land and finances available for intensifying cultivation. The most important of these factors is the overall availability of groundwater in an area; and the power supply situation vis-à-vis water availability in the wells.

If power supply restrictions limit pumping of groundwater by farmers, then it is very unlikely that as a result of adoption of conventional WSTs, farmers would expand the area under irrigation. Let us see how this happens. In the states of Punjab, Gujarat, Karnataka and Madhya Pradesh, power supply to agriculture sector is only for limited hours (GOI, 2002). It acts as a constraint in expanding the irrigated area, or increasing irrigation intensity, in those areas where groundwater availability and demand is more than what the restricted power supply can pump.

Since the available power supply is fully utilized during winter and summer seasons, farmers will be able to just irrigate the existing command with MI system. This is because the well discharge would drop when the sprinkler and drip systems connected to the well outlet start running, owing to increase in pressure developed in the system (please see equation below). In other words, the energy required to pump out and deliver a unit volume of groundwater increases with the introduction of MI system. The only way to overcome this is to install a booster pump for running the MI system. As electricity charges are based on connected load, farmers have least incentive to do this.

$$Q = \frac{\beta * 100 * \eta}{H}$$

Where, "BHP" is pump power in kilowatt/sec, "H" is the total head, "Q" is the discharge. η = combined electrical and hydraulic efficiency of pump set.

Such outcomes are expected in the alluvial areas of north Gujarat and Punjab. In this area, even in situations of availability of extra land, it won't be possible for farmers to expand the area under irrigated crops due to restrictions on power supply.

The other factor is the lack of availability of extra arable land for cultivation. This is applicable to areas land use and irrigation intensity is already high. Example is central Punjab. But, farmer might still adopt water-saving technologies for cash crops to raise yields or for newly introduced high-valued crops to increase their profitability. So, in such situations, adoption would result in reduction in aggregate water demand.

On the other hand, if the availability of water in wells is less than what the available power supply can abstract, with adoption of micro irrigation systems, the farmers are likely to expand irrigated area. This is the situation in most of the hard rock areas of peninsular India, central India and Saurashtra. Due to limited groundwater potential and over-exploitation, well water is very scarce in these areas. The available power supply is more than what is needed to abstract the water in the wells. Hence, farmers have strong economic incentive to go for MI systems other than yield enhancement (Dhawan, 2000). The reason is that the saved water could be used to expand the irrigated area and improve the economics of irrigated farming. In Michael region of central India, for instance, farmers use low cost drips to give pre sowing irrigations to cotton, before monsoon, when there is extreme scarcity of groundwater. This helps them grow cotton in larger area as water availability improves after the monsoon (Verma *et al.*, 2005), and hence there is no water saving at the aquifer level.

The third factor is the crops chosen. Often MI technologies follow a set cropping pattern. All the areas/pockets in the country where adoption of drip irrigation systems has undergone a "scale", orchard crops are the most preferred crops (Dhawan, 2000; Narayanamoorthy, 2004b). Therefore, while farmers adopt MI systems, the crops also change, normally from field crops to fruits[12]. While for many fruit crops, the gestation period is very large extending from 3-10 years (for instance, citrus, orange and mango), for many others like grapes, pomegranate and banana, it is quite short extending from one to two years. Also, farmers can go for intercropping of some vegetables and watermelon, which reduces their financial burden of establishing the orchards. This flexibility enables small and marginal farmers also to adopt MI systems, as found in north Gujarat and Jalgaon and Nasik districts of Maharashtra.

Access to credit and subsidy further increases MI adoption among small and marginal farmers. The irrigation water requirement of the cropping system consisting of field crops such as paddy, wheat, pearl millet/sorghum combinations is much higher than that of fruit crops such as pomegranate, gooseberry, sapota and lemon. Also for other orchard crops such as mango, the irrigation water requirements during the initial years of growth would be much less than that of these field crops. Therefore, even with expansion in cropped area, the aggregate water use would drop. Only in rare situations, the system design for one crop is adaptable for another crop. For example: the micro sprinklers that are used for winter potato, can also be used to irrigate summer ground nut and hence farmers opt for that crop.

3.2.2 Economic Impacts of MI Systems

There is enormous amount of research-based literature showing the positive economic impacts of water-saving irrigation devices. Many research studies available from India during the past one decade quantified economic benefits from drips. They are summarized in Table 9.

Synthesizing, there is very little data across agro-climatic conditions on the yield impacts of micro irrigation systems for the same crop. The research is heavily skewed towards drip irrigation systems, and there is hardly any data on the economics of other WSTs. As we have seen early, for a given crop, the yield as well as water-saving benefits of MI system could change across systems, so are the capital costs. Also, it could change across crops. But, the research is also heavily skewed towards orchard crops, banana, sugarcane and cotton. These crops still occupy a small percentage of the irrigated area in the country. Further, these economic analyses were not contextualized for the socioeconomic and institutional environment for which they were performed. The socio-economic and institutional environments determine the extent to which various physical benefits get translated into private and economic benefits. We would explain it in the subsequent paragraphs.

Normally, it has been found that drip irrigation is economically viable for horticultural crops and orchards such as banana, grapes, orange, coconut, and sugarcane (Dhawan, 2000: pp 3775; Sivanappan, 1994; Narayanamoorthy, 2003). The reason for this is that the crops are high valued and even a marginal increase in yield results in significant rise in value of

Table 9. Results available from past studies on economic viability of drip and sprinkler irrigation

Name of researchers	*Location*	*Nature of study*	*Results on*	
			Economic Viability	*Remarks*
Jadhav *et al.* (1990)	Pusa, Haryana	Socio-economic	5.16 and 2.96 for drip and furrow method, respectively, in tomato	
Muralidharan and others (1994)	Kolar, Karnataka	Socio-economic	B-C ratio not as good as in furrow irrigation for mulberry crop.	But, B-C ratio did not take into account the price at which water is traded in the region
Narayanamoorthy (1996)	Nashik, Maharashtra	Socio-economic (respondent survey)	Incremental return was Rs. 32400/ha in banana and Rs. 50180/ha in grapes. Reduction in cost of cultivation was Rs. 1300/ha in banana and Rs. 13400/ha in grapes	B-C analysis was based on direct costs and direct benefits and not based on incremental returns against incremental cost of drips

Narayanamoorthy (1997)	Nashik, Maharashtra	Socio-economic (respondent survey)	B-C Ratio ranged from 2.07 to 2.36 for banana and 1.48 to 1.80 for grapes with varying discounting rates	Do
Shivanappan (1994)	Tamil Nadu	Physical and Socio-economic	B-C Ratio ranged from 1.3 for sugarcane to 11.5 for grapes. The B-C ratio improved when the benefits of water saving was reckoned with	The incremental benefits calculated for the scenario of irrigated area expansion did not include the cost of establishing the crops in case of orchards
Reddy and Thimmegowda (1997)	Bangalore, Agricultural University Research Station	Experimental farm measurements	Average establishment cost was Rs.92522/ha for emitter drip irrigation, and Rs. 57482/ha for turbo tape. Turbo tape drip irrigation was found more profitable than emitter drip irrigation as indicated.	The pay back period was three years for turbo tape drip and five years for emitter drip irrigation for the main crop.

R. L. Shiyani and others (1999)	Four districts of Saurashtra in Gujarat viz., Junagadh, Rajkot, Amreli and Bhavnagar (Cotton)	Socio-economic survey	Significant differences in cost-B and cost-C between drip adopters and the farmers using surface method of irrigation. The major advantages of drip system over conventional method were: higher yield, higher profit, rise in labour productivity and reduction in unit cost of production	Other advantages of drip system included saving in water, reduction in weeding and labour cost, suitability for un-leveled and stony soils, increase in water use efficiency, decline in diseases and pests incidence and improvement in the quality of product
Palanisamy and others (2002)	Coimbatore, Tamil Nadu (Coconut)	Economic performance of drip irrigation	Additional cost of drips in coconut cultivation was Rs. 31,165/ha. The cost of cultivation went up by 19% in drip-	Reasons for improved financial viability were: higher price of coconut, 20 to

			irrigated coconut. The financial viability of drip irrigation system showed more than 30 per cent modified internal rate of return in the water scarcity condition.	30 % increase in yield; increased fertilizer use efficiency; reduction in expenditure on plant protection chemicals; 50% water saving; and labour saving to the tune of Rs. 3000/ha.
Luhach *et al.* (2003)	Haryana	Socio-economic survey of sprinklers adoption in wheat	Average net returns per ha from sprinkler irrigation was found to be 19.53% higher than that for pump irrigation. On an average, the net present value of sprinkler was found to be Rs. 7970, benefit-cost ratio was 1.97, and the internal rate of return was 17%	

Source: Synthesis of various studies by the authors.

crop output. Dhawan (2000) argues that higher value of crop output is realised also from improved price realization due to quality improvements on one hand and early arrival of the drip-irrigated crop in the market on the other. The same need not be true for other cash crops, and field crops.

For instance, the income benefit due to yield improvement depends on the type of crop. For cereals, it cannot be significant. A 10 per cent rise in yield would result in an incremental gain of 400-500 kg of wheat or Rs. 3000-Rs.3750 per ha of irrigated wheat. At the same time, a 10 per cent rise in yield of pomegranate, whose minimum yield is 60000 kg per ha per year, would result in an incremental gain of 6000 kg/ha or Rs.90000 per ha. Besides the incremental value of outputs, an important factor which influences the economic performance of drip system is the cost of installation of the system.

From the point of view of deciding on the investment priorities including the provision of subsidies, it is important to know the social benefits from drip irrigation. As Dhawan (2000) notes, cost-benefit analyses, which do not take into account social costs and benefits, are on weak conceptual footing as the government subsidies in micro irrigation systems are based on the premise that there are positive externality effects on the society due to water saving. In areas, where available water in wells is extremely limited, it is logical to take water-saving benefits and convert the same in monetary terms based on market price or in terms of additional area that can be irrigated. Same is the case with energy saving. But the same methodology cannot be applied to areas where access to water is not a limiting factor for enhancing the area under irrigation, or energy is not a scarce resource. But, such analysis are absent in India.

Given the range of variables—physical, socio-economic and financial—, that affect the costs and returns from crops irrigated by MI systems, it is important to carry out comprehensive analysis taking into account all these variables, across situations where at least the physical, socio-economic conditions change. Now, we would examine how the way these variables operate change under different situations.

As regards water saving, in many areas, the well owners are not confronted with the opportunity cost of wasting water. Hence, water saving does not result in any private gains. Where as in some hard rock areas like Kolar district in Karnataka, the amount of water that farmer can pump from the well is limited by the geo-hydrology. The price at which water is sold is also high in such areas (Deepak *et al.*, 2005), and the opportunity cost of using water is high in those areas. Hence, the amount of water saved would mean income saving for the adopters.

As regards benefit due to energy-saving, it is applicable to certain MI devices, especially low pressure systems and gravity systems such as drip tapes, micro tube drips and easy drips. But, farmers of many water-scarce regions are not confronted with marginal cost of using energy. Hence, for them energy saving does not result in any private gain. But, from a macro economic perspective, if one wants to examine the economic viability of the system, it is important to consider the full cost of supplying electricity to the farms while evaluating the economics of irrigation using the system. Also, we consider the price at which water is traded in the market for irrigation (ranging from Rs.1.5/m^3 to Rs.2.5/m^3 in north Gujarat to Rs.6/m^3 in Kolar) as the economic value of water[13] then any saving in water resulting from drip use could be treated as an economic gain. The real economic cost of pumping water would range from Rs. 1.5/m^3 in north Gujarat to Rs. 2/m^3 in Kolar district.

The private income benefit due to water saving is applicable to only those who purchase water on hourly basis. Dhawan (2000) cautions that over-assessment of private benefits are possible in certain situations where return flows from conventional irrigation are significant (Dhawan, 2000: pp 3777). But in regions where reduction in deep percolation means real water saving, it leads to private benefits. Here, for water buyers, the private income gain from the use of drip or sprinkler system depends on the price at which water is purchased (volumetric) and the reduction in water use achieved. There could be significant social benefits due to water saving in water scarce regions, owing to the reduced stress on precious water resources (Dhawan, 2000: pp 3775), resulting from reduced pumping. In situations like north Gujarat, such social benefits could not be over-emphasised.

As regards the cost, the capital costs could vary widely depending on the crop. For widely spaced crops (mango, sapota, orange and gooseberry) the cost could be relatively low due to low density of laterals and drippers. For closely spaced crops such as pomegranate, lemon, papaya, grapes, the cost could go up. For crops such as castor, cotton, fennel and vegetables, the cost would go further up as denser laterals and drippers would be required. Even for low cost micro tube drips, the cost per ha would vary from Rs. 12000 for sapota and mango to Rs.28000 for pomegranate to Rs.40000 for castor.

Keeping in view these perspectives and situations, economics of water-saving technologies can be simulated for four typical situations for alfalfa in Banaskantha district of north Gujarat based on real time data collected from four demo plots in farmers' fields. Alfalfa is an annual crop used as forage grown in north Gujarat region, including Banaskantha district.

The first level of analysis is limited to private cost-benefits (level 1). Yield increase and labour saving are the private gains here. The annual yield benefit was estimated by taking calculated daily yield increase (col. 3- col. 5 in Table 11) and multiplying by 240, which is the approximate number of days for which the fodder field yields in a year. The labour saving benefit was calculated by taking the irrigation equivalent (in daily terms) of total water saved (total volume of water saved/ discharge of pump in 8 hours) and multiplying it by the daily wage.

In the second level of analysis, the actual economic cost of using every unit of electricity is considered as a benefit from saving every unit of the energy (level 2). In this case, the energy saving and cost saving depend on two factors: the energy required to pump unit volume of groundwater, and the total volume of water saved. Here, it is assumed that no extra energy would be required for using the inline drip system, which is connected to the existing pumping devise[14]. In the third level of analysis, the unit price of water in the market was treated as economic gain from "actual saving" of every unit of water and was added to the cost of electricity to pump unit volume of water (level 3). This was multiplied by the total volume of water saved to obtain the total economic gain in excess of the gain from yield increase and labour saving. The fourth level of analysis for farmers who are irrigating with purchased water. Here in this case, the unit price of water could be considered as a private gain from saving every unit of water (level 4). In this case, the cost of construction of a storage tank and a 0.5 HP pump are added to the cost of installation of the system. The results are presented in Table 10.

An analysis of economics of some water-saving technologies (pressurized drips, sprinklers and micro tubes) was attempted on the basis of data on crop inputs and outputs, and capital investments collected from primary survey of adopters and non-adopters for Kachchh, Bhavnagar, Rajkot and Banaskantha districts. While Kachchh has arid climate, Bhavnagar and Rajkot have semi arid climate. The results are presented in Table 11. The analysis is based on the estimates of incremental returns from drip irrigation over the entire life of the system against the additional capital investment for the system. For calculating the present value of an annuity, a discount rate of 6% was used and the life of the system was considered as 10 years. The incremental returns considered are the average of two consecutive years. This was done to take care of the problems of yield reductions due to crop failure and price fluctuations. While estimating the incremental returns, the effect of differential input costs, and differential return were considered. The benefit cost analysis was carried out for three important crops in all the four districts irrigated by micro irrigation systems.

In the case Kachchh, the B/C ratio ranges from the lowest of 0.56 for castor to 6.0 for banana. Apart from castor, there was one more crop for which the B/C ratio was found to be less than 1.0 for mango also. For all other crops, the B/C ratio was more than 1.0. In the case of Banaskantha, the B/C ratio ranged from 1.37 for bajra to 5.2 for castor. In the case of Bhavnagar, the B/ C ratio ranged from 0.84 for bajra to 15.3 for mango. For crops in Rajkot, the B/C ratio ranged from 1.06 for chilly to 3.3 for

Table 10. Economics of Drip Irrigation in Alfalfa for Four Different Situations

lot o.	*Initial Cost of the System (US $)*	*Total Water Saving /Year (M^3)*	*Equivalent Energy Saving/ Year (K.W. hr)*	*Labour Saving /Year (person days)*	*Yield Increase From the entire plot (Kg)*	*Private Benefit/ Cost (Level 1)*	*Economic Benefit/ Cost Ratio (Level 2)*	*Economic Benefit/ Cost Ratio (Level 3)*	*Private Benefit/ Cost Ratio (for water buyers) (Level 4)*
	157.0	479.50	149.00	4.00	448.00	1.09	1.83	2.78	1.39
	136.0	111.30	92.30	6.00	409.00	1.29	1.48	1.74	0.99
	201.0	63.60	31.60	4.90	586.00	1.10	1.18	1.28	0.88
	168.0	468.00	232.80	6.00	414.00	1.05	1.73	2.59	1.33

Source: Kumar, 2007

cotton. Overall, two major findings emerge from the results of benefit-cost analysis. First: for cash crops and orchard crops, the B/C ratio often become very high but with wide variations across crops. For instance, in case of castor in Banaskantha, the B/C ratio is 5.2, whereas it is only 0.56 for the same crop in Kachchh. Second: for conventional field crops, the B/C ratios are generally low, but with low variation.

Table 11. Private costs and returns from micro irrigation in the selected districts

Crop	*Incremental net income (Rs)*	*Incremental annual cost of the system (Rs)*	*B/C Ratio*
Rajkot			
1. Chilly	17518.28	16792.63	1.06
2. Cotton	20064.84	6266.75	3.30
3. Groundnut	7574.25	9216.00	1.30
Banaskantha			
1. Alfalfa	49062.77	9998.76	4.90
2. Bajra	1787.88	1221.13	1.40
3. Castor	5373.78	1016.48	5.20
4. Mustard	6021.25	3970.70	2.00
5. Wheat	2305.95	2602.72	0.98
Kachchh			
1. Banana	54297.21	10949.73	6.00
2. Cotton	17303.65	11158.78	1.70
3. Lemon	34029.61	15677.26	2.70
4. Mango	8570.48	8386.90	0.94
5. Brinjal	42816.90	32608.70	1.30
6. Castor	18953.74	33840.17	0.56
Bhavnagar			
1. Groundnut	3509.98	685.47	5.10
2. Bajra	2155.14	2559.86	0.84
3. Jowar (Fodder)	38150.91	8861.06	4.30
4. Cotton	3719.35	2138.46	1.70
5. Mango	29901.90	1953.13	15.30
6. Lemon	3933.28	2822.49	1.40

Source: Authors' own estimates based on primary survey.

It is noteworthy that the incremental net returns were generally markedly higher for cash crops viz., ground nut, cotton, castor; and fruits viz., mango and banana than for food crops viz., bajra and wheat. This is in conformation with the work of earlier researchers (see Narayanamoorthy, 1997; Sivanappan, 1994; Narayanamoorthy, 2003). The incremental returns from cash crops, particularly fruits, could, however, fluctuate significantly depending on the price and yield fluctuations. At the same time, it is also equally striking to note that the benefit-cost ratios are good for even cereals given the fact that the capital cost of the system is high and the market value of the produce is not high Perhaps, this could be due to the reason that the farmers, who did not use the system faced significant yield losses due to water stress.

4. Potential Future Benefits from Micro-irrigation Technologies

This section is based on inference drawn from section 3 concerning the conditions under which micro irrigation system becomes a good bet technology.

4.1 Crops Conducive to Micro-irrigation Technologies

A rigorous analysis of published and unpublished literature shows that there are a wide range of crops that are conducive to micro-irrigation technologies from physical feasibility point of view. They could be classified to: 1] tree crops and orchards; 2] row crops; 3] plantation crops; 4] field crops; 5] vegetables; and 6] cash crops. A list of crops which are conducive to different water-saving irrigation technologies are presented in Table 12. However, this does not mean that micro irrigation systems would be economically viable for these crops in the regions mentioned.

4.2 Water-scarce River Basins that can benefit from Micro-irrigation Technologies

Though the economic viability of MI systems for a given crop would depend on a wide range of factors, such as natural environment (soils and climate), production conditions, market conditions, spread of the technology in an area and the type of price considered for economic evaluation (whether, farm gate price or market price) due to paucity of data on the actual

Table 12. Crops conducive to water-saving technologies in India and their Potential Spread

Crop Category	*Different crops conducive for WSTs*	*Type of WSTs that can be used*	*Regions**
Tree crops and orchards	Mango, Guava, Gooseberry, Pomegranate, Sapote, Orange, Coconut, Banana, Date palm, Grapes, Papaya, Citrus and Kinnow, Drumstick	Drips (for all); and also Sprinklers (Banana, Mango) and plastic mulching in case of extreme water stress	Maharashtra, Andhra Pradesh, Kerala, Karnataka, Tamil Nadu, and Punjab
Row field crops	Potato and Groundnut	Drips; and also mulching (for groundnut and potato)	Gujarat, Maharashtra and Punjab
Plantation Crops	Coconut, Coffee, Tea, Teak	Drips (for coconut and teak); and sprinklers (for tea and coffee)	Kerala and Karnataka (coconut, tea and coffee), Orissa (tea); Tamil Nadu (coconut)
Field Crops	Wheat, Pearl millet, Sorghum, Maize, Alfalfa, Mustard	Overhead sprinklers (wheat, pearl millet, maize and sorghum) and mini and micro sprinklers for alfalfa	Punjab, Haryana, Gujarat, Maharashtra, Rajasthan and Madhya Pradesh, Andhra Pradesh, and Karnataka

Crop Category	*Different crops conducive for WSTs*	*Type of WSTs that can be used*	*Regions**
Fruit/Vegetables	Tomatoes, Cucumbers, Capsicums, Brinjal, Gourds, Chilly, Cabbage, Cauliflower, Strawberry	Drips, and plastic mulching	Maharashtra, Gujarat, Rajasthan, Andhra Pradesh, Tamil Nadu, Karnataka
Cash crops	Cotton, Fennel, Castor, Sugarcane, Vanilla and Cumin, betel vines	Drips for sugarcane; fogger sprinklers for Vanilla; and micro sprinklers for cumin	Maharashtra, Tamil Nadu and Gujarat (for cotton, sugarcane and ground nut), Gujarat for cumin and fennel, Orissa and central India for betel vines, and Kerala for vanilla

Note: Drips include pressurized drips (integrated drips, emitters, drip tapes); easy drips; micro tube drips; Regional priority only indicates, any of these crop types could be grown there and not all the crops under the category conditions for which the evaluation is performed, general conclusions are drawn on the conduciveness of the basins to the technologies based on the available data and the knowledge about the regions' physical and socio-economic conditions and institutional settings.

That said, there are many basins that can benefit from MI devices. But, the extent to which it can contribute to overall improvement in basin water productivity would depend on: 1] the total area under crops that are conducive to micro irrigation devices in the basin; 2] the types of sources of irrigation of those crops, i.e., whether lift irrigated or gravity irrigated; 3] the climatic conditions in the basin; and, 4] the geo-hydrological conditions.

We have seen that the crops that are served by gravity irrigation are least likely to be covered under MI systems due to physical, socio-economic and institutional constraints. Hence, large areas of Haryana, Uttar Pradesh, and Punjab offer no potential for scaling up of micro irrigation systems as mostly they are covered under canal systems. Over and above, paddy, one of the major crops grown in these areas, is also not conducive to water-saving irrigation devices. Though sprinklers can be used for wheat, the water-saving and yield impacts are not likely to be significant enough to motivate farmers to go for it. Nearly 55% of the groundwater in Haryana is of poor quality with salinity and alkalinity, and the problems are more severe for deeper aquifers in the region. The use of groundwater for irrigation itself is marginal, making micro irrigation system adoption difficult. In Bihar, leaving aside the problem of low appropriateness of the prevailing cropping system (comprising wheat and paddy), power crisis would be a major stumbling block for adoption of sprinklers which are energy-intensive.

As regards climate, most of Gangetic-Brahmaputra-Megha basin covering most parts of Uttar Pradesh, Bihar, and north east has sub-humid and cold climate, and the extent of water-saving possible through MI system adoption could be quite insignificant.

If we consider factors such as physical availability of water, physical conditions of water supply and land use, cropping systems, groundwater table conditions, the basins where MI system adoption could take off and where it would result in enhancement in basin level water productivity are: west flowing rivers north of Tapi (river basins of Saurashtra, Kachchh and Luni in Rajasthan); Banas, Sabarmati, south-western parts of Punjab and Haryana in Indus; Cauvery basin; Krishna basin; Pennar basin; Vaghai basin; Narmada; downstream areas of Tapi; Mahanadi and Godavari.

The enhancement in water productivity would come from two phenomena. 1. Reduction in the amount of water depleted with no effect on crop consumptive use. 2. Raising the yield of all the crops that are grown in these basins. Nevertheless, within these basins, there are areas where the groundwater table is very shallow, and climate is sub-humid. They include: south and central Gujarat, which are falling in the downstream areas of Tapi and Narmada.

The western Ghat areas in Kerala, Karnataka, Maharashtra and Goa provide very favourable environment for adoption of micro-irrigation devices due to the presence of tree & fruit crops and plantation crops—coconut, arecanut, coffee, tea, mango and banana. The semi arid, hard rock areas of Tamil Nadu, Karnataka, Andhra Pradesh, Maharashtra and most parts of Gujarat, provide favourable environment for adoption of MI systems owing to limited groundwater potential; the dominance of well irrigation; and dominance of tree crops, fruit crops, cash crops, row crops and vegetables as mentioned above. At the same time, there would be real saving in water due to the fact that the groundwater table is falling in these regions.

The available data on adoption of micro irrigation systems in different states of India during the past four years is a testimony to what has been discussed in the preceding paragraphs. The highest area under drip irrigation is in Maharashtra (22358 ha). This is followed by Andhra Pradesh (17556 ha), Karnataka (16731 ha) and Gujarat and Rajasthan. But, at the aggregate level, micro irrigation accounts for nearly 1.6% of India's total irrigated area, against 21% in the United States, and 30% (8% under drips and 22% under sprinklers) in Australia.

4.4 Area that can be brought under MI Technologies in Major Indian States

Map 1 shows the area under different crops that are conducive to MI devices in different states of India. The empirical basis for estimating this is: 1] the gross irrigated area under such crops; and 2] the percentage of net irrigated area under well irrigation in the respective states. Such approach has the inbuilt assumption that percentage area under well irrigation is uniform across crops. This may not be true. In fact, it has been found that in surface irrigated areas, farmers normally take water-intensive, but less water-sensitive crops. It considered only 16 major states, and had excluded the minor states (13 nos.) and Union Territories. Further, it has excluded area under crops viz., wheat, mustard, rapeseed, pearl millet

Map 1: Estimated Area under Crops Conducive to Water Saving Irrigation Technologies

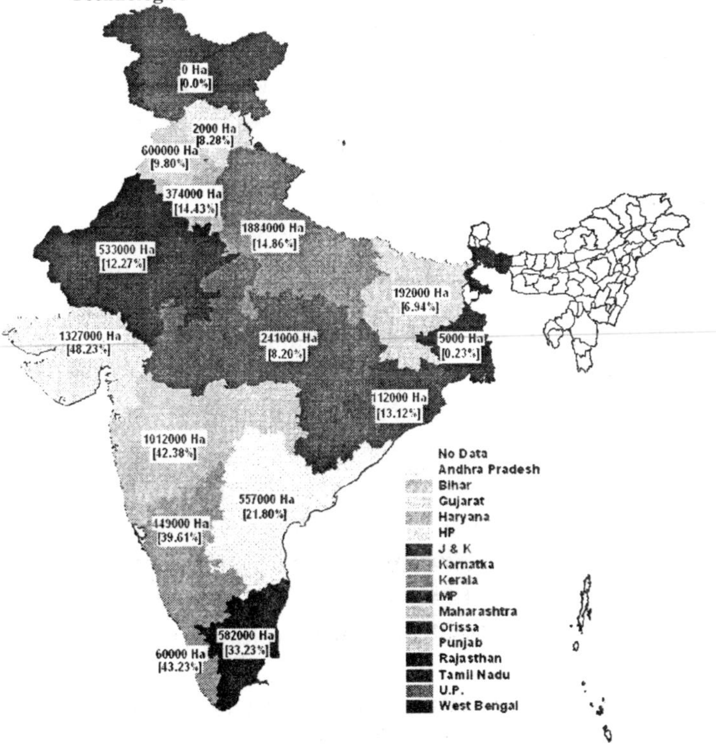

Figures in parenthesis represent percentage area under the crop

and sorghum which can be irrigated using sprinklers, but with poor results in terms of water-saving, and had included only those which are amenable to drips and plastic mulching.

The total area under crops that can be brought under MI technologies is 7.93 million ha. The map shows that Uttar Pradesh has largest area (1.884 M ha) under crops amenable to WSTs. It is followed by Gujarat with 1.327 M ha, and Maharashtra with 1.012 M ha.

4.5 Basins and Cropped Area Conducive to Adoption of Micro-irrigation Technologies

In order estimate the figures of "total irrigated cropped area that would benefit from MI systems", we have superimposed the cropped area that are conducive to MI systems, and the basins where MI adoption would lead to real water saving, and water productivity improvements. We would explain the logic behind this.

The earlier analysis has shown that peninsular and western India had substantial area under crops that are conducive to MI technologies. It has also shown that Central and north and central India have very little area under such crops. The exception is Uttar Pradesh, which accounts for nearly 25% of the area that is conducive to MI systems. The basins in peninsular, western and central India have natural environments (soil, geo-hydrology, climate), wherein MI adoption can actually result in real water saving and basin level water productivity improvement. But, in Ganga-Brahmaputra basin, in which UP falls, adoption is going to be poor due to poor rural electrification; relative water abundance; shallow groundwater in most areas; and very low size of operational holdings of farmers. Even if this region adopts MI systems on a large-scale, it may result not in reduction in depleted water, but a little difference in crop yields, with the resultant increase in basin level water productivity being meagre. Western part of Mahanadi is another area that would be conducive to MI systems. Hence, Ganga-Brahmaputra-Meghna) have to be excluded from our analysis.

Hence, the cropped areas that will benefit from MI system would be from: 1] basins of all east-flowing rivers of peninsular India; 2] basins of west-flowing rivers north of Tapi in Gujarat and Rajasthan; Mahanadi; some parts of Indus basin covering south-western Punjab; and west flowing rivers of South India. Hence, the total would be 5.844 m ha (7.930-2.086) of cropped area. This is the absolute potential, and the real adoption would depend on several socio-economic and institutional factors.

Now, let us look at the area estimates provided by Narayanamoorthy (2004b), and the task force on MI in India. Narayanamoorthy (2004b) provided an estimate of 21.27 m. ha as the net area under all irrigated crops that can be brought under drip systems in India, with an upper figure of 51.42 m. ha including area under those crops, which are currently rain-fed. But this analysis did not consider the several physical and socio-economic factors that would ultimate determine the viability of drips for these crops. Whereas the task force on MI had estimated a figure of 69 m. ha as the area suitable for MI systems in India. It is quite clear from such a high figure that the task force estimates had included all regions and area irrigated by different types of irrigation systems, therefore not considered the physical (technical, and hydro-meteorological), and socio-economic constraints in the adoption of MI systems.

4.6 Quantification of Potential Future Impact of MI Systems on Water Requirements

In order to analyze the impact of MI devices on aggregate water requirement for crop production in India, we started with the data provided in Table 2 in which data on water use efficiency[15] impact of drip irrigation for various crops are presented. A total of six crops, for which country-level data on irrigated crop area are available, were considered for estimating the future water-saving benefits. Then the data on aggregate output from these crops are obtained. Assuming that the same output for the respective crops is to be maintained in future, the future water requirement for growing the crops could be estimated by dividing the improved water use efficiency figures by the crop output.

The reduction in water requirement for crop $_i$= Present Output of Crop $_i$ [1/Current Water Productivity -1/Improved Water Productivity]

The procedure can be repeated for all crops.

Table 13. Aggregate Reduction in Water Requirement for Crop Production Possible with Drip Irrigation Systems

Sr. No.	*Name of Crop*	*Current Yield (ton/ha)*	*Expected Yield Coming from the Potential States* (Million ton)*	*Water Productivity (Kg/m³)*	*Improved Water Productivity (Kg/m³)*	*Reduction in Crop Water Requirement (BCM)*
1.	Sugarcane	128.0	170.0	5.950	18.09	31.00
2.	Cotton	2.600	4.391	0.303	1.080	10.42
3.	Groundnut	1.710	2.840	0.340	0.950	1.453
4.	Potato	23.57	34.47	11.79	17.21	0.127
5.	Castor	1.260	1.350	0.340	0.670	0.497
6.	Onion	9.300	12.20	1.544	2.700	0.963
7.	Total	44.46				

* States where MI systems are likely to be adopted. This is obtained by multiplying the average crop yield under conventional irrigation (as provided in Table 4) with the sum of the estimated area under that crop in each state. The water productivity figures are estimated from the yield and water consumption figures provided for the respective crops in Table 3 of this report.

While estimating the crop area that are likely to be brought under drips, the area under the respective crops in water-abundant states viz., UP, Bihar, West Bengal, Haryana and north eastern states were subtracted. The aggregate reduction in crop water requirement due to the adoption of drip systems was estimated to be 44.46 BCM. It can also be seen from Table 13 that highest water-saving could come from the use of drips in sugarcane, followed by cotton. This is the maximum area that can be covered under the crops listed in well-irrigated areas, provided all the constraints facing adoption are overcome through appropriate institutional and policy environments. In the subsequent section, we would discuss what these policies are.

5. Major Findings

1. In India, the extent of adoption of MI devices is just 1.6% of the total irrigated area. Adoption is also heavily skewed vis-à-vis geographical spread and crops.

2. The available literature shows that drip irrigation leads to substantial saving in applied water over conventional method of irrigation, yield improvements, and improvements in water use efficiency. The extent of field level water saving is the highest for orchards. The available data are from experimental farms; and social research. Both have limitations. In the first case, issue is of replicability and in the second case, the reliability and adequacy of data.

3. There are methodological issues involved in the estimation of water-saving and water productivity impacts of MI systems. The available estimates are based on the assumption that all the water applied to the crop is depleted. But, in view of the fact that MI devices are mostly adopted in semi arid and arid regions with deep and falling water table conditions, such assumptions are permissible.

4. Analysis of the potential contribution of MI systems in India in reducing the aggregate demand for water in crop production involves three complex considerations: 1] the extent of coverage of MI systems that can be achieved at the national level; 2] the extent of real water saving possible with MI system adoption at the field level; and 3] what farmers do with the water saved through MI systems, and the changes in the cropping systems associated with adoption.

5. The factors that limit the expansion of MI technologies in India are many. Some of them are: (1) lack of independent source of water and pressurizing device for many farmers; (2) poor quality of groundwater in many semi arid and arid regions; (3) the mismatch between water delivery schedules in surface irrigation systems, and irrigation schedules required in MI systems; (4) cropping systems that dominate field crops in semi arid regions; (5) dominance of small and marginal farmers, and

small plot sizes; (6) low opportunity costs of pumping groundwater due to lack of well-defined water rights; (7) negative technical externalities in groundwater use; viii] poor extension services; and (8) poor administration of subsidies.

6. The field level water saving due to MI systems depend on: (a) the geo-hydrological environment; (b) crop type; (c) agro-climate; (d) type of MI technology. Water saving impacts would be high for drip systems, particularly under arid to semi arid climate, for widely spaced row crops, when groundwater table is deep. While MI system would result in field-level water saving in various degrees, depending on the situation, its impact on aggregate water use would depend on groundwater availability vis-à-vis power supply situation, the crops farmers choose with MI, and the extra land available for cultivation.

7. A comprehensive analysis of economics of different WSTs for different crops across Gujarat shows that B/C ratios are highly influenced by crop choices and largely limited to high value crops (fruits and some vegetables), which have further capital investment requirements apart from the irrigation system.

8. The river basins that are likely to be benefited by and are also conducive to MI systems are: western part of Indus in Punjab and Haryana; west-flowing rivers north of Tapi; east-flowing rivers south of Tapi; west-flowing rivers south of Tapi in the Western Ghats; Sabarmati; and Mahanadi. In these basins, extensive adoption of efficient irrigation technologies would result in overall enhancement in basin-level crop water productivity. The total well-irrigated area that can be potentially brought under MI systems from 16 major states of India is estimated to be 5.6 m ha.

9. The total potential reduction in crop water requirement with the full adoption of drip systems in six selected crops is estimated to be 44.46 BCM. It can also be seen that highest reduction in water requirement could come from the use of drips in sugarcane, followed by cotton. Both the estimates are much lower than the estimates provided by Narayanamoorthy (2004b) and that by the Task Force on Micro Irrigation in India.

6. Institutional and Policy Alternatives for Spreading Micro-Irrigation Technologies

The most ideal policy environment for promotion of MI technologies in well irrigated areas would be pro-rata pricing of electricity. As we have seen in the previous chapter, this would create direct incentive for efficient water use (Kumar, 2005). But, to what extent the MI technologies would reduce energy use and therefore pro-rata pricing creates incentive for adoption of MI devices depends on the crop type and the type of technology—whether pressurized system or gravity drip system—, used for the crop. The reason is not all MI technologies are energy efficient. Hence, bringing non-conventional (non-pressurized) drip systems under the ambit of subsidies is very important, once pro-rata pricing of electricity is introduced. It would also force farmers in areas irrigated by diesel engines to adopt such MI systems as it could save diesel and reduce input costs.

While in the long run, total metering and consumption-based pricing would be the most desired scenario to emerge (Kumar, 2007), the governments can start with metering of agricultural consumption. Cash incentives or heavy subsidy for MI devices could be provided to farmers who are willing to use them, provided they minimize electricity consumption. This cash incentive could be inversely proportional to the total energy use and directly proportional to the percentage area under MI system. This would create incentives for farmers to maximize the coverage of MI systems in their irrigated crops, particularly those which are less energy intensive; and limit the total irrigated area.

Improving power supply—both quality and duration—, is extremely important for boosting adoption of pressurized MI devices in many areas. Such areas include alluvial north Gujarat and south-western Punjab. One could argue that with improved power supply, groundwater use could go up. But, in reality, with improved hours of power supply, the quality of irrigation would go up, enabling farmers to realize the full potential of MI systems. The actual impact of improved power supply regime on sustainability would depend on the type of crops farmers grow with MI systems, and the availability of extra land for area expansion[16].

All these policy measures would help address the issues in well-irrigated areas. Still, a large chunk of the irrigated area (23.606 M ha in 1999-00 in India, source: Ministry of Agriculture and Cooperation, GOI), which is from surface sources, would be left untouched. In addition to amendments in administration of subsidies and improvements in extension activities, the way to bring these areas under MI systems is to either change the delivery practices or to increase the economic incentives.

The water delivery systems need to be designed in such a way that farmers can directly connect the source to their distribution system. The irrigation schedules need to be reworked in such a way that the duration between two turns becomes much shorter than the present 2-3 weeks. In the most ideal situation, the supply has to be perennial. This can happen in the most advanced stage of irrigation systems design and would take time. Over and above, it can be thought about only in case of new schemes. One of the reasons why the farmers in Israel adopt micro irrigation systems at such a large-scale (with 95% of the irrigated crops are under drip systems) is that the surface water is delivered in their fields under pressure through pipes.

Economic incentives for MI adoption in canal commands can be improved by increasing the price of irrigation water. High prices for irrigation water would affect cost saving as a result of applied water saving. Alternatively, the cost of building the intermediate storage systems can be reduced through proper design of subsidies. In command area of Indira Gandhi Canal Project, most of the farmers are using intermediary storage tanks and locally it is known as "*Diggi*". The farmers are using electric pump for lifting this water and they irrigate crops whenever they required. After seeing the benefits of such interventions on reducing the pressure on the resource, government has started providing subsidy for construction of "*Diggi*". Many farmers are using sprinklers to irrigate their crops from the tank water.

Apart from saving the cost of water, the differential economic returns farmers get under lift irrigation over canal irrigation (IRMA/UNICEF, 2001; Kumar and Singh, 2001) and the differential return in drip irrigated crops would be the strongest incentive for farmers to go for intermediate storage systems. The justification for subsidizing the systems is that the private benefit-costs ratio would not be very attractive with very high capital cost of the system and the additional infrastructure, whereas the social benefits accrued from saving the scarce water resources would be high when compared against the social costs. The differential returns could be due to the better control over water delivery possible with lift (IRMA/UNICEF, 2001) or due to the increased ability to grow cash crops such as cotton, banana, and fruits and vegetables in the command areas. With this, the actual area that could be brought under MI systems would be larger than the estimates we have provided for the potential area under MI system.

Improving the administration of subsidies is necessary to increase the welfare impacts. The farmers should be made to pay the full cost of the system initially, and subsidies be paid in instalments based on periodic review of system performance. As manufacturers have to sell the system at the market price, it would compel them to improve the competitiveness of their products, and also provide good technical input services. The rural credit institutions can advance loans to farmers for purchase of MI systems so as to maximize coverage of small and marginal farmers. In Gujarat, a new model for promoting MI devices is being implemented by the state government through a state-owned company called Gujarat Green Revolution Company (GGRC). Under this model, the subsidy is paid by GGRC to the farmer in instalments, and the results are very encouraging. Not only that the adoption of MI devices is fast, but significant percentage of the adopters belongs to small holder category, having less than 2.0 ha of land, and they use it for cash crops viz., cotton, ground nut, potato and vegetables.

On the other hand, there is a need for creating a separate agency for promoting MI in each state to increase the speed of processing of application from farmers. The agency can work in tandem with the manufacturers and farmers to enable timely technical inputs to the farmers. In areas where agricultural processing units are concentrated, provision of all critical inputs including subsidies would not be a problem, as they could come from these processing units. The example is that of sugarcane and grape grower cooperatives of Maharashtra. But, in areas where demand for drip irrigation is scattered vis-à-vis crops and geographical spread, this would be an issue. The new agency should facilitate survey of farmers' fields by the manufacturer, and get the designs and estimates prepared along with the most desirable cropping system. This would also help farmers procure the system well in advance of the crop season to make full benefit of it. Within a year after the creation of GGRC, a total of 30,000 ha of crop land had already been brought under drips in the state.

7. Conclusions

Adoption of MI systems is likely to pick up fast in arid and semi arid, well-irrigated areas, where farmers have independent irrigation sources, and where groundwater is scarce. Further, high average land holdings, large size of individual plots, and a cropping system dominated by widely spaced row crops, which are also high-valued, would provide the ideal environment for the same. The extent of real water-saving and water productivity improvements at the field level through adoption of MI systems would be high for widely spaced row crops, in arid and semi arid conditions, when the groundwater table is deep or aquifer is saline. In hard rock areas with poor groundwater potential, MI adoption would result in improved efficiency of water use, but would not reduce the total groundwater draft.

In semi arid and arid areas which face severe groundwater scarcity, the economics of MI systems would be sound for high-valued cash crops. In areas where electricity charges are not based on power consumption, and opportunity cost of using water is zero, the saving in energy and water achieved through MI system do not get translated into economic benefits. Hence, economics of MI system will not be sound in such areas. But, the evaluation studies of are skewed towards drip systems, and do not capture the effect of changing physical, socio-economic and institutional settings on the economic dynamic.

The future potential of MI systems in improving basin level water productivity is primarily constrained by the physical characteristics of basins vis-à-vis the opportunities they provide for real water-saving at the field level, and area under crops that are conducive to MI systems in those basins. Preliminary analysis shows very modest potential of MI systems to the tune of 5.69 m ha, with an aggregate impact on crop water requirement to the tune of 43.35 BCM possible with drip adoption for six selected crops. Creating appropriate institutions for extension, designing water and electricity pricing policies apart from building proper irrigation and power supply infrastructure would play a crucial role in facilitating large-scale adoption of different MI systems. The subsidies for MI promotion should be targeted at regions and technologies, where MI adoption results in real water and energy saving at the aggregate level.

References

Ahmad, M. D., I, Masih and H. Turral (2004) Diagnostic analysis of spatial and temporal variations in crop water productivity: A field scale analysis of the rice-wheat cropping system of Punjab, Pakistan, *Journal of Applied Irrigation Science*, 39 (10).

Amarasinghe, Upali, Bharat R. Sharma, Noel Aloysius, Christopher Scott, Vladimir Smakhtin, Charlotte de Fraiture, A. K. Sinha and A. K. Shukla (2005) *Spatial Variation in Water Supply and Demand across River Basins of India*, IWMI Research Report 83, Colombo, Sri Lanka.

Barker, Randolph, David Dawe and Arlene Inocencio (2003) "*Economics of Water Productivity in Managing Water for Agriculture*," in Jacob Kijne and others (Eds.) *Water Productivity in Agriculture: Limits and Opportunities for Improvement*, Comprehensive Assessment of Water Management in Agriculture. UK: CABI Publishing in Association with International Water Management Institute.

Behera, B.P. and N. Sahoo, (1998) Economic evaluation of a drip irrigation system in Orissa. *Environment and Ecology*, Vol. 16(2): 297-299.

Brewer, J., Shashi Kolavalli, A.H. Kalro, G. Naik, S. Ramnarayan, K.V. Raju and R. Shakthivadivel (1999) Irrigation Management

Transfer in India: Policies, Processes and Performance. New Delhi and Calcutta: Oxford & IBH.

Carter, Richard, Melvyn Kay and Keith Weatherhead (1999) Water Losses in Smallholder Irrigation Schemes, *Agricultural Water Management*, 40 (1): 15-24.

Central Ground Water Board (1998) Groundwater Problems of Mehsana District. Report, Central Ground Water Board, West-Central region, Ahmedabad.

Chavez, H. and F. Andrew (1974) Drip irrigation increase yields, lowers water costs. *Citrus and Vegetable Magazine*, Vol. 38: 1,6 and 18.

Dahake, S.G., S. P. Lambe, H.V. Kalpande; D.M. Nikhade and V.V. Kalpande (1998) Utility perception of orange growers about drip irrigation system. *Jouranal of Soils and Crops*, Vol. 8(2): *154-156.*

Desale, P.G., P.P. Pawar and R.P. Patil (2003) Economics analysis of drip irrigation for banana. *Indian Journal of Agricultural Economics*, July-September, Vol. 58, No. 3, p. 506.

Deepak, and others (2005) Water Demand Management: A Strategy to Deal with Water Scarcity, paper presented at the 4th Annual Partners' Meet of IWMI-Tata Water Policy Research Programme, February

Dhawan, B. D. (2000) "Drip Irrigation: Evaluating Returns". *Economic and Political Weekly*, pp 3775-3780, October 14.

Frederick, K. D. (1993) *Balancing Water Demand with Supplies: The Role of Management in a World of Increasing Scarcity*, Technical Paper 189, Washington D. C: World Bank.

Gaonkar, Rekha and Shashikala Sarmalkar (2003) Policies for sustainable use of water. *Indian Journal of Agricultural Economics*, July-September, Vol. 58, No. 3, p. 508.

Government of Gujarat (1996) Water Resource Planning for the State of Gujarat- Phase III, Vol. II, Main Report.

Government of India (1994) Drip irrigation in India, Indian National Committee on Irrigation and Drainage, Ministry of Water Resources, Government of India, New Delhi.

Government of Gujarat (1999) "Report of the Committee on Estimation of Ground Water Resource and Irrigation Potential in Gujarat State: GWRE – 1997", Department of Narmada, Water Resources and Water Supplies, Gandhinagar.

Government of India (2002) "Annual Report (2001-02) of the Working of State Electricity Boards and Electricity Departments 2001-2002," Planning Commission-Power & Energy Division, May 2002.

Hapase, D.G., A.N. Mankar; A.N. Salunkhe; V.M. Salokhe; Gajendra Singh and S.G. Illangantileke (1992) Techno-economic evaluation of drip irrigation for sugarcane crop. In Proceedings of an International Agricultural Engineering Conference, held in Bangkok, Thailand on 7-10 December, 1992, Vol. III, pp. 897-904.

Inamdar, P.P., J. R. Pawar and D.L. Sale (1995) Economic efficiency of bi-wall drip irrigation in sugarcane production: a case study in Ankalkhop village in Sangli district of Maharashtra. *Bharatiya Sugar*. Vol. 22(2): 43-48.

Ingle P.O. and N.A. Sagane (1992) Constraints in the use of drip irrigation systems : a case study. *Journal of Maharashtra Agricultural Universities,* Vol. 17(2) :294-297.

IRMA/UNICEF (2001) White Paper on Water in Gujarat, Report submitted to the Department of Narmada, Water Resources and Water Supplies, Government of Gujarat, Gandhinagar.

Jadhav S.S., Gutal G.B. and A.A. Chougule (1990) Cost economics of the drip irrigation system for tomato crop. In Proceedings of the International Congress on the Use of Plastics in Agriculture, New Delhi, 26th February – 2nd March, 1990.

Keller, A., J. Keller and David Seckler (1996) *Integrated Water Resources Systems: Theory and Policy Implications.* Research Report 3, Colombo: International Water Management Institute.

Kijne, Jacob, Randolph Barker and David Molden (2003) Improving Water Productivity in Agriculture: Editors' Overview, in Jacob Kijne and others (Eds.) *Water Productivity in Agriculture: Limits and Opportunities for Improvement*, Comprehensive Assessment of Water Management in Agriculture. UK: CABI Publishing in Association with International Water Management Institute.

Kumar, M. D. (2002a) Integrated Water Management in the Face of Growing Scarcity and Threatened Groundwater Ecology: Constraints and Opportunities, discussion paper, IWMI-TATA Water Policy Research programme.

Kumar, M. Dinesh (2002b) Reconciling Water Use and Environment: Water Resources Management in Gujarat, Report of the Hydrological Regime Subcomponent of the State Environmental Action Programme, submitted to Gujarat Ecology Commission, Vadodara.

Kumar, M. Dinesh (2003a) "Food Security and Sustainable Agriculture in India: The Water Management Challenge," Working Paper # 60, International Water Management Institute, Colombo, Sri Lanka.

Kumar, M. Dinesh (2003b) "Micro Management of Groundwater in North Gujarat, Water Policy Research Highlight # 5: IWMI-Tata Water Policy Programme, Anand.

Kumar, M. Dinesh (2005) Impact of Electricity Prices and Volumetric Water Allocation on Groundwater Demand Management: Analysis from Western India, *Energy Policy*, 33 (1).

Kumar, M. Dinesh (2007) *Groundwater Management in India: Physical, Institutional and Policy Alternatives*, New Delhi: Sage Publications.

Kumar, M. Dinesh and O. P. Singh (2001) Market Instruments for Demand Management in the Face of Scarcity and Overuse of Water in Gujarat, Western India, *Water Policy*, 5 (3): 387-403.

Kumar, M. Dinesh, Katar Singh, O.P. Singh and R. L. Shiyani (2004) Impacts of Water Saving and Energy Saving Irrigation Technologies in Gujarat, Research Report 2, India Natural Resources Economics and Management Foundation, Anand.

Luhach, M.S., R.K. Khatkar, and D.P. Malik (2003) Economic viability of sprinkler irrigation: An empirical analysis, *Indian Journal of Agricultural Economics*, July-September, Vol. 58, No. 3, p. 489.

Minasia A. N., A.I. Karaghouli and S.K. Habeeb (1994) An economic analysis of drip irrigation systems: A choice among alternatives, Plasti culture, 101: 23-27.

Molden, David, R. Sakthivadivel and Zaigham Habib (2001) Basin-*Level Use and Productivity of Water: Examples from South Asia*, IWMI Research Report 49, Colombo: International Water Management Institute.

Muralidhara, H. R., D.S. Gundurao, A.M.Sarpeshkar, and R. Ramaiah (1994) Is drip irrigation viable for mulberry cultivation: an economic analysis. *Mysore Journal of Agricultural Sciences*, 28(3): 256-260.

Narayanamoorthy, A. (1996) Impact of drip irrigation on consumption of water and electricity. *Asian Economic Review*, 38(3): 350-364.

Narayanamoorthy, A. (1997) Economic Viability of Drip Irrigation: An Empirical Analysis from Maharashtra. *Indian Journal of Agricultural Economics*, October-December, 52 (4), pp. 728-739.

Narayanamoorthy, A. (2004a) Impact Assessment of Drip Irrigation in India: The Case of Sugarcane, *Development Policy Review*, 22 (4): 443-462.

Narayanamoorthy, A. (2004b) Drip irrigation in India: can it solve water scarcity? *Water Policy*, 6 (2004): 117-130.

Narayanamurthy, A. and R. S. Deshpande (1997) "Economics of Drip Irrigation: A Comparative Study of Maharashtra and Tamil Nadu". Mimeo, Gokhale Institute of Politics and Economics, No. 47, Pune.

Palanichamy N.V., K. Palanisamy and T.R. Shanmugam (2002) Economic performance of drip irrigation in coconut farmers in Coimbatore. *Agricultural Economics Research Review*, Conference Issue, pp. 40-48.

Puranik, R.P., S.R. Khonde and P.L. Ganorkar (1992) Constraints and problems as perceived by non-adopters and adopters of drip irrigation system. *Agricultural Situation in India*, Vol. XLVII, No.1 April, pp. 33-34.

Rangachari, R., Nirmal Sengupta, Ramaswamy R. Iyer, Pranab Banergy, and Shekhar Singh (2000) Large Dams: India's Experience, Final Report, prepared for the World Commission on Dams, Cape Town, South Africa, Secretariat of World Commission on Dams.

Rao, P.S. (2003) Study on efficient use of irrigation water device: a case study. *Indian Journal of Agricultural Economics*, July-September, Vol. 58, No. 3, p. 504.

Reddy, D.V.S. and S. Thimmegowda (1997) Economic analysis of different drip irrigation systems of main and ratoon hybrid cotton. *Mysore Journal of Agricultural Sciences*, Vol. 3 1(1):17-22.

Shiyani R.L., D.B. Kuchhadiya and M.V. Patat (1999) Economic impact of drip irrigation technology on cotton growers of Saurashtra region. *Agricultural Situation in India*, 56 (7): 407-412..

Todd, David K. (2003) *Groundwater Hydrology*, Second Edition, John Wiley and Sons (Asia) Pte Ltd. Singapore.

Verma, Shilp, Stanzin Tsephal and Tony Jose (2005) Pepsee Systems: Farmer Innovations under Groundwater Stress, *Water Policy*, 6:4 (2004): 303-318.

Waykar, K.R., B.K. Mali, Y.C. Sale and A.B. Bhosale (2003). Drip irrigation system: A sustainable way for sugar production. *Indian Journal of Agricultural Economics*, July-September, Vol. 58, No. 3, pp. 498-499.

Footnotes

1. See Allen et al, (1997) for definitions of non-beneficial evaporation, non-recoverable deep percolation
2. Watermelon is often grown in intercropping with orchard crops, reducing the capital cost of drips significantly.
3. The total area under horticultural crops and vegetables is only 5.04 per cent of the net irrigated area in the country in 2001-02. It is highest in Maharashtra, both in percentage (19.04%) and aggregate terms (0.75 M ha).
4. They are: 1] crop area based pricing of surface water for irrigation; 2] flat rate system of pricing of electricity or free electricity followed by many Indian states for farm sector. Only Gujarat and Orissa had partially introduced metering of electricity for farm wells.
5. These are not formal water markets, but pump rental markets. Here the well owners are not confronted with the opportunity cost of tapping water from the aquifer.
6. For instance, a survey of 19 tube well owners carried out in Daskroi taluka of Ahmedabad district showed that the total hours of pumping including that for providing irrigation services to the neighbouring farmers is in the range of 80 hours and 2930 hours. Most of them are found to be in the range of 1000 hours. But, the hours for the farmers could run the pump is as high as 3600.
7. It refers to total amount of water diverted from the source for irrigation and not the amount of water applied in the field
8. Deep percolation is due to the drainage below the root zone, which can find its way to perched water table or true groundwater table. Deep percolation is common in all surface methods of irrigation such as border irrigation (both leveled and unleveled small and large border), furrow irrigation and flooding.
10. Soil types, climate and hydrology can affect water losses. Surface irrigation is likely to be more efficient on vertisols than sandy soils. Undulating or sloping land may dictate the use of drip or sprinkler irrigation which can then be managed with less water loss than surface techniques. Unpredictability complicates management and normally reduces efficiency. Total irrigation is easier to schedule and manage than supplementary irrigation because of the unpredictability of natural rainfall (Carter *et al.*, 1999)

11. If power supply is more than what is required to pump the available water from wells, then water saving can lead to expansion in irrigated area. Whereas, if power supply is less than what is required to pump the available water from wells, then water saving per unit area cannot result in area expansion (Kumar, 2002)

12. Farmers bring about significant changes in the cropping systems of farmers with the adoption of drips. When drips are adopted for orchards, farmers are found to permanently abandoning cultivation of traditional crops such as paddy and wheat. A most recent example is Nalgonda district in Andhra. Farmers generally start with small areas under orchards and install drips. After recovering the initial costs, the general tendency of farmers is to bring the entire cultivated land under orchards, and put them under drip irrigation. Thi s is because orchards require special care and attention and putting the entire land under orchards makes farm-management decisions easier. However, the same tendency of area expansion is not seen when MI systems are used for other cash crops such as cotton and sugarcane.

    In the case of cotton, it is difficult for farmers to take up any crop that can be irrigated with drips after the harvest in the end of winter. This is due to the lack of flexibility in the design of the conventional MI systems. Due to the high capital cost, it is best suited to permanent plantings or crops having roughly the same planting space as frequent removal and rolling back can cause damage to online drips. Exceptions are porous pipes used for sub-surface irrigation. In the cotton growing areas, far mers normally roll back the system and cultivate the traditional crops in summer only if water is available. But, early sowing of cotton is found to be common among farmers who have installed drip irrigation, as they are able to manage their pre-sowing irrigation with very little water available from wells (Verma *et al.*, 2005). With improved planting patterns (paired rows, pit system) farmers install almost permanent drip systems for sugarcane crop.

13. Though the actual economic value of the groundwater would be equal to the economic surplus generated by the use of that water for irrigation, which would vary according to the type of crops farmers grow, this would be a reasonable assumption that can lead to more conservative estimates of economic benefits of water saving.

14. The system being designed and installed for small plots of 500 m with an operating pressure requirement of 0.4kg/cm for the inline drips, all the farmers who used the system ran them under the residual head.
15. We treat them as water productivity values as the modified values of WUE capture the net effect of improved water application and improved agronomic practices.
16. In areas where the entire cultivable land is under irrigation, adoption of MI devices would result in reduction in groundwater use at the farm level. Subsidies are required here to promote MI adoption as it would lead to social benefits from reduced stress on groundwater.

6

Can Virtual Water Trade be a Panacea for Global and Regional Water Scarcity Problems?

ABSTRACT

The argument that economies that face acute water scarcity problems can and should meet their water demand for food through cereal imports from water-rich countries; and that virtual water trade can be used to achieve water securities has become dominant in the discussions on ways to deal with global food and water scarcity problems. The underlying rationale in the virtual water trade argument is "global water use efficiency" and "distribution of scarcity". This is based on the assumption that all the humid, water-rich countries are at an advantage in economic terms in producing food grains as compared to the arid and semi-arid countries.

Analysis of country level data on renewable freshwater availability and net virtual water trade of 146 nations across the world shows that a country's virtual water trade is not determined by its water situation. Some countries have the advantage of high "economic efficiency" in food production and have surplus water, but resort to food import, whereas some water scarce countries achieve high virtual water trade balances. Further, virtual water trade increased with increase in gross cropped area. Many of the humid, water-rich countries will not be in a position to produce surplus food and feed the water scarce nations; and virtual water often flows out of water-poor, land rich countries to land-poor water-rich countries. This means that "distribution of scarcity" and "global water use efficiency", are goals that are difficult to achieve through virtual water trade in a practical sense.

The important policy inferences emerging from the analyses are two. First: assessing the food security challenges posed to nations in future purely from a water resource perspective provides a distorted view of the food security scenario. National policies on food security should take into account "access to arable land" apart from water availability. Second: analysis of water challenges posed by nations purely from the point of view of renewable water availability and aggregate demands will be dangerous. Access to water in the soil profile, which is determined by access to arable land, would be an important determinant of effective water availability. Regional virtual water (food) trade, as it is occurring in India today, does not have positive implications for global water use efficiency. In regions that are characterized by imbalances in water availability in demand, physical transfer of water could be attempted as it increases the ability of land-rich regions to produce surplus food. Increase in productivity of land, and incremental economic value realized from the transfer of water might justify the cost of such water transfers.

Key Words: Virtual Water Trade, Global Water Use Efficiency, Global Land Use Efficiency, Distribution of Scarcity, Total Water Sufficiency, Effective Agricultural Water Use, Per Capita Arable Land, Water Richness, Economic Value of Water.

1. "Virtual Water Trade" Changing the Global Debate on Water Scarcity

The recent past has seen several initiatives to provide analytical rigour to the dialogue on future global concerns in water. The major inspiration behind all these initiatives is the diametrically opposite views held by international scholars on the issue of "global water scarcity" (Allan, 1997), which had in a way become a deadlock in the discussions on effective future water management choices. While several of them believe that with rising population and depleting freshwater ecosystems, global water scarcity is imminent and would eventually affect many countries sooner or later (for instance Postel, 1996; Raskin *et al.*, 1997; Seckler *et al.*, 1998), several others hold optimistic views about global freshwater situation.

Table 1: Per Capita Arable Land and Cropping in North Gujarat and South and Central Gujarat – 1998-99

Name of Region	*Per Capita Arable Land (Ha)*	*Net Sown Area/Arable Land (%)*	*Percentage Area under Irrigation*	*Cropping Intensity (%)*	*Irrigation Intensity (%)*	*Per Capita Gross Cropped Area*
North Gujarat	0.188	93.40	44.00	126.0	125	0.223
South and Central Gujarat	0.124	77.60	42.60	111.0	120	0.108

Source: Authors' own calculations based on data provided on land use classification of Gujarat State http://www.indiastat.com/

While the methodology adopted by these global initiatives for assessing future water scenarios have differed—in terms of drivers of change in the water demand and supply conditions—, (see Seckler *et al.* 1998) often leading to creation of uncertain scenarios (based on Allan 1997: Table 1.3 pp. 20), they all tried to address a common concern, i.e., whether there would be sufficient water in different countries and continents to meet their future water needs, largest among them being water for food production, thereby achieving total self-sufficiency in water (Allan 2003b: p. 1).

The term "virtual water" was introduced in 1993 by Prof. Tony Allan to indicate the amount of water made available in the global system through agricultural commodity trade. Prof. Allan interpreted the amount of water present in cereals, milk and livestock in terms of the amount of water used to produce it (Allan 2003a: p. 4). The concept was introduced as a powerful economic tool to ameliorate water scarcity problems of national economies (Allan 1997). Later on several researchers argued in similar lines that water scarce regions can achieve high global water use efficiency by importing products that have high virtual water content embedded in it and exporting products that have very low water content embedded (for instance Warner 2003; Hoekstra and Hung 2002; Chapagain and Hoekstra 2003).

The argument that food import is a strong indicator of level of water deficit that economies face; and that all economies around the world which face acute water scarcity problems can and should meet their water demand for food through cereal imports from water-rich countries has become dominant in the discussions on ways of facing global water challenges (Allan 1997: p. 4; Warner 2003: p.127). This has almost become a truism because some of the largest virtual water importing countries, the Middle East and North Africa, face serious water deficits and some of the virtual water exporting countries are water-rich.

While the underlying rationale in the virtual water trade argument is "global water use efficiency" and "distribution of scarcity" (Allan 1997; Delgado *et al.* 2003; Warner 2003), the assumption is that all the humid, water-rich countries are at an advantage in economic terms in producing food grains as compared to the arid and semi-arid countries; and that the comparative advantage essentially comes from more favourable climatic conditions that reduce evapo-transpiration, and availability of water as the "free good" in the form of soil moisture that reduces the irrigation water requirements. But, this is only one side of the truth.

It is true that when a crop which has high embedded water is grown in a humid, water-rich country and traded with a arid or semi-arid country in return for a crop which has high economic efficiency (in Rs/m^3), there would be a "net water gain" for the water scarce country as virtual water flows out of the water-rich country. With food imports, countries/regions achieve a net gain in water, which otherwise would have to be used from their own internally available resources (Chapagain and Hoekstra 2003: p. 1; Parveen and Faisal undated). But the operational aspect of this concept needs to be looked into. Such an analysis would go far beyond mere agro-climatic variations and comparative water advantages, which scholars have already considered.

It would be dangerous if we view virtual water trade with optimism as an "act of balancing water" without a proper understanding of the real reasons behind it. Such a high optimism is evident from Prof. Allan's argument that there would be sufficient water in the global system for water deficit countries and that water would essentially come from water-rich countries if we leave aside the mega question of availability of sufficient freshwater on earth for future populations (for instance see Allan 1997: p. 2). As a matter of fact, many countries are moving away from the policy of self-sufficiency in food production to food imports due to the fear of being unable to meet water demands from other sectors (Meinzen-Dick and Bruns 2000).

There are factors other than mere climate and water surplus that would determine the success of converting this idea of virtual water trade into a practical problem-solving tool for water stressed countries, just as according to Earle and Turton (2003), there are factors that cause reliance on virtual water.

While the virtual water trade concept is closely related to notion of comparative economic advantage, farm level decisions regarding crop production and marketing would be influenced by public policy regarding the economy, international trade and the prices of inputs and outputs (Wichelns, 2003). Even in water scarce countries, there are major political economic considerations in allocating water resources across sectors and within sectors (Parveen and Faisal undated; Warner, 2003). Virtual water trade would also depend on the geopolitics of the region. But, the purpose of this contribution is to examine whether the much talked about water management goals such as "global water use efficiency" and "distribution of scarcity", as argued by many scholars, are really achievable through virtual water trade.

Globally, research studies dealing with virtual water have largely viewed food trade as a tool for mitigating the stress caused by scarcity of water needed for food production (see for instance Allan 1997; Hoekstra 1998; Parveen and Faisal undated; Earle and Turton 2003; Meissner 2003), barring Warner (2003) which argued that virtual water analysis should consider non-water factors as trade in food and other water containing products not only concerns virtual water, but virtual land, virtual labour etc. They also view food insecurity problems experienced by many countries as a problem associated with water shortage or lack of technologies to utilize it, while Maroum (2003) attributed it to local policy factors also. Amarasinghe *et al* (2005) showed, in the context of India, that many water-scarce basins are net exporters of food grains, whereas many water-rich basins have to import food to meet their consumption requirements.

Finally, there are water management objectives that virtual water transfer does not address. The most important of which is water productivity. Even for crops that have high water use efficiency, water productivity could be much low resulting from inefficient use of irrigation water. Unfortunately, the distinction between water use efficiency and water productivity is often not explicitly stated in irrigation management literature (Grismer, 2001). This results in little attention being paid to the mechanisms for improving actual field efficiency in water use. Though over the past 25 years, there have been significant improvements in efficiency of water use in irrigation globally leading to leveling off of water use (source: Gleick (1998) as cited in Sorooshian *et al.* 2002), it has mostly been in developed countries (Sorooshian *et al.*, 2002).

2. The Study Objectives and Methodclogy

The major objectives of the chapter are: (1) to test the validity of the assumption that virtual water flows out of water-rich regions to water deficit regions based on analysis of global realities with regard to virtual water trade; (2) to provide a rigorous analysis of the natural and socioeconomic factors that drive global virtual water trade; (3) to draw useful conclusions for the ongoing global debate on water-food security nexus, particularly on factors concerning national policy making with regard to food security and water management; and 4] to provide a first cut analysis of the potential of using virtual water trade as an operational policy for addressing regional water deficits.

The study involved analyses of linkage between virtual water trade and: (1) renewable water availability; (2) agricultural water withdrawal; (3) net and gross cultivated land; (4) net and gross irrigated area; (5) Gross Domestic Product; (6) Human Development Index; and (7) per capita income in different countries. We ran regressions taking parameters such as agricultural land, gross cultivated land, gross irrigated land, per capita gross domestic product and human development index as independent variables jointly or separately, against virtual water trade (dependent variable). The study also analyzed the linkage between: cultivated land and apparent and effective agricultural water withdrawal (dependent variable); and "water richness" and access to agricultural land. The analyses were carried out using country level data on the above figures deduced for population unit.

3. Data Sets, Analyses and Discussion

We have used the data on renewable freshwater availability, water withdrawal for agriculture, agricultural land and irrigated land provided by Food and Agriculture Organization (2000)'s

FAOSTAT and AQUASTAT which are available for a set of 200 countries. We have obtained the estimates of net virtual water trade balance for 213 countries from Chapagain and Hoekstra (2003), which provided the average figures of virtual water trade (import/export) for the period 1995-1999. The country level data on irrigated land, obtained from FAO (2000) concern net irrigated area. In order to estimate gross irrigated area, we have used the irrigation intensity figures estimated by Seckler *et al.* (1998). But these estimates were available for only 113 countries. For the rest of the countries, we assumed the irrigation intensity as 100%. From the figures of renewable water availability provided in FAO AQUASTAT (2000), we arrived at the per capita renewable freshwater using the average population figures (1995-1999) provided in Chapagain and Hoekstra (2003). In the same way, figures of agricultural water use, agricultural land, irrigation and net virtual water export were also estimated in per capita term. The values of HDI and ppp adjusted GDP for different countries and were obtained from UNDP (2003).

We have also estimated the soil water use for agriculture for all the countries since such figures are non-existent from water accounts. In order to estimate the soil moisture available for crop use, the only two parameters considered were annual rainfall and gross cultivated land. The mean annual rainfall figures (for the period from 1961-1990) for all the 131 countries were obtained from FAOSTAT and AQUASTAT data sets. It was assumed that the total soil moisture use would be a function of rainfall magnitude and area brought under cultivation. However, a direct relation between rainfall magnitude and soil moisture would be unrealistic. Beyond a point, the soil moisture levels would not increase with rainfall magnitude. We have assumed a maximum soil moisture level of 100 mm for high rainfall countries (more than 1000 mm), 75 mm for countries with medium rainfall (500-1000mm), 50 mm for countries with low rainfall (between 200-500 mm) and 30 mm for countries with extremely low rainfalls (0-200 mm). However, in arriving at the minimum soil moisture level (i.e., 30 mm), the lowest rainfall which a country receives (Egypt receives a mean annual rainfall of 51 mm and is lowest in the world) was considered. These estimates were subsequently added to figures of blue water use for agriculture. The figures thus estimated were termed as "effective agricultural water use".

3.1 Does Renewable Water Availability influence Virtual Water Trade?

To begin with we wanted to examine whether any relationship exists between water availability in a country and the extent of virtual water trade that the country is engaged in. We started with the assumption that a country, which is rich in water resources in terms of per capita renewable water, would tend to produce food much in excess of its own domestic requirements and export to countries that face water deficits in relation to food production. For the analysis, the sample size was 131. The per capita renewable water availability ranged from a lowest of 10.4 m^3/annum for Kuwait to a highest of 481806 m^3/annum for Suriname. Out of these 131 countries, nine are falling in the absolute water scarce category, four in the water scarce category and 14 in the water stressed category. The rest 114 countries are water abundant according to Falkenmark's index of physical water scarcity. The absolute water scarce countries are Kuwait, Qatar, Bahrain, Algeria, Malta, Yemen, Israel, Jordan and Barbados.

The analysis showed that no correlation exists between relative water availability in country and the virtual water trade or the volume of water embedded in the food and food products traded. There are many water-rich countries that are still resorting to food imports in an extensive way. There are a total of 65 countries belong to water-rich category that have trade deficit in virtual water. The amount of water imported in the virtual form is more than exported. The trade deficit ranges from a lowest of 4.9 m^3/capita/annum to 838 m^3/capita/annum. For instance, Japan, which has a renewable water availability of 3390 m^3/capita, is heavily dependent on cereal imports for its domestic consumption and the water equivalent of this amount to 645 m^3/capita annually. Many extremely water-rich countries (example: Portugal with 7718 m^3/capita and Indonesia with 13,708 m^3/capita) record high virtual water imports.

On the contrary, there are several countries which are not really water-rich, but are on the verge of approaching the water stress mark. Examples are Afghanistan, Malawi, India, Thailand and Denmark. Their renewable water availability is below 3000 m^3/capita mark, but export food grains, livestock, poultry and livestock products. The food grain export from India during 2000-01 stood at 2.39 million tones (GOI, Undated). It is a known fact that countries like India are already facing acute water stress in many pockets. For the depletion of groundwater resources and degradation of land through their intensive use, the all time record achieved in cereal production in India would not have been possible.

The very fact that "virtual water" flows out of a relatively water scarce semi-arid country to a cold and humid country itself indicates that the goals of improved "global water use efficiency" and distribution of scarcity does not get realized through virtual water trade as it happens today in the global context. This does not mean that water availability does not act as a variable in the food production function in a country context. It only means that "total water sufficiency" does not necessarily mean food self-sufficiency in a practical sense. Following explanations would help a better appreciation of the argument.

A country can be water-rich through two ways. In the first case, the magnitude of rainfall, runoff and groundwater recharge a unit land area receives becomes very high (examples are Finland, Japan, Indonesia and Malaysia). In the second case, the rainfall, runoff and groundwater recharge rates are very low, but the amount of land which receives it (catchment area) is high owing to low population densities. Example is Canada which receives 537 mm of rainfall; but has very high land area available, an average of 32 ha/capita. Even with very low rainfalls, the amount of water that gets captured increases due to large catchments

Now, let us think of a graph showing per capita renewable water Vs per capita arable land for a group of countries. Chart AB and A^1B^1 given in Figure 1 show two diametrically opposite trends in access to arable land with increase renewable water availability. The most ideal situation where water richness leads to food self-sufficiency is the one in which the per capita water availability is reasonably high to take care of the food production

Figure 1: Renewable Water, Arable Land and Virtual Water Export

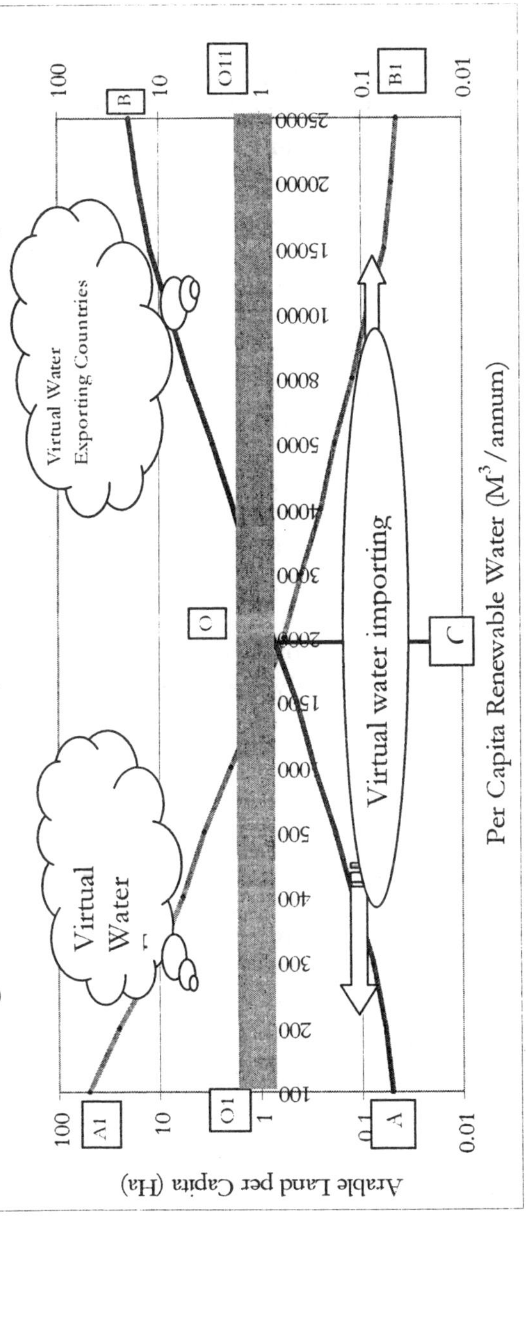

requirements (of course this would also be determined by the climatic conditions) and also the available arable land is sufficient to use up the available water resources for growing crops. This is shown by the point O in the graph, which is the intersection of line AB and line A^1B^1. Now there could be several countries that have lower per capita renewable water and arable land than the minimum required. All those countries will fall within the zone shown as AO^1OC if we consider both the charts. They would have to resort to virtual water import for food. On the other hand, many countries will have more than the minimum per capita renewable water and arable land. Those countries under natural circumstances be able to produce excess food and hence will have a virtual water trade surplus. Those countries would fall in the zone shown as BOO^{11}. These are the simple sets of conditions.

Now there could be some countries which have very low per capita water availability, but at the same time higher arable land. There would also be in a position to produce surplus food irrespective of water deficit. This is because they could harness the soil moisture, a factor, which is not considered in the conventional assessment of water deficit of nations. The amount of water accounted by the soil moisture would increase with rise in per capita arable land resources. Such countries would fall in the zone shown as A^1OO^1. Exceptions are countries which have extreme climates, especially deserts. To cite a few are Saudi Arabia, United Arab Emirates. On the other hand, there could be several countries that have very high per capita renewable water resources, but extremely limited arable land. Such countries will be in a position to use up only a fraction of their available water resources for crop production. This is because there are limits on the intensity with which a given amount of arable land could be brought under cultivation imposed by the crop cycle. Such countries will have to resort to food imports. They would eventually fall in the zone shown as $O^{11}OCB^1$. Because of this reason, no clear relationship exists between renewable water availability and virtual water trade. In nutshell most of the countries satisfy those conditions that are more favourable for food imports. The line O^1O^{11} will be rather thick owing to the fact that quite a few countries with varying degree of per capita arable land and per capita renewable water resources would have trade balance in virtual water.

3.2 Does Arable Land Control Virtual Water Trade Dynamic?

We start with the basic assumption that virtual water trade would be primarily determined by the amount of water which countries divert or draw for agriculture, provided we ignore the effects of climatic variations. The second assumption is that availability of arable land would be an important factor that would influence the amount of water that countries would draw from the man made water resource systems and soil profile, provided they have sufficient water resources in the form of surface water, groundwater and soil moisture levels.

If these assumptions are valid, then access to arable land will be an important factor that would draw the contours of global food trade and hence define virtual water flow directions. But, in reality how far this parameter (i.e., availability of arable land) influences the virtual water trade would depend on the relative positioning of different countries with respect to: (1) effective renewable water resources that takes into account the soil moisture; and (2) prevailing climatic conditions in the country, effective rainfall and potential evapo-transpiration being the two most important factors. To elaborate, the effect of arable land on virtual water trade would depend on the significance of soil moisture use in relation to total water use for agriculture, across similar climates.

We used data of a total of 131 countries to carry out the analysis out of a total of 143 countries for which concerned data were available. In the case of virtual water import, the figures were shown as negative. Regression analyses were carried out separately for analyzing the effect of: (1) net cultivated land; (2) gross cultivated land; (3) agricultural water withdrawal (blue water); (4) gross irrigation; (5) agricultural land, agricultural water withdrawal and gross irrigation; and (6) agricultural land and gross irrigation, on virtual water trade.

While doing the analysis, we have purposively excluded twelve countries from our sample. They are either those which are having extreme climatic conditions (hot deserts, cold regions) or those which show exceptionally high figures of virtual water trade balance or deficit in per capita terms, but in reality do very little trading of virtual water due to small population or those in which unique economic structures. They are Saudi Arabia, United Arab Emirates, the Netherlands, Ireland, Iceland, New Zealand, Mauritania, Mongolia, Turkmenistan, Chad, Guyana and Sri Lanka. The first two were excluded because of the desert ecosystems prevailing in the region as well as the lack of dependence of these oil rich economies on agriculture and allied activities. Turkmenistan and Mangolia were excluded because of the desert climate where as Iceland was excluded due to the extremely cold climates, which makes farming ecologically non-feasible. Sri Lanka was excluded because the figures of virtual water trade (import) available for this country did not represent the normal situation and were for the years during which the country faced extreme droughts.

The analyses showed that none of the parameters as adequately explains virtual water trade of a country as the gross cropped area. The per capita gross agricultural land explains virtual water trade to an extent of 40.3% (R^2 = 0.403) at one per cent level of significant. The second parameter, which explained virtual water trade, was net cultivated land in which case the R^2 value was 0.40. The analyses showed that with increase in either per capita gross cultivated land or net cultivated land, there was increased possibility for a country to have surplus in virtual water trade.

The regression equation is:

Virtual water export in cubic metre/capita/annum (VWE) = -188.527+144.756*(Gross Cultivated Land in Ha)

It is clear from the equation that a country's virtual water trade deficit will reduce by 144.756 m^3/capita/annum if the per capita gross agricultural land increases by one hectare, provided the other factors that explain virtual water trade magnitude remains the same.

Many countries having very low per capita gross cultivated land had significant virtual water trade deficits. Examples are

Albania (0.36 ha), Bangladesh (0.12 ha), Italy (0.36 ha), Indonesia (0.25 ha), Japan (0.08 ha), Korean D.P. Republic (0.19 ha), Malaysia (0.38 ha), Nepal (0.27 ha), Philippines (0.20 ha), and United Kingdom (0.29 ha). These are relatively water-rich countries, some of them extremely water-rich.

Many countries having high per capita gross agricultural land recorded virtual water trade surpluses. Examples are Afghanistan (1.55 ha), Australia (24.24 ha), Canada (1.91 ha), Paraguay (4.61 ha), Sudan (4.57 ha), Syria (1.00 ha), Uruguay (1.57 ha), and United States (1.62 ha). Some of these countries rank high in virtual water exports and are also water-rich (Canada and USA). But they use only a small fraction of their "blue water". The absolute use of "blue water" for agriculture is also low (137m^3 and 712m^3 per capita respectively) as compared to that of relatively water scarce virtual water exporting countries such as Uruguay and Afghanistan (915m^3 and 886m^3 per capita respectively). A major share of their agricultural water use should be coming from soil moisture, which is determined by the area under crops.

There are several other variables that could influence virtual water trade magnitude, other than cultivated land. The most important among them is agro-climate. Certain countries by virtue of their unique climatic conditions would be able realize full genetic potential of certain crops as compared to certain other countries resulting in higher yields for every unit of cultivated land. Example is the Philippines, which gets exceptionally high paddy yields. Lack of adoption of modern crop technologies which directly affects the crop yields could be another factor. Patterns of domestic food consumption could be another factor. However, we have not considered these variables for the present analysis. The graphical representation of variations in virtual water export of different countries with per capita gross cropped land (logarithmic values) is given in Figure 2. From the graph, it is evident that there are a few countries that have high per capita land availability, but still import food. This could be due to the extreme climatic conditions prevailing in these countries, which act as negative externalities for crop production (countries in the middle east and Sub Saharan

Figure 2: Gross Cropped Land Vs Virtual Water Export

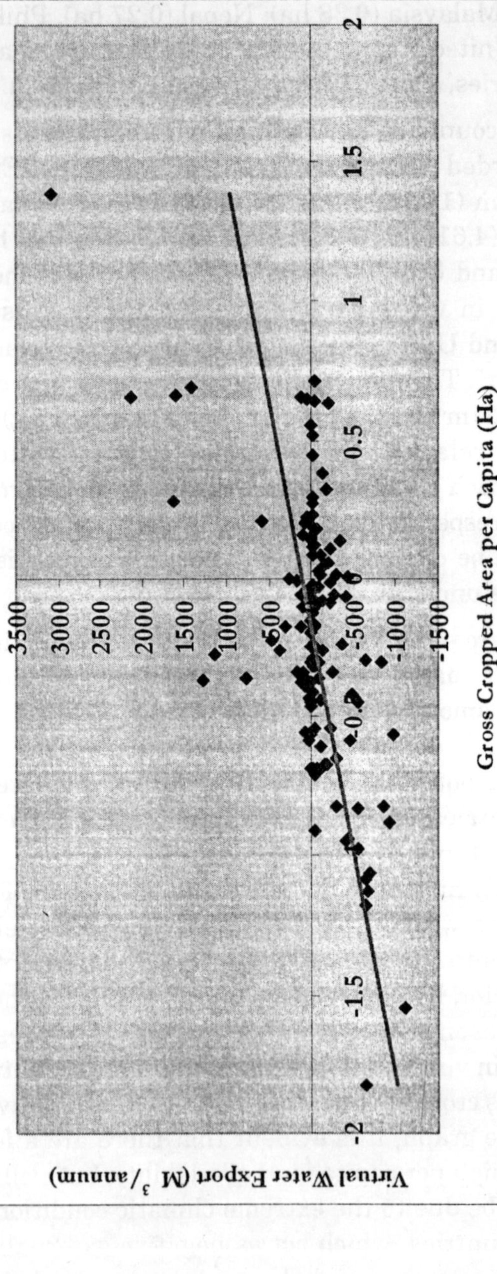

Africa), poor adoption of crop technologies (countries in East Africa), and higher levels of consumption of meat and meat products that are higher up in the food chain (countries such as Spain and China). On the other hand, India has very low per capita arable land (0.26 ha), but is food self-sufficient and produce surpluses. One reason could be the unique consumption habits of majority of Indian population, where the consumption of food items that are higher up in the food chain, particularly meat and meat products, is quite low[1]. Another reason could be the successful adoption of green revolution technologies and intensive development of irrigation facilities.

The reason for this strong correlation between cultivated land and virtual water trade is increased ability to tap the water in the soil profile with increase in per capita agricultural land. Though Prof. Allan highlights the importance of soil water in producing new biomass, he argued that it was abundant in temperate climates to permit it to be exported to water-poor countries (Allan 1997). Also increased per capita agricultural land increases the ability to utilize the renewable water resources (groundwater and surface water) available in man made and natural water resource systems. The increased agricultural water withdrawal thus made leads to more virtual water trade, these are the main assumptions we started with. The linear regression performed for analyzing the effect of agricultural land on the figures of water withdrawal for agriculture showed no effect. But as we have already discussed, these figures only show the blue water withdrawal. It does not take into account the green water usage by these countries. For many water scarce countries, which are rich in arable land, soil moisture use is a significant component of the total water use for agriculture. Therefore, we ran the regression between gross cultivated land and effective agricultural water use. The analysis showed a strong correlation. Gross cultivated land explained effective agricultural water use to an extent of 94.6% ($R^2 = 0.946$) at one per cent level of significance.

The regression equation was estimated as

Effective Water Use in Agriculture (WUA) = 296.42 + 787* Gross Cultivated Land

The graphical representation of the variation in effective water withdrawal with gross cultivated land (logarithmic values) is given in Figure 3. From the graph one can see that in the sample we have chosen, there are no countries with have per capita land area above 5 ha except Australia. But, it was felt that Australia would be extremely important because of the extent of virtual water export it does annually.

There is a remarkably high level of correlation between gross cropped area and effective water withdrawal for agriculture, especially when we consider the following two facts: 1] irrigation has very little impact in terms of expanding the cropped area for many countries as only a small fraction of the cultivated land is under irrigation in most of the countries[2]; and 2] there are major climatic factors that affect irrigation water withdrawal for a unit of irrigated land and they may vary across the 131 countries considered sporadically. But, one could argue that since soil moisture use, a component of effective water use in agriculture, was estimated using agricultural land area as one of the variables, such a relationship is quite possible. But it is interesting to note here that its effects on gross agricultural water use cannot be significant as soil moisture is not a major share of the effective water use in agriculture for all the countries, and instead it varies from a lowest of 1.7%. In 41 out of the 131 countries, estimated soil water use is less than 50% of the effective agricultural water use. Therefore, one should assume that to an extent agricultural land influences blue water use and not water availability.

3.3 Relation between Access to Arable Land and Water Richness

Further analysis investigated into the strong direct relationship between agricultural water withdrawal and cropped area. The idea was to analyze whether there are climatic reasons for effective increase in water withdrawal for agriculture with increase in cropped area. For this we considered the annual rainfall magnitude and per capita cropped area. The analysis showed an inverse exponential relationship between magnitude of rainfall and per capita agricultural land. Rainfall explained access to agricultural land in per capita terms to an extent of

15.1% (R^2 =0.15) and was at one per cent level of significance. This only meant that there is a great probability for countries with larger per capita arable land to have poor rainfall conditions and vice versa. In fact, many countries with large areas of crop land in per capita terms had very low rainfalls, though several countries with smaller areas of crop land in per capita terms were also low rainfall countries. The per capita crop land in Australia is 24.02 ha while the annual rainfall in this largely drought-prone country is only 534 mm. Kyrgyzstan had an annual rainfall of 381 mm, but a per capita crop land of 2.21 ha. Many countries that receive high rainfalls annually had very poor access to cultivable land. Examples are Bangladesh, Indonesia and Malaysia.

Low rainfall areas also experience droughts. Due to these factors, dependence on water in the soil profile and irrigation increases. Also, with widespread use of electrical and mechanical pumps over the past 100 years worldwide, rate of groundwater utilization has become unprecedented in many regions of the world. The communities manage to tap groundwater stocks accumulated over several hundreds of years for irrigation, excessively, with consequences such as depletion and land subsidence (Sorooshian *et al.* 2002: pp 319). When drought hits, dependence on it increases to stabilize crop yields. Hence, effective water withdrawal is higher in regions with larger cropped area.

Analysis of regional water balance can help provide insights into this linkage. In Gujarat, one of the semi-arid western States in India, the renewable water availability varies from 1932 m^3/capita/annum in the South and Central Gujarat, which has semi-arid to humid climatic conditions, to a lowest of 427 m^3/capita/annum in semi-arid North Gujarat. The renewable water availability in Kachchh, which is an arid region, is 875 m^3/capita/annum. In contrast to this water availability situation, water withdrawal for agriculture (as per estimates for 1997) was highest for north Gujarat (448m^3/capita/year) and lowest (375 m^3/capita/year) for South and Central Gujarat (IRMA/UNICEF 2001). South and Central Gujarat is water-rich also in terms of annual rainfall. The mean of the average annual rainfall

Figure 3: Gross Cropped Area Vs Eff. Agricultrual Water Use

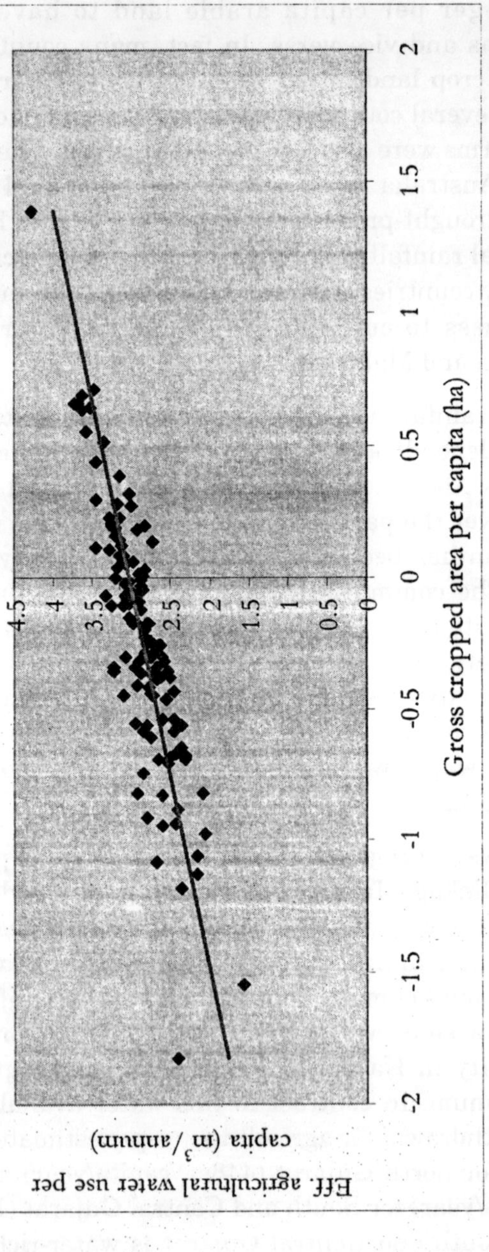

(1901-1990) is about 809 mm in erstwhile Kheda district and 1839 mm in Valsad district (Kumar 2002: pp 26 on the basis of GAU 1997). The biggest constraint in utilizing the available water for agriculture in the region is not climate or poor utilization potential created, but poor availability of land which keeps the irrigation demand low. The per capita arable land in South and Central Gujarat is only 0.124 ha against 0.188 ha in North Gujarat. Further, lesser fraction of the arable land is brought under cultivation in South and Central Gujarat (77.6%) as compared to north Gujarat (93.4%) interpreted as percentage sown area (Column # 3 in Table 1). This may be attributed to socio-ecological factors. Most parts of South and Central Gujarat fall in a high rainfall region wherein monsoon rains are spread over longer period of time, might affect the ability of people to carry out farming operations on time.

Farmers here are already growing highly water intensive crops such as sugarcane, banana and paddy of which the first two are long duration crops. On the other hand, farmers in north Gujarat are already into low water-consuming, short duration crops viz., cumin and mustard. These crops have much higher water use efficiency as compared to sugarcane, paddy and banana. Short duration crops also help them increase the cropping intensities. Now, not only is cultivation, but also is irrigation more intensive in north Gujarat resulting (Table 1). High per capita arable land, and intensive use of land through the use of short duration crops and irrigation effectively increases the per capita gross cropped area (0.223 ha). This results in higher agricultural water withdrawal as shown in IRMA/UNICEF (2001).

Therefore, even with highly water efficient crops, the total effective agricultural water use in a water scarce country could much higher than that in a water-rich country due to intensive land use for crop production. Water-intensive dairy production in north Gujarat—estimated to be 3.2 m^3 for a litre of buffalo milk and 2.5 m^3 for a litre of crossbreed cow milk—, a large chunk of which is exported to other regions in Gujarat, is leading to virtual water exports from the region (Singh 2004). Whereas possibilities of intensive land use through short-duration crops are very little in countries falling in high rainfall regions due to factors relating to agro-ecology and socio-ecology.

A recent analysis by Amarasinghe and others (2005) also shows that the more arid water-scarce basins in north and north western India such as Indus and some basins of peninsular India are net exporters of food grains to water-rich sub-humid basins (Amarasinghe *et al.*, 2005). A major reason for this is the availability of sufficient amount of arable land in the semi arid regions supported by agricultural modernization, as against poor availability of arable land compounded by agro ecological problems in the water-rich sub-humid regions (Kumar, Sivamohan and Narayanamoorthy, 2008).

4. Rethinking on Global Food and Water Security Challenges

The past research attempts on global food security were centered on water security. The proponents of virtual water concept have tried to relate food self-sufficiency to "total water sufficiency" (for instance, see Allan (1997) and Hoekstra (1998)). Scholars have comes up with indices to assess different dimensions of water scarcity. Malin Falkenmark developed physical indicators to assess different levels of water scarcity that a country/region could face. Paul Raskin *et al.* (1997) used total water diversion in relation to the total renewable water resources as an indicator of water scarcity. They do not take into account factors, such as access to arable land. All these indices have their basis in quantification of minimum water needed to produce food for human consumption and to meet the socioeconomic needs and the amount of renewable water resources that countries are endowed with. An exception is Ohlsson (1998), which evolved a social water scarcity index where in attributes such as "social ingenuity" and "institutional maturity" were used to explain how regions and nations can counteract resource scarcity to move to a more "water extensive production" and a more sensible and just distribution pattern.

Our analysis shows that "total water sufficiency" alone does not guarantee food self-sufficiency, but access to arable land would except under extreme climatic conditions. While it does not contradict the received wisdom that a minimum amount of water would be needed to meet the food production need, it suggests that the assessment of "minimum water availability" should also include water in the soil profile and therefore, the per capita arable land also should be factored into while assessing water sufficiency and not renewable water alone.

In nutshell, first, assessing the future food security challenges of nations purely from a water resource perspective does not provide a holistic but a distorted view of the food security scenario as it does not provide the vital information needed for a meaningful discussion on food security and food policy. There is a need to recognize the fact that many countries import food not because they lack "total water sufficiency", but do not have sufficient arable land to be put to cultivation. Therefore, what matters more is "how much land is available for utilizing that water" for crop production.

Second: assessing water management challenges posed by nations purely from the point of view of renewable water availability and aggregate demands will be dangerous, reason being that such an analysis would often end up in suggestions for allocation of available water to economically more efficient uses than agriculture in situations of demand exceeding supplies. Access to water in the soil profile, which is determined by access to arable land, would be an important determinant of effective water availability for food production, from which a major portion of the aggregate demand comes. While global water use efficiency is difficult to achieve, field level water use efficiency could be enhanced. In fact there are many arid regions in the world that still rely on virtual water imports, but have high potential to increase their farm revenue by using their internal water resources for growing water efficient crops and increase export revenue which in turn can be used for grain imports (see Al-Weshah (2000) for Jordan and Israel; Earle and Turton (2003) for Egypt and Meissner (2003) for SADC states; Yang (2002) for northern China).

5. Virtual Water Trade Vs Regional Water Transfers

Now let us examine the implications of these two arguments for a water scarce country, characterized by regional variations in water endowments, for making policy choices between "regional virtual water trade" and "water transfer". For this, we consider a food importing country. China, SADC countries and Spain are some of the countries/regions in the world that are characterized by major variations in water endowments, and rely on food imports. In Haihe watershed of northern China, the per capita renewable water availability is 358 m^3/annum against 3327m^3/annum in Zhujiang watershed of South China (Yang 2002: p. 2 based on Figure 1), whereas the country average is 2195m^3/capita/annum (Yang 2002: p. 1).

We have to start with a reasonable assumption that water-rich regions have lesser amount of arable land as compared to water scarce regions in per capita terms, based on the evidences provided in the earlier section, and that arable land in such regions is already put to maximum use. From food self-sufficiency point of view, it might make sense for the country to transfer water from the "water-rich" region to the "water scarce region" even if it may be at the cost of bringing down the net renewable water of the "water-rich" region below the acceptable levels defined by "total water sufficiency". This is because of two reasons: water in the soil profile, which is not considered in assessing renewable water availability, would still be available; and water sufficiency for food production directly relates to availability of arable land. Water transfer would increase utilization of water resources for crop production at country level. With increased water availability for irrigation, the area under cultivation might also go up significantly resulting from increased land use intensity. Going by the chart AB in Figure 1, the country would move from "virtual water importing" to "virtual water exporting category". At the same time, the agricultural production potential in the water-rich region would remain unaffected. This would benefit the economy, employment and people's livelihood.

If is so, it could be advanced as a counter-argument against those who oppose inter-basin water transfer projects (on the ground that they could deprive water-rich areas of their share of renewable water and therefore livelihoods), and support virtual water import[3]. It is because these project would not merely attempt to reduce the major regional variations in natural water endowments; but would address the issues of the untapped potential of water for crop production and other economic activities, and the demand-supply balance (for instance see Yang 2002: p. 2; GOI 1999).

As regards India, southern peninsula has vast amount of arable land that could be brought to intensive cultivation, if water is provided (GOI 1999). Similarly, northern Chinese provinces that are now facing severe water shortage, have been practicing intensive irrigated agriculture (Yang 2002). By embarking on major water transfer projects, the water management goal being achieved is improving the productivity of land in water scarce regions apart from equalizing "water richness". It has been established that irrigation water use efficiencies in arid and semi-arid, water scarce regions are much higher than that in humid, water-rich regions. All these arguments build a strong case for physical water transfer.

We will now show that regional virtual water trade from the perspective of global water use efficiency and scarcity distribution will have little practical relevance. It is revealing that many water-rich regions still remain as importer of food, and naturally water scarce, semi-arid regions feed them. Bihar, which is one of the water-rich states in India in terms of per capita water availability, has been an importer of food grain for quite some time. The naturally water-scarce, semi-arid and arid regions are agriculturally more prosperous indicated by high productivity, primarily through irrigation (examples are Indian and Pakistan Punjab, southern Peninsula and western parts of India), whereas the water-rich, semi-humid regions of eastern India, including Bihar, have remained agriculturally backward. It has already been established that the "factor productivity of irrigation" has been much higher for all regions of India than the eastern parts (Evenson *et al.* 1999). Another important reason for the food deficit of Bihar is the small per capita landholding of the order of 0.092 ha (Kumar 2003: p. 5), which combined with agronomic factors limit the scope of using the abundant water resources within the region.

There is another big reason for supporting physical transfer of water from water-rich regions to water-scarce regions. It is the higher economic value realized from the use of water in agriculture in naturally water–scarce regions. A recent study in western Punjab and eastern UP shows that higher economic value is realized from the use of every unit of water in western Punjab, which is water-scarce and land rich when compared to eastern UP, which is water-rich and land-scarce. The average economic output from a unit of water was Rs.14.05/m^3 in western Punjab, against Rs. 11.65/m^3 in eastern UP. In eastern UP, the net returns from every unit of land cultivated was much higher than that in western Punjab. In western Punjab, the farmers allocate a greater proportion of their irrigation water for growing crops and doing dairying which give higher returns per unit of water, whereas in eastern UP, farmers allocate a greater proportion of their land for growing crops which give high income return per unit of land. Water productivity was not a consideration in choosing crops there (Kumar et al., 2008).

While transfer of surplus water from water-rich regions to water scarce regions does not need a better economic rationale than increasing the productive use of the un-utilized water, the notable fact is that such transfers for agriculture lead to realization of greater economic value. The increase in land productivity achieved through bringing rain-fed crops under irrigation will have to justify the investments for transfer of surplus water from water-rich regions to water deficit regions. The "incremental value realization" might demand reallocation of more than the real "volumetric surplus" available within the water surplus region to a water-scarce region. But such additional transfers have to satisfy two conditions. First: the incremental value realized exceeds the cost of such transfer. Second: mechanisms exist for compensating for the economic and livelihood losses suffered by the water-rich region (Kumar et al., 2008).

This does not mean that water deficit countries/regions should embark on water transfer projects as a blanket policy. Wherever possibilities exist virtual water trade should be encouraged. But for a region, which is well-endowed with good arable land, it would be the natural choice to bring in water from a water-rich region to improve the efficiency of use of land, and thereby also efficiency of use of water from the natural environment which remains under-utilized in surplus regions. But, this does not mean that on-farm water use efficiency can be ignored. In fact, physical efficiency of irrigation water use is extremely low in third world countries resulting from absence of proper pricing leading to reduced water productivity. It has been found that when confronted with the scarcity value of water, farmers make efforts to improve the efficiency with which water is used. In north Gujarat, farmers who pay for groundwater on volumetric basis, and farmers whose groundwater allocation is rationed in volumetric terms (shareholders of tube well partnerships) achieve much higher water productivity (in kg/m^3) for the same crop as compared to well owners who neither pay for groundwater nor electricity on actual consumption basis (Kumar 2005: p. 39-51).

6. Major Findings of the Study

1. The proponents of virtual water trade have largely viewed global food grain trade as a mechanism for addressing the deficit of water needed for producing crops for their consumption. They argue that virtual water import could be an effective economic system that can be water deficit economies around the world for accessing water from the global system to ameliorating problems of water deficit.

2. The cross country analyses of virtual water trade involving 131 samples show that renewable water availability does not have any bearing on virtual water trade volume. Many countries that are water-rich are extremely poor in arable land resources and hence are not able to fully utilize the available blue water for crop production. Very few countries have the advantage of high arable land, and total water sufficiency to be able to create surpluses in agriculture, and thus be part of virtual water exporting countries.

3. Further analyses show that virtual water flow dynamic is controlled more by the access to arable land than access to renewable freshwater. Gross cropped area explains virtual water trade to an extent of 40% with one per cent level of significance.

4. Increase in access to arable land leads to increase in "effective water withdrawal" in agriculture, irrespective of the strong mismatch between water richness and land richness. This is explained by two factors: many countries that are rich in arable land are "water-poor", which in turn increases the irrigation water requirement; and water drawn from the soil profile increase with cultivated land.

5. Virtual water often flows out of "water-poor", but "land-rich" country to "water-rich" and "land-poor" countries. Therefore, "global water use efficiency" and "distribution of scarcity" are difficult goals to be achieved through virtual water trade in the practical sense. When virtual water flows into a water-rich country, what is being achieved is improved land use efficiency.

6. Assessing the future food security challenges posed to nations purely from a water resource perspective provide a distorted view of the food security scenario. It may bring in complacency for water-rich nations; while unwanted pessimism for water scarce nations. Access to arable land equally or even more concerns country's food security and therefore should be integrated with other considerations in national food and water policy making.

7. Assessing the water management challenges posed by nations purely from the point of view of renewable water availability and aggregate demands will be dangerous. Access to water in the soil profile would be an important determinant of effective water availability for food production, from which a major portion of the aggregate demand comes. This could add a potentially new dimension to the global water scarcity debate.

8. The dominant water management paradigm suggested for water scarce countries that are characterized by major regional variations in the resource endowment and still relying on food imports is virtual water transfer. But, this could spell doom if arable land is limited in the "well endowed" area. Under such circumstances, inter-regional water transfer could be justified as a measure to equalize "water richness" per unit of arable land thereby enabling productive use of both land and water for crop production at the country level. Transfer of water in addition

to the "volumetric surplus" available in the water-rich region also might be desirable as it helps improve the economic outputs from the use of water.

7. Conclusions and Policy Implications

The virtual water trade argument, to an extent, has influenced regional debates on setting policy priorities to deal with water shortages for food production that are likely to occur in future in the context of South Asia, some of the states of SADC and China. Our analyses show that while "global water use efficiency" and availability of blue water for food production could be important concerns that influence country water policies of water-poor nations, they could not be the decisive factors. Availability of arable land that effectively increases the potential for tapping water in the soil profile therefore effective water availability, and "degree of dependence" of a country on water for economic growth and its population for livelihood are important considerations.

Regional virtual water (food) trade from a global water use efficiency perspective will have limited relevance. It may appear as a constraint in expanding the scope of using virtual water as a tool for addressing regional water problems. But, this can be converted into an opportunity provided: we change the rationale for virtual water trade from "water use efficiency" and "distribution of scarcity" to "land use efficiency"; adopt "productivity potential of water" as the water management goal; and we consider regional water transport as a technically feasible option. The idea is to physically transfer the water to naturally water scarce regions; put it to use; and then transfer food grains produced to the "water-rich" and "land-poor" regions. The volume of virtual water embedded in food export can be treated as an exchange for taking water out of surplus areas. This will help avert any inter-state conflicts that could result decisions to transfer water from the water-rich states.

Another important merit of such transfer arrangements is that the water scarce regions that are used to intensive use of their endogenous water for livelihood will continue to have their irrigation-based livelihoods, an important concern in virtual water trade. Massive transfer of water to these water starved regions and its subsequent use for irrigation would also result induced groundwater recharge. The impact will be double: first, water transfer will reduce groundwater pumping, and the return flows from irrigation would increase recharge thereby reducing the stress on groundwater. The increase in land productivity achieved through bringing rain-fed crops under irrigation will have to justify the investments for transfer of surplus water from water-rich regions to water deficit regions. But, as Kumar *et al.* (2008) notes, the amount of water to be transferred could be more than the real volumetric surplus available within the water-rich region, if the incremental value realized in the water-scarce region exceeds the cost of such additional water transfer, and mechanisms exist for compensating for the economic and livelihood losses suffered by the water-rich region through such transfers.

The foregoing analysis, however, provided economic rationale for water projects. In the next chapter we would see the reasons other than mere economic growth for investing in water sector, particularly in infrastructure and institutions. It shows that it is necessary for reducing hunger and poverty, and achieving progress in human development.

References

Allan, J. A. (1997) Virtual water: A long term solution for water short Middle Eastern economies?' Paper presented at the 1997 British Association Festival of Science, University of Leeds, 9 September 1997.

Allan, J. A. (2003a) Virtual Water Eliminates Water Wars? A Case Study from the Middle East, Virtual water trade, proceedings of the international expert meeting on virtual water trade, edited by Hoekstra, A. Y., Value of water research report series # 12.

Allan, J. A. (2003b) Virtual Water-the Water, Food, Trade Nexus, Useful Concept or Misleading Metaphor?, Discussion paper, *Water International*. 28 (1) pp 4-10.

Al-Weshah, Radwan A. (2000) Optimal Use of Irrigation Water in the Jordan Valley: A Case Study, *Water Resources Management* 14: 327–338, 2000, pp 327 -338.

Amarasinghe, Upali, Bharat R. Sharma, Noel Aloysius, Christopher Scott, Vladimir Smakhtin, Charlotte de Fraiture, A. K. Sinha and

A. K. Shukla (2005) *Spatial Variation in Water Supply and Demand across River Basins of India*, IWMI Research Report 83, Colombo, Sri Lanka.

Chapagain A.K. and A.Y. Hoekstra (2003) Virtual water trade: A quantification of virtual water flows between nations in relation to international trade of livestock and livestock products, Virtual water trade, proceedings of the international expert meeting on virtual water trade, edited by Hoekstra, A. Y., Value of water research report series # 12.

Delgado, Christopher, Mark Rosegrant, Henning Steinfeld, Simeon Ehui and Claude Courbois (2003) Livestock to 2020: The Next Food Revolution, Food, Agriculture and Environment Discussion Paper 28. International Food Policy Research Institute.

Earle A. and A. Turton (2003) The virtual water trade amongst countries of the SADC, Virtual water trade, proceedings of the international expert meeting on virtual water trade, edited by Hoekstra, A. Y., Value of water research report series # 12.

Evenson, Robert E., Carl E. Pray and Mark W. Rosegrant (1999) *Agricultural Research and Productivity Growth in India*, Research Report 109, International Food Policy Research Institute.

Food and Agriculture Organization (2000) FAOAQUASTAT database on line on water and agriculture. http://www.fao.org/ag/agl/aglw/aquastat/dbase/

Food and Agriculture Organization (2000) FAOSTAT on line database Agricultural. http://apps.fao.org/page/collections

Gleick, P. H. (1998) *The World's Water 1998-1999*. Washington D. C: Island Press.

Government of India (1999) *Integrated Water Resource Development a Plan for Action* – Report of the National Commission for Integrated Water Resource Management, Volume – I, Government of India, Ministry of Water Resources, New Delhi

Government of India (undated) *Annual Report 2002-03*, Ministry of Commerce and Industry, Government of India. (http://www.indiastat.com/)

Government of Gujarat (undated) *District-wise classification of land-use in Gujarat – 1998-99*, Department of Agriculture, Government of Gujarat (http://www.indiastat.com/).

Grismer, E. M. (2001) Regional cotton lint yield and water value in Arizona and California. *Agricultural Water Management*, 1710, 1-16.

Haddadin, M. J. (2003) Exogenous Water: A Conduit to Globalization of Water Resources, Virtual water trade, proceedings of the international expert meeting on virtual water trade, edited by Hoekstra, A. Y., Value of Water Research Report Series # 12.

Hoekstra, A.Y. (1998) Perspectives on water: An integrated model-based exploration of the future. International Books, Utrecht, the Netherlands.

Hoekstra A.Y. (2003) Virtual water: An introduction, Virtual water trade, proceedings of the international expert meeting on virtual water trade, edited by Hoekstra, A. Y., Value of Water Research Report Series # 12.

Hoekstra, A.Y. and P. Q. Hung (2002) Virtual water trade: A quantification of virtual water flows between nations in relation to international crop trade, Value of Water Research Report Series No.11, IHE, Delft, the Netherlands.

Hoekstra, A.Y. and P.Q. Hung (2003) Virtual water trade: A quantification of virtual water flows between nations in relation to international crop trade, Virtual water trade, proceedings of the international expert meeting on virtual water trade, edited by Hoekstra, A. Y., Value of Water Research Report series # 12.

IRMA/UNICEF (2001) *White Paper on Water in Gujarat*, report prepared for the government of Gujarat.

Kumar, M. Dinesh (2002) Reconciling Water Use and Environment: Water Resources Management in Gujarat, Report of the Hydrological Regime Subcomponent of the State Environmental Action Programme, submitted to Gujarat Ecology Commission, Vadodara.

Kumar, M. Dinesh (2003) Food Security and Sustainable Agriculture in India: The Water Management Challenge, IWMI Working Paper 60. Colombo: IWMI.

Kumar, M. Dinesh (2005) Impact of Electricity Prices and Volumetric Water Allocation on Energy and Groundwater Demand Management: Analysis from Western India, *Energy Policy*, 33 (1) 39-51.

Kumar, M. Dinesh, Ajaya Kumar Malla and Sushanta Kumar Tripathy (2008) Economic value of water in agriculture: comparative analysis of a water-scarce and a water-rich region in India, *Water International*, 33 (2): 214-230.

Maroum, M. El-Fadel (2003) The Concept of Virtual Water and Its Applicability in Lebanon, Virtual water trade, proceedings of the international expert meeting on virtual water trade, edited by Hoekstra, A. Y., Value of Water Research Report Series # 12.

Meissner R. (2003) Regional food security and virtual water: Some environmental, political, and economic considerations, Virtual water trade, proceedings of the international expert meeting on virtual water trade, edited by Hoekstra, A. Y., Value of Water Research Report Series # 12.

Meinzen-Dick, Ruth S. and Bryan Randolph Bruns (2000) Negotiating Water Rights: Introduction, in Bryan Randolph Bruns and Ruth S. Meinzen Dick (Eds.) Negotiating Water Rights, Vistar and Intermediate Technology Publications: IFPRI-ADB Book.

Mori, K. (2003) Virtual water trade in global governance, Virtual water trade, proceedings of the international expert meeting on virtual water trade, edited by Hoekstra, A. Y., Value of Water Research Report series # 12.

Ohlsson, L. (1998) Water and Social Resource Scarcity - An Issue Paper Commissioned by FAO/AGLW. Presented as a discussion paper for the 2nd FAO E-mail Conference on Managing Water scarcity. WATSCAR 2.

Parveen, Saila and I. M. Faisal. undated. Trading Virtual Water between India and Bangladesh: A Politico-economic Dilemma.

http://www.siwi.org/waterweek2003/Workshop%207%20Oral(28).htm

Postel, Sandra (1996) Dividing the Waters: Food Security, Ecosystem Health, and the New Politics of Scarcity, World Watch Paper No. 132. Washington D.C, World Watch Institute, 1996, cited by Elmusa (1997) pp. 194.

Raskin, P., P. Gleick, P. Kirshen, G. Pontius, and K. Strzepek. 1997. *Water futures: Assessment of long-range patterns and problems*, Comprehensive assessment of the freshwater resources of the world, Stockholm Environment Institute, Stockholm, Sweden.

Rockström, J. and L. Gordon (2001) Assessment of green water flows to sustain major biomes of the world: implications for future eco hydrological landscape management, *Phys. Chem. Earth (B)* 26: 843-851.

Seckler, David, Upali Amarasinghe, David Molden, Rashika De Silva and Randolph Barker (1998) World Water Demand and Supply, 1990 to 2025: Scenarios and Issues, Research Report # 19, Colombo, Sri Lanka: International Water Management Institute.

Singh, O. P. (2004) Water Productivity of Milk Production in North Gujarat, Western India, Proceedings of the *2nd Asia Pacific Association of Hydrology and Water Resources (APHW) Conference*, Vol. 1: 442-449.

Sorooshian, Saroosh, Martha P. L. Witaker and Terri S. Hogue (2002) Regional and global hydrology and water resource issues: The role of international and national programmes, water policy article. *Aquatic Sciences*, 64 (2002) 317-327.

United Nations Development Programme (2003) *Human Development Report – 2003*, Oxford university press, New York.

Warner, J. (2003) Virtual water – virtual benefits? Scarcity, distribution, security and conflict reconsidered, Virtual water trade, proceedings of the international expert meeting on virtual water trade, edited by Hoekstra, A. Y., Value of Water Research Report Series # 12.

Wichelns, D. (2001) The role of 'virtual water' in efforts to achieve food security and other national goals, with an example from Egypt. *Agricultural Water Management* 49(2):131-151.

Wichelns, D. (2003) The Role of Public Policies in Motivating Virtual Water Trade, With an Example from Egypt, Virtual water trade, proceedings of the international expert meeting on virtual water trade, edited by Hoekstra, A. Y., Value of Water Research Report Series # 12.

Yang, H. (2002) Water, environment and food security: a case study of the Haihe River basin in China. http://www.rioc.org/wwf/Water_in_China_Haihe.pdf

Zehnder, A.lexander J. B. and Armin Reller (2002) Water Issues. *Editorial*. http://www.oekom.de/verlag/german/periodika/gaia/pdf/lese2002_04.pdf

Footnotes

1. Average meat consumption in India is only 4 kg/capita/annum against 33 kg/capita/annum in China as per FAO estimates for 1993. Again, the percentage contribution of calorie intake from animal products is only 7 in India against 15 for China (source: Delgado *et al.* 2003). While it takes nearly one cubic metre water for producing one kilogram of wheat, the conversion factor for beef is 6 kg. A diet with 20% meat and daily calorie intake of 2500 kcal per person results in a virtual water consumption of an additional 3300 litres of water per person per day (Zehnder and Reller 2002).

2. The intensity of irrigation expressed as a percentage of net cultivated land was estimated to be less than 10% in 92 out of the 131 countries chosen for the analysis.
3. In the case of China and SADC states, scholars have mooted the idea of food import. The countries that have recently ventured into mega water transfer projects are China, Spain and India. These projects aim to transfer water from water-rich areas to areas that are water-scarce, but have long tradition of vibrant irrigated production. These projects aim to transfer water from water-rich areas to areas that are water-scarce, but have long tradition of vibrant irrigated production.

7

Why We Should Invest in Water Infrastructure and Institutions?

ABSTRACT

In this chapter, we first analyze the nature of linkage between water situation of a country, vis-à-vis access and use, water environment and institutional capabilities in the water sector on economic growth. For this, data on sustainable water use index derived from WPI; human development and per capita GDP (ppp adjusted) for 145 countries, and data on global hunger index (GHI) for 117 countries are analyzed. In order to illustrate how creating water storages supports economic growth of countries which fall in hot and arid, tropical climates index, data on per capita dam storage were analyzed for 22 countries.

The regression analyses between SWUI and per capita GDP show that improving the water situation, vis-à-vis improved access to and use of water, institutional capabilities in water sector and improved water environment, through investments in water infrastructure, creating institutions and making policy reforms, can support economic growth of a nation. This is explained by the regression between SWUI and HDI, which showed that increase in SWUI raised the indicators of human development, paving the foundation for growth. This strong linkage can be partly explained by the reduction in malnutrition and infant mortality with improvement in water situation as indicated by the strong inverse relationship between SWUI and GHI. Whereas regression between per capita GDP and decomposed HDI shows that a country's progress in human development has little to do with its economic prosperity, and that a country can achieve good indicators of development even at low levels of economic growth, through welfare oriented policies which encourage investments in water, health and education infrastructure. This means, economic growth is not a pre-requisite for solving water related problems. Instead, countries should invest in water infrastructure, institutions and policy reforms to achieve human development and sustain economic growth. Further analysis shows that hot and arid tropical countries, the investment in large water storages had helped support economic growth. Also, it seems to reduce malnutrition and incidence of child mortality.

Key Words: *Water Poverty Index, Sustainable Water Use Index, decomposed Human Development Index, per capita GDP, Global Hunger Index, per capita dam storage.*

1. Introduction

As water scarcity hits many developing regions of the world, internationally, there is a renewed interest in understanding how growing threats to water security affects future progress in human development and economic growth of nations (see Grey and Sadoff, 2005). The international development debate is, however, heavily polarized between those who believe that policy reforms in the water sector would be crucial for bringing about progress in human development and those who believe that economic growth itself would help solve many of the water problems, which countries in their economic transition and many backward regions, are facing today (HDR, 2006: pp. 66). Such debates, that are often not healthy, are causing delays in deciding investment priorities in water sector, particularly in the developing world (Biswas and Tortajada, 2001). The underlying concern here is that water insecurity could decouple economic growth and progress in human development.

There is rich theoretical discussion on the returns on investment by countries in water infrastructure and institutions (Sadoff and Grey, 2005). Many scholars and international agencies have provided robust evidences to the effect that water security can catalyze human development and growth (World Bank, 2004; 2006a & b; Braga *et al.*, 1998; Briscoe, 2005). But, the number of regions for which these evidences are available is too limited for evolving a global consensus on this complex issue. Till recently, there were no authentic and comprehensive database on various factors influencing water security for sufficient number of countries which are at different stages of human development and economic growth. This contributed to the complexity of the debate. The water poverty index (WPI), conceived and developed for countries by C. Sullivan (2002), and the international comparisons now available from a recent work by Laurence, Meigh and Sullivan (2003) for 145 countries enable us to provide an empirical basis for enriching the debate.

But, the WPI is a composite index consisting of five sub-indices, viz., water access index, water use index, water endowment index, water environment index and institutional capacities in water sector. In order to realistically assess the water situation of a country, which can capture the crucial attributes like access to water for various uses; level of use of water in different sectors; condition of the water environment; and technological and institutional capacities in water sector, a new index called Sustainable Water Use Index (SWUI) is derived from WPI. The paper provides empirical analysis using global database on SWUI and many other water and development indicators to enrich the debate "how water security is linked to human development and economic growth".

2. Objectives and Hypothesis

The objectives of the paper are to: (i) analyze the nature of linkage between water situation of a country, comprising improved water access and use, water environment and institutional capacities in the water sector, and economic growth of a nation; and (ii) understand the role of large water storages in boosting economic growth and changing human development indicators of countries which fall in hot and arid, tropical climates.

We have three propositions. First: improving the water situation through investments in water infrastructure, institutions and policies would help ensure economic growth through the human development route. Second: nations can achieve reasonable progress in human development even at low levels of economic growth, through investment in water infrastructure, and welfare policies. Third: countries need to invest in building large water storages to support economic prosperity, and ensure water security for social advancements.

The hypotheses are: (1) improved water situation supports economic growth through the human development route; and (2) countries, which are in tropical climates with aridity, can support their economic growth through enhancing per capita reservoir storage that improves their water security.

3. Analysis and Data Sources

The values of Sustainable Water Use Index were calculated by adding up the values of four of the sub-indices of Water Poverty Index, viz., water access index, water use index, water environment index and water capacity index.

The first hypothesis is tested using a regression of global data on: Sustainable Water Use Index (SWUI), and data on per capita GDP (ppp adjusted); SWUI and GHI; and SWUI and HDI. Since regression between SWUI and HDI showed a strong relationship (R^2= 0.79), the causality, i.e., whether SWUI influences GDP growth or vice versa, can be tested by running regression between per capita GDP and a decomposed HDI, which contain the indices for health and education. The underlying premise is that if economic growth drives water situation, then it should change the indicators of human development that are independent of income levels, such as health and education, and that which are inter-related with water situation. The second hypothesis is tested by analyzing the link between per capita GDP (ppp adjusted) and per capita dam storage (m^3/annum) of 22 selected countries falling in hot and arid tropical climate.

Data on per capita GDP and HDI were obtained from Human Development Report 2006. Data on GHI[1] for 117 countries were obtained from Wiesmann Doris (2007). Data on WPI for 145 countries were obtained from Laurence et al. (2003). Data on dam storage and human population in 22 countries were obtained from FAO AQUASTAT-2006.

4. Water and Economic Growth

Before we begin to answer this complex question of "what drives what", we need to understand what realistically represents the water richness or water poverty of a country. A recent work by Kellee Institute of Hydrology and Ecology which came out with international comparisons on water poverty of nations had used five indices, viz., water resources endowment; water access; water use; capacity building in water sector; and water environment, to develop a composite index of water poverty (see Laurence, Meigh and Sullivan, 2003).

Among these five indices, we chose four indices to be important determinants of water situation of a country, and the only sub-index we excluded is the water resources endowment. We consider that this sub-index is more or less redundant, as three other sub-indices viz., water access, water use and water environment take care of what the resource endowment is expected to provide. Our contention is that natural water resource endowment becomes an important determinant of water situation of a country only when governance is poor and institutions are ineffective, adversely affecting the community's access to and use of water, and water environment. Examples are the droughts in Sub-Saharan African countries. This argument is validated by a recent analysis which showed strong correlation between rainfall failure and economic growth performance in these countries. That said, all the four sub-indices we chose significant implications for socio-economic conditions, and are influenced by institutional and policy environment, and therefore have human element in them. Hence, such a parameter will be appropriate to analyze the effect of institutional interventions in water sector on economy.

All the sub-indices have values ranging from 0 to 20. The composite index developed, by adding up the values of these indices, is called sustainable water use index (SWUI). It is being hypothesized that that the overall water situation of a country (or SWUI) has a strong influence on its economic growth performance. This is diametrically opposite to the hypothesis postulated by Shah and Koppen (2006), where in they have argued that economic growth (GDP per capita), and HDI are determinants of water access poverty and water environment.

It is important to provide empirical evidence to this. Worldwide, experiences show that improved water situation (in terms of its access to water; levels of use of water; the overall health of water environment; and enhancing the technological and institutional capacities to deal with sectoral challenges) leads to better human health and environmental sanitation; food security and nutrition; livelihoods; and greater access to education for the poor (see for instance UNDP, 2006). This aggregate impact can be segregated with irrigation having direct impact on rural poverty (Bhattarai and Narayanamoorthy, 2003; Hussain and Hanjra, 2003); irrigation having impact on food security, livelihoods and nutrition (Hussain and Hanjra, 2003), with positive effects on productive workforce; and domestic water security having positive effects on health, environmental sanitation, with spin off effects on livelihoods and nutrition (positive), school drop out rates (negative) and productive workforce.

According to the Human Development Report (2006), only one in every five people in the developing world has access to an improved water source. Dirty water and poor sanitation account for vast majority of the 1.8 million child deaths each year (almost 5,000 every day) from diarrhoea- making it the second largest cause of child mortality. In many of the poorest countries, only 25% of the poorest households have access to piped water in their homes, compared with 85% of the richest. Diseases and productivity losses linked to water and sanitation in developing countries amount to 2% of GDP, rising to 5% in Sub-Saharan Africa—more than the aid the region gets. Women bear the brunt of responsibility for collecting water, often spending up to 4 hours a day walking, waiting in queues and carrying water; water insecurity linked to climate change threatens to increase malnutrition to 75–125 million people by 2080, with staple food production in many Sub-Saharan African countries falling by more than 25%.

The strong inverse relationship between SWUI and the global hunger index (GHI), developed by IFPRI for 117 countries, provide a broader empirical support for some of the phenomena discussed above. In addition to these 117 countries for which data on GHI are available, we have included 18 developed countries. For these countries, we have considered zero values, assuming that these countries do not face problems of hunger. The estimated R square value for the regression between SWUI and GHI is 0.60. The coefficient is also significant at one per cent level. It shows that with improved water situation, the incidence of infant mortality (below five years of age) and impoverishment reduces (Figure 1). In that case, improved water situation should improve the value of human development index, which captures three key spheres of human development such as health, education and income status.

That said all the sub-indices of HDI have strong potential to trigger growth in economy of a country, be it educational status; life expectancy; or income levels. When all these factors improve, they could have a synergetic effect on the economic growth. Hence, the "causality" of water as a prime driver for economic growth can be tested if we are able to establish correlation between water situation and HDI. This we would examine at a later stage in this paper.

Before that, we would first look at how water situation and economic growth of nations are correlated. Regression between sustainable water use index (SWUI) and ppp adjusted per capita GDP for the set of 145 countries shows that it explains level of economic development to an extent of 69 per cent (see Figure 2). The coefficient is significant at one per cent level. We must mention here that Laurence, Meigh and Sullivan (2003) had estimated an R^2 value of 0.81 for WPI and HDI (source: Table 2: page 5, Laurence et al., 2003). Figure 2 shows that the relation between SWUI and per capita GDP is a power function. Any improvement in water situation beyond a level of 50 in SWUI, leads to exponential growth in per capita GDP.

This only means that for countries to be on the track of sustainable growth path, the following steps are needed: (1) investment in infrastructure, and institutional mechanisms and policies to: (a) improve access to water for all sectors of use and across the board, (b) enhance the overall level of use of water in different sectors, and (c) regulate the use of water, reduce pollution and provide water for ecological services; and (2) investment in building human resources and technological capabilities in water sector to tackle new challenges in the sector. Regression with different indices of water poverty against economic growth levels shows that the relationship is less

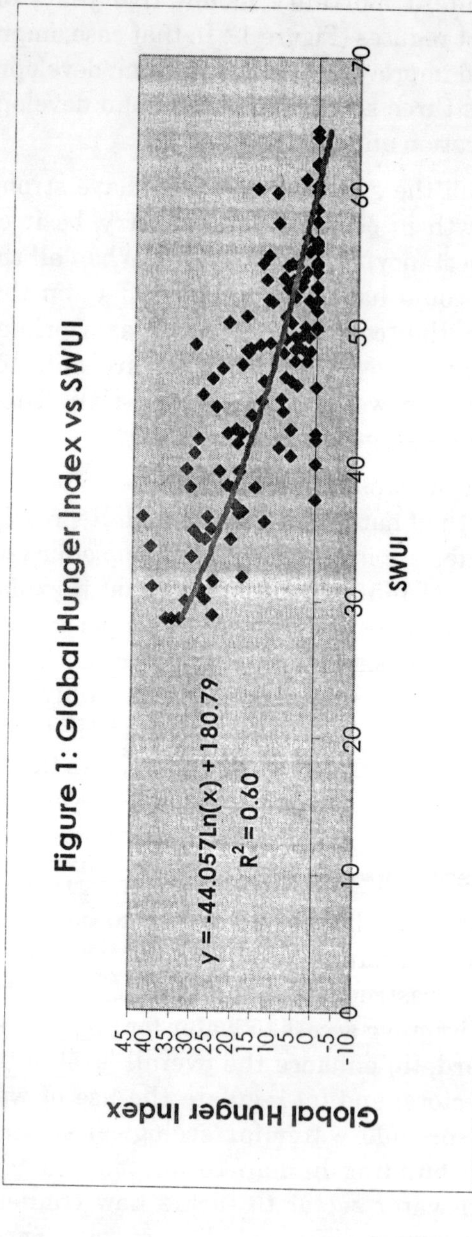

Figure 1: Global Hunger Index vs SWUI

Figure 2: Sustainable Water Use Index Vs GDP Growth

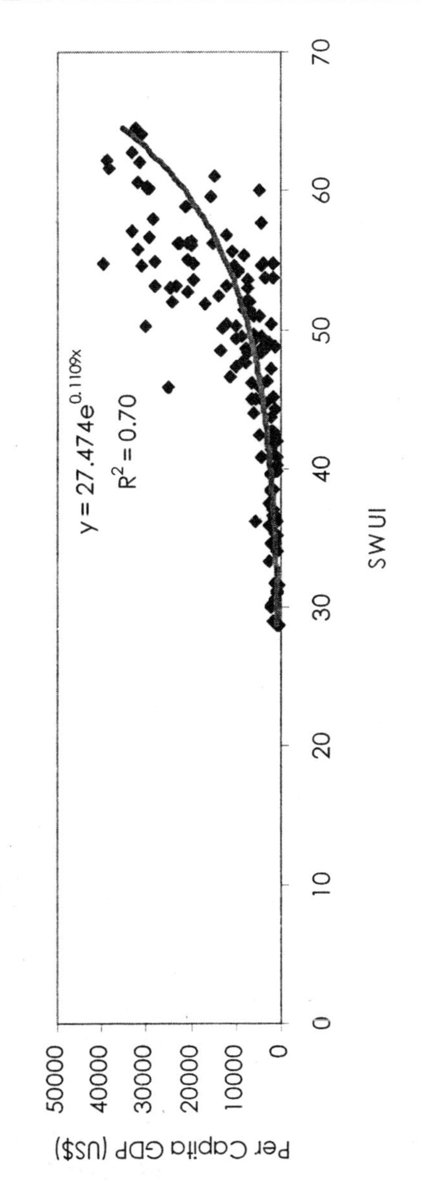

strong, meaning all aspects (water access, water use, water environment and water sector capacity) are equally important to ensure growth.

Major variations in economic conditions of countries having same levels of SWUI (in the range of 53-56), can be explained by the economic policies of which the country pursues. Some countries of central Asia viz., Uzbekistan, Kyrgyzstan and Turkmenistan and Latin American countries viz., Ecuador, Uruguay, Colombia and Chile have values of SWUI as high as North America and northern European countries, but are at much lower levels of per capita GDP. While North America and north, west and southern European countries have capitalist and liberal economic policies, these countries of old soviet block and Latin America have socialist and welfare oriented policies.

4.1 Can Economic Growth Drive Water Security?

International development discussions are often characterized by polarized positions on whether money or policy reform is more crucial for progress in human development (various authors as cited in HDR, 2006: pp 66). If the stage of economic development determines a country's water situation rather than vice versa, the variation of human development index, should be explained by variation in per capita GDP, rather than water situation in orders of magnitude. We have used data for 145 countries to examine this closely. The regression between shows economic growth levels (expressed in per capita GDP ppp adjusted) explains HDI variations to an extent of 85 per cent). This is in spite of the fact that HDI already includes per capita income, as one of the sub-indices.

Subsequently, analysis was carried out using decomposed values of HDI index (after subtracting the GDP index). The regression value came down to 0.69 (R^2=0.69) when the decomposed index, which comprises education index and life expectancy index, was run against per capita GDP (Figure 3). What is more striking is the fact that 16 countries having values of per capita income below 2,000 dollars per annum have medium levels of decomposed index. Again 42 countries having per capita GDP (ppp adjusted) less than 5,000 dollars per annum have medium levels of decomposed human development index. As Figure 3 shows, significant improvements in HDI values (0.30

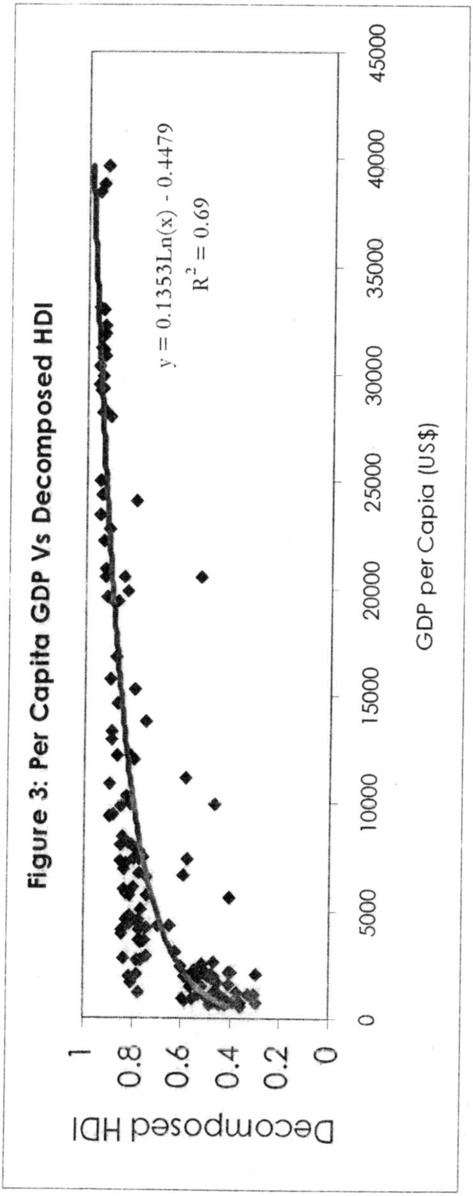

Figure 3: Per Capita GDP Vs Decomposed HDI

to 0.9) occur within the small range in per capita GDP. The remarkable improvement in HDI values with minor improvements in economic conditions, and then "plateauing" means that improvement in HDI is determined more by factors other than economic growth. Our contention is that the remarkable variation in HDI of countries belonging to the low income group can be explained by the quality of governance in these countries, i.e., whether good or poor.

Many countries that show high HDI also have good governance systems and institutional structures to ensure good literacy and human health. For instance, Hungary in eastern Europe; some countries of Latin America viz., Uruguay, Guatemala, Paraguay, Nicaragua and Bolivia; and countries of erstwhile Soviet Union viz., Turkmenistan, Kyrgykistan and Armenia have welfare-oriented policies. They make substantial investment in water, health and educational infrastructure, and have good governance practices[2].

Incidentally, many countries, which have extremely low HDI, have highly volatile political systems and ineffective governance, and are characterized by corruption in government. In spite of huge external aid, consequently, the investments in building and maintenance of water infrastructure are very poor in these countries. Sub-Saharan African countries, viz., Angola, Benin, Chad, Eritrea, Ethiopia, Burundi, Niger, Togo, Zambia and Zimbabwe; and Yemen from Middle East belong to this category. Sub-Saharan Africa has the lowest irrigated to rain-fed area ratio of less than 3% (FAO, 2006, Figure 5.2: pp 177), where as Ethiopia has the lowest water storage of 20 m^3/capita in dams (World Bank, 2005). How water security decoupled human development and economic growth in many regions of the world were illustrated in the recent human development report (HDR, 2006: pp. 30-31).

The overall public expenditure on health and education is extremely low in these African countries and Yemen when compared to the many other countries which fall under the same economic category (below US $ 5,000 per capita per annum). Over and above, the pattern of public spending is more skewed towards military (source: based on data provided in HDR, 2006,

Table 19: pp 348-351). Besides, access to water supply and sanitation is much higher in the countries which have higher HDI, as compared to those countries which have very low HDI (based on data in HDR, 2006, Table 7, pp306-309).

High incidence of water-related diseases such as malaria and diarrhoea, high infant mortality, high school drop out rate mainly due to lack of access to safe drinking water; and scarcity of irrigation water in rural areas, poor agricultural growth, high food insecurity, malnutrition etc. are characteristic of these regions (HDR, 2006). Consequently, their HDI is very low, as also shown by the international literature which illustrates how water insecurity decouples human development from economic growth.

At the same time, regression between *water situation* (expressed in terms of sustainable water use index) and HDI shows that it explains variation in HDI in a much better way than the level of economic development (Figure 4). This is in spite of the fact that human development index as such does not include any variable that explicitly represents access to and use of water for various uses; overall health of water eco-system; and capacities in the water sector as one of its sub-indices. The R square value was 0.79 against 0.69 in the earlier case when per capita GDP is run against decomposed HDI. Also, the coefficient is significant at one per cent level. It means that variation in human development index can better be explained by *water situation* in a country, expressed in terms of sustainable water use index, than the ppp adjusted per capita GDP. Now, such a strong linear relationship between sustainable water use index and HDI explains the exponential relationship between sustainable water use index and per capita GDP as the improvements in sub-indices of HDI contributes to economic growth in its own way (i.e., per capita here is the education index, and is the health index).

While an alternative to analyze the impact of a country's water situation on its economic growth performance is to look at the historical data on: cumulative investments in water sector, water access and use by population in different sectors, change in water environment, and economic conditions for individual

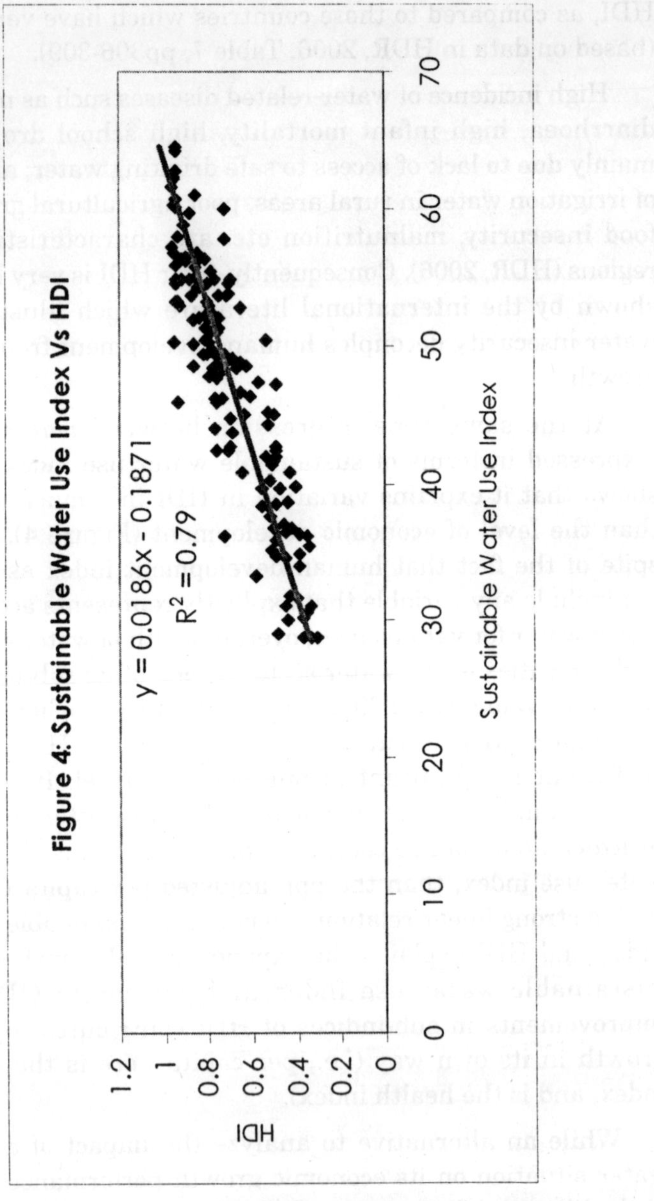

Figure 4: Sustainable Water Use Index Vs HDI

nations, such data are seldom available on a time series basis. Under such a circumstance, the best way to go ahead is to analyze the impact of natural water endowment, i.e., rainfall on economic growth in a situation where investments in infrastructure and institutions and governance mechanisms for improving water access and use and water environment are poor. The reason is that under such situations, the water access, water use, and water environment would be highly dependent on natural water endowment.

There cannot be a better region than Sub-Saharan Africa to illustrate such effects. A recent analysis showed a strong correlation between rainfall trend since 1960s and GDP growth rates in the region during the same period, which argued that the low economic growth performance could be attributed to long term decline in rainfall which the region experienced (Barrios *et al.*, 2004). Such a dramatic outcome of rainfall failure can be explained partly by the failure of the governments to build sufficient water infrastructure. Sub-Saharan Africa has smallest proportion of its cultivated area (< 3%) under irrigation (HDR, 2006). Due to this reason, reduction in rainfall leads to decline in agricultural production, food insecurity, malnutrition, loss of employment opportunities and an overall drop in economic growth in rural areas.

The foregoing analyses suggest that improving water situation of a country, which is represented by sustainable water use index, is of paramount importance if we need to sustain economic growth in that country. It would be rather an improper logic to consider that a country can wait till its economy improves to a certain level to start tackling its water problems. While the natural water endowment in both qualitative and quantitative terms cannot be improved through ordinary measures, the water situation can be improved through economically efficient, just and ecologically sound development and use of water in river basins.

5. Storage Development and Economic Growth

Now, water development has an important role in improving the access to and use of water, the two pre-requisites for improving the water situation (expressed in terms of SWUI) of a region, though intensive water development in river basins might reduce indicators on the water environment front. The amount of storage that needs to be created to improve access to and use of water depends on the type of climatic conditions. In temperate and cold climates, the demand of water for irrigation, which is the largest user of water in most regions with agricultural base, would be negligible when compared that in tropical and hot climates. Hence, the storage requirements would be much lower, mainly limited to that for meeting domestic/municipal water needs and water for manufacturing. Hence, it makes logic to explore links between storage development for meeting various human needs and economic growth only in tropical and hot climates.

The sheer scale of water infrastructure in rich countries is not widely appreciated (HDR, 2006: pp-155). Many developed regions of the world that experience tropical climates had high water storage in per capita terms. The United States, for instance, had created a per capita storage capacity of nearly 6000 m^3. In Australia, the 447 large dams alone provide a per capita water storage facility of nearly 3,808 m^3 per annum or a total of 79,000 MCM per annum. Aquifers supply another 4,000 MCM per annum. Against this, the country maintains a use of nearly 1,160 m^3 per capita per annum for irrigation, industry, drinking and hydropower, with irrigation accounting for 75% of the use (source: www.nlwra.gov.au/atlas). China, one of the fastest growing economies in the world, has per capita reservoir storage capacity of 2,000 m^3 per annum through dams, and an actual storage of nearly 360m^3 per capita. This is in spite of the great technological advancements made by most of these countries in improving water use efficiencies, particularly in sectors such as irrigation and industry.

When compared to these impressive figures, India, which is still developing, has a per capita storage of only 200m^3 per annum. Though a much higher level of withdrawal of nearly 600 m^3 per capital per annum is maintained by the country, a large percentage of this (231 BCM per annum or nearly 217 m^3 per capita per annum) comes from groundwater draft. But, there are increasing evidence to suggest that this won't be sustainable.

Many semi arid areas are already facing problems of groundwater over-draft, with serious socio-economic and ecological consequences as discussed in the recent work by Kumar (2007). Ethiopia, the poorest country in the world, has a per capita storage of 20 m^3 per annum. These facts also strengthen the argument that economic prosperity that a country can achieve is a function of available water storage per unit of population.

The per capita water storage and the per capita GDP (ppp adjusted) for a group of 22 countries is given in Figure 5. One can see a strong relationship between level of storage development and country's economic prosperity. The R square value is 0.55 (Figure 6), and the coefficient is significant at one per cent level. Such a relationship is understandable. Water storage infrastructure reduces risks, and improves water security.

Investments in hydraulic infrastructure had in many cases supported economic prosperity and social progress, though in some cases had caused environmental damage (HDR, 2006, based on various authors: pp140). Since 1920, the US Army Corps of Engineers had invested a sum of $ 200 billion on flood management and mitigation alone, yielding a benefit of $ 700 billion. The Tennessee Valley Authority, which built dams for hydropower, transformed the flood-prone, impoverished part of the Valley, with some of the worst human development indicators of the United States, into an agriculturally prosperous region. In Japan, heavy post war investments in infrastructure supported rapid development of hydropower, flood control and irrigated agriculture. The returns from these investments were tremendous. Until World Water II, the floods and typhoons had resulted in losses often amounting to 20% of GNI, whereas since the 1970s, the losses never exceeded 1% of the GNI (HDR, 2006: pp 156).

The returns on investments in building water storages were more visible in India. The recent analysis using panel data on gross irrigated area and rural poverty rate for 14 states showed poverty reducing effect of irrigation, with lowest rate of poverty found in Punjab which had the highest level of gross irrigated

Figure 5: Per Capita GDP & Dam Storage in Selected Countries

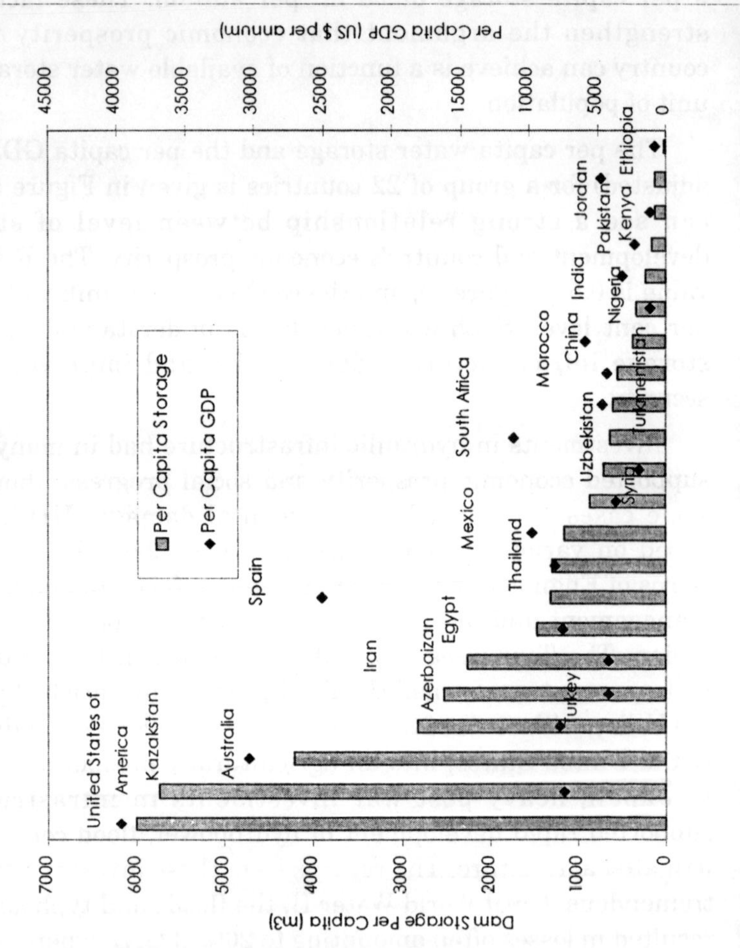

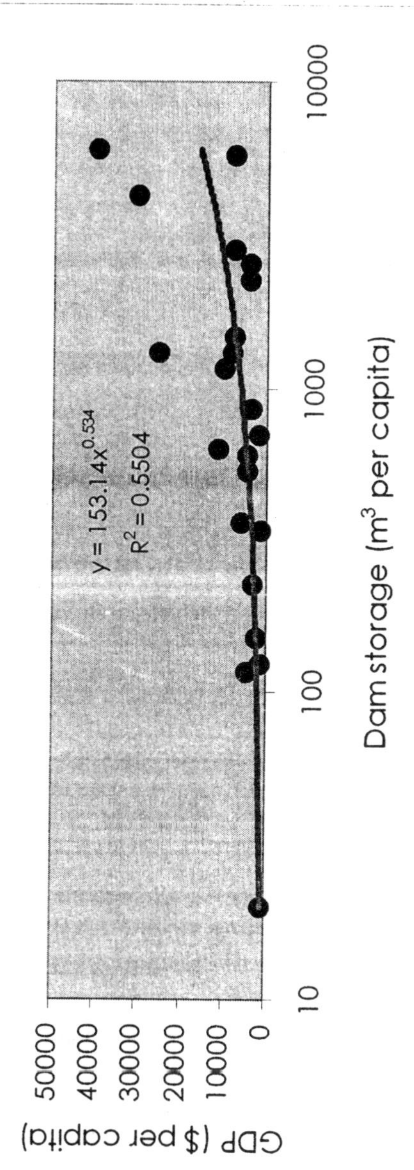

Figure 6: Per Capita GDP vs Per Capita Dam Storage

area, which reduced over time from 1973-74 to 1993-94 (Bhattarai and Narayanamoorthy, 2003). The Bhakra-Nangal Project had transformed the economy of Punjab. The almost perennial water supply from the project enabled farmers in this region to intensify cultivation with irrigated paddy and wheat, making it the country's bread basket. Now, 90% of the cropped area in the state is irrigated, three quarter of it going to paddy and wheat. Despite comprising less than 2% of the geographical area, Punjab accounts for 10% of rice production and 20% of wheat production in India. Agriculture accounts for 40% of the state GDP in the state, which has the highest per capita GDP amongst all Indian states (Cummings *et al.*, 2006).

The potential positive impact of water infrastructure on economic growth in regions that experience seasonal climates, rainfall variability and floods and droughts can be better demonstrated by the economic losses that water-related natural disasters cause in such regions which lack them badly. For instance, deviation in per capita GDP from the normal values during the 20-year period from 1980-2000 correlated with departure of annual rainfall from normal values (World Bank, 2006a). In Kenya, economic losses due to floods during 1997-98 were to the tune of 11% of the national GDP, where as that due to droughts during 1998-2000 was 16% of the GDP (World Bank, 2004a and World Bank 2006b).

But, there are many critiques to the argument based on per capita storage. According to Vandana Shiva, a renowned eco-feminist from India, the norms used for estimating per capita water use is fraudulent, and a way to push the large dam agenda by the World Bank. According to her, the many millions of ponds and tanks in rural areas of India themselves capture a lot of water and supplies it to the rural population in a more democratic and decentralized way than the large dams do. But, the contribution of such storage in augmenting our water supplies is often over-estimated by environmentalists. In the case of Australia, the National Heritage Trust's report of the audit of land and water resources say, the many millions of farm dams in Australia create a total storage of 2,000 MCM per annum, against 79,000 MCM by large dams (www.nlwra.gov.au/atlas).

Nevertheless, the overall impact of water storages on economic growth would depend on the nature of uses for which the resources are developed, the effectiveness of the institutions that are created to allocate the resource and the nature of institutional and policy regimes that govern the use of the resource. As we have seen in the case of incidence of hunger, in Zambia and Zimbabwe, use of water storages for hydropower generation had not helped improve the overall economic condition of the people also. Though the per capita water storage in Israel is quite low (nearly 150 m^3 per annum), the efficiency with which water is used in different sectors is extremely high. Nearly 90% of the country's irrigated area is under micro irrigation systems. A large portion of the water used in urban areas is recycled and put back to use for irrigation. Water is not only priced on volumetric basis, water allocation to agriculture is rationed.

One could as well argue that access to water could be better improved through local water resources development intervention including small water harvesting structures, or through groundwater development. As a matter of fact, environmental activists advocate decentralized small water harvesting systems as alternatives to large dams (see Agarwal and Narain, 1997). Small water harvesting systems had been suggested for water-scarce regions of India (Agarwal and Narain, 1997; Athavale, 2003), and the poor countries of Sub-Saharan Africa (Rockström *et al.*, 2002). But, recent evidence suggests that they cannot make any significant dent in increasing water supplies in countries like India due to the unique hydrological regimes, and can also prove to be prohibitively expensive in many situations (Kumar *et al.*, 2006). Also, to meet large concentrated demands in urban and industrial areas, several thousands of small water harvesting systems would be required. The type of engineering interventions[3] and the economic viability of doing the same are open to question. Recent evidence also suggests that small reservoirs get silted up much faster than the large ones (Vora, 1994), a problem for which large dams are criticized world over (see McCully, 1996).

As regards groundwater, intensive use of groundwater resources for agricultural production is proving to be catastrophic in many semi arid and arid regions of the world, including some developed countries like Spain, Mexico, Israel, Australia, and parts of United States (Kumar, 2007), and developing countries such as India, China, Pakistan, Yemen and Jordan (HDR, 2006), though some of the developed countries like United States and Australia have achieved some degree of success in controlling it through establishment of management regimes (Kumar, 2007) with physical and institutional interventions like in western US, or through physical interventions alone like in Israel.

But, it is important to recognize the fact that in the basins that are facing problems of environmental water scarcity and degradation in the world (see Smakhtin, Revenda and Doll, 2004) due to large water projects, river-flows are appropriated and transferred for various consumptive needs. Some of these basins are the Colorado river basin in the western US; Yellow river basin in northern China; Aral sea basins, viz., Amu-Darya and Syr Darya in Central Asia; Indus basin in Pakistan and India; basins of northern Spain; Nile basin in northern Africa; basins of Euphrates, Tigris; the Jordan river; Cauvery, Krishna and Pennar basins of peninsular India; river basins of western India including Sabarmati, Banas and Narmada, located in Gujarat, Rajasthan and Madhya Pradesh in India. Most of the water demands they meet are agricultural[4]. They are also agriculturally prosperous regions. They not only meet the food requirements of the region, but also export significant chunk of the food to other regions of the world, including some of the water-rich regions, within the country's territory (Amarasinghe *et al.*, 2005 for Indus basin and peninsular region in India; Kumar and Singh, 2005 for many water-scarce countries of the world; Yang, 2002 for China).

Strikingly, wherever aquifers are available for exploitation, these regions had experiencing problems of groundwater over-draft, though some developed countries had developed the science to deal with it. The most glaring examples are aquifers in western United States, aquifers in the countries of the Middle East including Yemen, Iran and Jordan; aquifers in Mexico; north China plains (Molden *et al.*, 2001); alluvial aquifers of

Indus basin areas in India; hard rock aquifers of Peninsular India; and aquifers in western and central India (GOI, 2005).

For the presence of large surface water projects, the negative impacts agricultural growth in these regions, might have caused on groundwater resources might have been far more serious. In fact, it is this surface water availability, which to a great extent helps reduce dependence of farmers as well as cities on groundwater. For instance, imported water from Indus basin through canal in Indian and Pakistan Punjab sustain intensive groundwater use in the regions, through continuously providing replenishment through return flows from surface irrigation (Ahmed *et al.*, 2004; Hira and Khera, 2002; Kumar, 2007). Water imported from the Central Valley Project in California is used to buy back the groundwater rights of farmers using water from Ogallala aquifer in Kansas and Texas. Water imported from a large reservoir named Sardar Sarovar in Narmada basin in Southern Gujarat in India had started supplying water to rejuvenate the rivers in environmentally stressed basins of north Gujarat (Kumar and Ranade, 2004).

6. Impact of Storage Development on Hunger

As one would expect, storage development has a direct impact on malnutrition, and infant mortality, which is captured in GHI. Here again, we have assumed zero values of GHI for developed countries viz., United States, Australia and Spain for which data on GHI are not available. Regression shows an R square value of 0.59 (Figure 7). As Figure 7 indicates, the relationship between per capita storage and GHI is inverse, logarithmic. The regression coefficient is significant at one per cent level. It means greater water storage reduces the chances of human hunger. This inverse relationship can be explained this way. For the countries, which we have chosen for the analysis, the ability to cultivate the available arable land intensively would increase with the amount of water storage facilities available. As HDR (2006: pp 174) notes, "Water security in agriculture pervades all aspects of human development". Increased availability of irrigation water reduces the risk of crop failure; enhances the ability of farmers to produce more crops to improve their own domestic food consumption of food, and

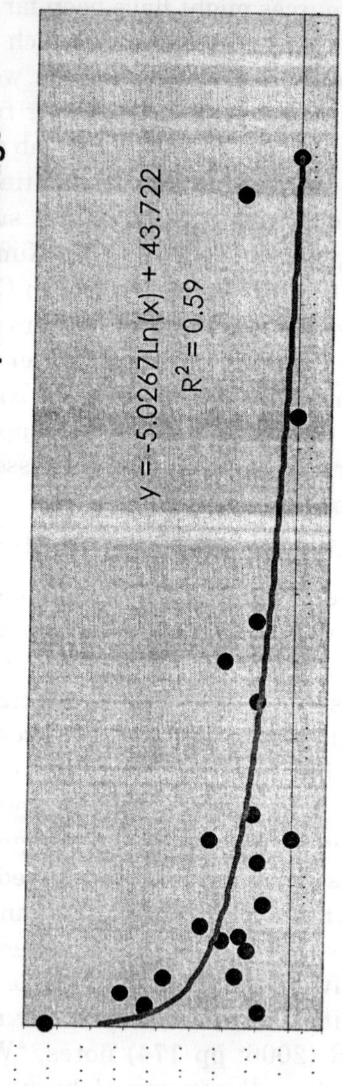

Figure 7: Global Hunger Index Vs Per Capita Dam Storage

take care of the cash needs. Also, increased irrigated production improves food and nutritional security of the population at large by lowering cereal prices in the region in question as the gap between cereal demand and supplies is reduced (Hussain and Hanjra, 2003 as cited in HDR, 2006: p. 175).

This was more evident in India than anywhere else, where irrigation expansion through large storages had contributed nearly 47 million tons of additional cereals to India's bread basket (Perry, 2001: pp 104). Shah and Kumar (2008) made a rough estimate of the positive externality it created in terms of lowering food prices for the consumers in India as US $ 20 per ton of cereals. One could also argue that rich countries could afford to import food. But, what is important is that water had played a big role for these countries to achieve a certain level of economic growth and prosperity, by virtue of which they can now afford to import food instead of resorting to domestic production. The exceptions are some of the oil rich countries of the Middle East, which do not have an agrarian base, but are economically prosperous.

Contrary to what is found in the case of these 22 countries, there are countries which have large storages, but have very high GHI. They are Zambia and Zimbabwe. They were not included in our analysis. These countries use their water storages for creating hydro-power, which is sold to the South Africa, and they earn revenue out of it. Most of it comes from just one hydropower dam, named, Kariba built in 1955-59 in Zambezi river basin. Hence, storage development does not lead to increased agricultural production in these countries. The GHI values are very high for these countries, which is 31.77 for Zambia, and 23.2 for Zimbabwe (Wiesmann, 2006). In such a situation, the impacts on food security would generally be seen only after many years. But in the case of these Sub-Saharan African countries, three decades of droughts and rainfall reduction had significantly affected the hydropower generation as well (McCully and Wong, 2004).

7. Summary of Findings

The findings from the foregoing analysis can be summarized as follows. Improving the water situation, vis-à-vis improved access to and use of water, institutional capabilities in water sector and improved water environment, through investments in water infrastructure, creation of institutions and introduction of policy reforms, can trigger economic condition in a nation. This occurs through the human development route, as shown by the consistent improvement in human development indicators with increase in values of SWUI. This strong linkage can be partly explained by the reduction in malnutrition and infant mortality, with improvement in water situation as indicated by the strong inverse relationship between SWUI and GHI for 117 countries.

Further, progress in human development has very little to do with their economic growth, and that they could achieve good indicators of development even at low levels of economic growth, through investment in water infrastructure and welfare-oriented policies. Many countries of the erstwhile Soviet Union, and communist countries of Latin America, which have low income, spend a significant portion of public funds in health and education, against many poor countries of Sub-Saharan Africa, which spend much less for health and education and more for military.

Countries which fall in tropical semi arid and arid climate, can improve their economic conditions through enhancing the reservoir storage. This potential impact be explained by increased water security that comes with greater water storage. This reduces the risks associated with natural calamities such as droughts and floods. Such natural calamities, which cause huge economic losses, are characteristic of these countries. For such large surface water development, the negative impacts agricultural growth would have induced on groundwater resources in such regions would have been far more serious. Nevertheless, the impact of storage could depend on the nature of uses for which the resources are developed, the effectiveness of the institutions that are created to allocate the resource and the nature of institutional and policy regimes that govern the use of the resource. Those countries having high per capita water storage also have very few people living in hunger.

9. Conclusions

Scholars have provided robust evidence to the effect that water security catalyses human development and economic growth. But, number of regions for which these evidence are available is too limited for evolving a global consensus on this complex issue. Water poverty index, conceived and developed by C. Sullivan (2002), and the international comparisons now available from Laurence, Meigh and Sullivan (2003) for 147 countries enable us to provide an empirical basis for the argument. A new index called SWUI was derived from WPI using four of its five sub-indices to assess the water situation of a country, vis-à-vis access and use of water, water environment and institutional capabilities in the water sector. Analysis was carried out using data on SWUI, GHI, HDI, per capita GDP and per capita water storage in dams to understand the nature of linkage between water situation of a country and its economic growth.

Findings show that economically poor countries, which also show very poor indicators of human development, need not wait till the economic conditions improve to address water sector problems. Instead, they should start investing in building water infrastructure, create institutions and introduce policy reforms in water sector that could lead to improved water situation vis-à-vis access to and use of water, water environment and institutional capabilities. Only, this can support progress in human development, and sustain economic growth, through poverty reduction; food security, improved livelihoods and nutrition, with positive effects on productive workforce; and domestic water security with positive effects on health, environmental sanitation, with spin off effects on livelihoods and nutrition, school drop out rates and productive workforce. But, a pre-requisite for hot and arid tropical countries is that they invest in large water resource systems to raise the per capita available storage. This will help them fight hunger and poverty, malnutrition, infant mortality, and reduce the incidence of water-related disasters.

References

Agarwal, Anil and Sunita Narain (1997) *Dying Wisdom: Rise and Fall of Traditional Water Harvesting Systems*, Centre for Science and Environment, New Delhi.

Ahmad, M. D., I, Masih and H. Turral (2004) Diagnostic analysis of spatial and temporal variations in crop water productivity: A field scale analysis of the rice-wheat cropping system of Punjab, Pakistan, *Journal of Applied Irrigation Science*, 39 (10).

Amarasinghe, Upali, Bharat R. Sharma, Noel Aloysius, Christopher Scott, Vladimir Smakhtin, Charlotte de Fraiture, A. K. Sinha and A. K. Shukla (2005) *Spatial Variation in Water Supply and Demand across River Basins of India*, IWMI Research Report 83, Colombo, Sri Lanka.

Athavale, R. N. (2003) *Water Harvesting and Sustainable Supply in India*, published for Environment and Development Series, Centre for Environment Education, Rawat Publications, Jaipur and New Delhi.

Barrios, Salvador, Luisito Bertinelli and Eric Strobl (2004) Rainfall and Africa's Growth Tragedy, paper.

Bhattarai, Madhusudan and A. Narayanamoorthy (2003) Impact of irrigation on rural poverty in India: an aggregate panel data analysis, *Water Policy*, 5 (2003): 443-458.

Biswas, Asit K. and Cecilia Tortajada (2001) Development and large Dams: A Global Perspective, *International Journal of Water Resources Development*, 17 (1).

Braga B., O. Rocha and J. Tundisi (1998) Dams and the Environment: The Brazilian Experience, *International Journal of Water Resources Development*, 14 (2).

Briscoe, John (2005) "India's Water Economy: Bracing up for a Turbulent Future," key note address at the 4th Annual Partners' Meet of IWMI-Tata Water Policy Research Program, Institute of Rural Management Anand, 26-29 February, 2005.

Cummings Jr. R., S. Rashid and A. Gulati (2006) Grain Price Stabilization Experiences in Asia: What Have We Learned?, Food Policy, 31 (4): 302-312.

Dharmadhikary, S. (2005) Unraveling Bhakra: Assessing the Temple of Resurgent India, Manthan Adhyayan Kendra, New Delhi.

Doris, Wiesmann (2006) *Global Hunger Index: A basis for cross country comparison*, International Food Policy Research Institute, Washington D. C.

D'Souza, D. (2002) Narmada Dammed: *An Enquiry into the Politics of Development,* New Delhi: Penguin Books India.

Food and Agriculture Organization of the United Nations (FAO) (2006) The AQUASTAT database. Rome. [www.fao.org/aq/agl/aglw/aquastat/dbase/index.stm]

Government of India (2005) Dynamic Ground Water Resources of India, Central Ground Water Board, Ministry of Water Resources, Government of India, August.

Hira, G. S. and K. L. Khera (2000) Water Resource Management in Punjab under Rice-Wheat Production System, Department of Soils, Punjab Agricultural University, Ludhiana.

Hussain, Intizar and Munir Hanjra (2003) "Does Irrigation Water Matter for Rural Poverty Alleviation? Evidence from South and South East Asia," *Water Policy*, 5 (5): 429-442.

Human Development Report (2006) Human Development Report-2006, New York: United Nations.

Kumar, M. Dinesh (2007) *Groundwater Management in India: Physical, Institutional and Policy Alternatives*, New Delhi: Sage Publications.

Kumar, M. Dinesh and Rahul Ranade (2004) Large Water Projects in The Face Of Hydro Ecological and Socioeconomic Changes in Narmada Valley: Future Prospects and Challenges, *Journal of Indian Water Resources Society.*

Kumar, M. Dinesh and O. P. Singh (2005) Virtual Water in Global Food and Water Policy Making: Is There a Need for Rethinking? *Water Resources Management*, 19: 759-789.

Kumar, M. Dinesh, Shatanu Ghosh, Ankit Patel, O. P. Singh and R. Ravindranath (2006) Rainwater Harvesting in India: some critical issues for basin planning and research, *Land Use and Water Resource Research*, 6 (2006): 1-17.

Laurence, Meigh and C. Sullivan (2003) Water Poverty of Nations: International Comparisons, Kellee University, Wallingford, UK.

Mc Cully, Patrick (1996) Climate Change Dooms Dams, *Silenced Rivers: The Ecology and Politics of Large Dam*, Zed Books, London.

Mc Cully, Patrick and Susanne Wong (2004) Powering a Sustainable Future: The Role of Large Hydropower in Sustainable

Development, paper prepared for the UN Symposium on Hydropower and Sustainable Development.

Molden, D. J., Upali Amarasinghe and I. Hussain (2001) "Water for Rural Development, "Working Paper 32, International Water Management Institute, Colombo.

Pearce, D. W. and Warford, J. (1993) *World Without End: Economics, Environment, and Sustainable Development*. (published for the World Bank) London and New York: Oxford University Press.

Perry, C. J. (2001) World Commission on Dams: Implications for Food and Irrigation, Irrigation and Drainage, 50: 101-107.

Rockström, J., Jennie Barron and Patrick Fox (2002) Rainwater management for improving productivity among small holder farmers in drought prone environments, *Physics and Chemistry of the Earth*, 27 (2002): 949-959.

Sadoff, Claudia and David Grey (2005) "Water Resources, Growth and Development," a Working Paper for Discussion, prepared by The World Bank for the panel of Finance Ministers, the UN Commission for Sustainable Development, 18 April, 2005.

Smakhtin, Vladimir, Carmen Revenda and Petra Doll (2004) "Taking into Account Environmental Water Requirements in Global-Scale Water Resources Assessments," Comprehensive Assessment Report 2, Comprehensive Assessment Secretariat, Colombo.

Shah, Tushaar and Barbara van Koppen (2006) Is India Ripe for Integrated Water Resources Management? Fitting Water Policy to National Development Context, Special Articles, *Economic and Political Weekly*, August 5, 2006.

Shah, Zankhana and M. Dinesh Kumar (2008) In the Midst of the Large Dam Controversy: Objectives, Criteria for Assessing Large Water Storages in the Developing World, *Water Resources Management*, 22: 1799-1824.

Sullivan, Caroline (2002) Calculating Water Poverty Index, *World Development*, 30 (7): 1195-1211.

Vora, B. B. (1994) Major and Medium Dams: Myth and the Reality, *Hindu Survey of the Environment*, Kasturi & Sons, Chennai.

World Bank (2004) *Towards a Water Secure Kenya: Water Resources Sector Memorandum*, Washington D. C.

World Bank (2005) "Pakistan Water Economy: Running Dry", Report 34081-PK. South Asia Region, Agriculture and Rural Development Unit, Washington D.C.

World Bank (2006a) *Managing Water Resources to Maximize Sustainable Growth: A Country Water Resources Assistance Strategy for Ethiopia*, Washington D. C.

World Bank (2006b) *Hazards of Nature, Risk to Development*, An IEG Evaluation of World Bank Assistance to Natural Disasters, Independent Evaluation Group, Washington D. C.

Footnotes

1. Indicator of the proportion of the population living in undernourished conditions and the child mortality rate (see Wiesmann, 2006).
2. For instance, the USSR had invested in a major way for building hydraulic infrastructure in central Asia (HDR, 2006). As a result, they attain high HDI even at low level of economic growth.
3. Complex engineering interventions would be required for collecting water from such number of small water harvesting and storage systems, and then transporting to a distant location in urban areas.
4. In Murray Darling basin, 90% of the annual flows are diverted for agricultural use.

8

Summary and Conclusions

The book began with a discussion on the current water crisis in India; the nature of debate on water management alternatives and identified the key knowledge gaps. We argue that while there are several solutions in popular parlance, there are serious knowledge gaps about "what solutions work and under what conditions". Such knowledge gaps result in certain myths about what can solve India's water scarcity problems. They can be classified into those concerning "supply management" and those concerning "demand management". On the supply management side, one dominant myth is that roof water harvesting would ensure domestic water security in naturally water-scarce regions, and can be treated as an alternate water supply option for poor rural and urban households which do not have good access to public water supply. The second one is that rainwater harvesting and local groundwater recharging offer great potential as an alternate source of augmenting water supply in naturally water-scarce regions to provide the much needed irrigation to crops experiencing water stress, thereby mitigating the impacts of droughts. Further, local recharge using harvested runoff can improve groundwater conditions in these regions.

On the demand management side, the following are the dominant myths. First: pricing of electricity in farm sector, though is a theoretically sound proposition for managing electricity use in agriculture and groundwater, is unviable. Metering electricity consumption, which is a pre-requisite for introducing consumption based tariff, would involve huge transaction costs. If this is passed on to the consumers, it would affect the economic prospects of farming, and therefore would be unpopular (Shah *et al.*, 2004). Second: micro irrigation systems have a great potential in India, and almost all the irrigated land in the country could be brought under it, barring paddy. Significant saving in water could be possible through the use of micro irrigation. Third: virtual water trade can be used as an economic instrument for dealing with water shortages for food production by water-deficit countries and regions, through the import of food from water-rich countries and regions; and virtual water trade can be an alternative to large-scale water transfer projects which food importing regions are getting engaged in.

The analysis presented in chapter 2 show that the roof water harvesting systems are not alternative to public systems in urban and rural areas of regions receiving low rainfall. Hydrological opportunities for RWHS are very poor in urban and rural areas under low rainfall conditions. They are also prohibitively expensive in terms of cost per unit volume of water harvested. The systems offer very little scope in ensuring domestic water security for urban housing stocks of low and middle-income groups. At the same time, they offer tremendous potential for independent bungalows having large roof area. However, their physical feasibility is very poor in urban areas. Their economic viability as a supplementary source of domestic water supply seems to be poor in urban areas, when compared to augmenting the supplies from the existing public systems.

The incredibly low rates charged for domestic supplies by urban water utilities, and government subsidies for RWHS would only lead to urban elite increasing their access to water supplies, while the burden on water utilities would remain unchanged. This will lead to greater inequities in access to water supplies. At the same time, in rural areas with dispersed populations and hilly areas, they may be economically viable as a supplementary source to already existing public water supply schemes. But as its impacts are not likely to be uniform across classes, government subsidies are not desirable. In hilly regions receiving high rainfalls, they would not only offer great scope in terms of hydrological benefits, but also would be economically sound. Hence, government investment for conventional public water supply schemes could be replaced by heavy subsidies for installation of RWHS which appear to be economically more viable.

Chapter 3 dealt with the hydrological opportunity and economics of rainwater harvesting in general, with particular focus on naturally water-scarce regions. The data include: rainfall magnitudes, variability in rainfall, rainy days and its variability, runoff, infiltration and geology. It also reinforces the rigour in this analysis by using primary data collected from two small river basins in India where intensive water harvesting activities were undertaken. The primary data used include daily rainfall, stream flows, number and capacity of water harvesting structures and groundwater level fluctuations.

The analysis presented showed that in water-scarce regions of India, runoff harvesting does not offer any potential for groundwater recharge or improve water supplies at basin scale. The issues can be summarized as follows. First: RWH efforts lack emphasis on potential local supplies and the demand it has to cater to. While local supply potential is low in most water scarce regions, with poor reliability. The demand for water far exceeds the supply potential in the naturally water-scarce regions. Secondly, there are complexities involved in economic evaluation of RWH, due to lack of scientific data on inflows, runoff collection and storage efficiency, beneficiaries, value of the incremental benefits generated and scale considerations. A rigorous analysis of data available from pilot experiments of CGWB showed that local water harvesting/recharging is prohibitively expensive in terms of cost per unit volume of water, and economically unviable if used for irrigated crop production.

With higher degrees of basin development, the marginal benefit from water harvesting at the basin level reduces, while marginal cost increases. Third: in many basins, there is a strong "trade off" between maximizing hydrological benefits and improving cost effectiveness. Fourth: many water-scarce basins are characterized by wide disparity in demand between upper catchments and lower catchments, due to which there is a trade off in maximizing benefits of upstream water harvesting with optimizing basin-wide benefits. Fifth: in many water-scarce basins, local water harvesting only divides the hydrological benefits rather than augmenting. Finally, lack of integration between surface water system and groundwater system reduces the potential of artificial recharging in hard rocks which also coincide with water-scarce regions.

Thus, the schemes of the government, NGOs and donors for water harvesting and local groundwater recharge in naturally water-scarce regions of Indian need to be planned with a lot of caution. In many instances intensive water harvesting might create a lot of negative externalities rather than bringing benefits to the society.

The fourth chapter covered the impact of introducing marginal cost for electricity and raising electricity tariff on equity, efficiency and sustainability of groundwater use in agriculture, and the overall net returns from farming. The analysis used primary data on farming systems of electric and diesel well commands (both owners and water buyers) in eastern UP and South Bihar covering 480 farmers. It also used data from two categories of electric well owners in north Gujarat: one who paid for electricity on flat rate basis; and the other who paid electricity charges on the basis of actual consumption, covering 120 farmers.

Our analysis shows that introducing marginal cost for electricity motivate farmers to use water more efficiently at the field level from physical, agronomic and economic point of view through careful use of irrigation water, use of better agronomic inputs and optimizing costly inputs. Also, it would motivate farmers to use water more efficiently at the farm level through careful use of irrigation water in crops; better agronomic inputs; optimizing costly inputs for crops; careful selection of crops and cropping patterns, and livestock composition that give higher return from every unit of water and low water consuming crops. It also showed that higher cost of irrigation water affected by higher energy cost will not lead to lower net return from every unit of water used as the farmers modify farming system itself in response to increase in energy cost.

The analysis also showed that changing the power tariff structure from flat rate to pro-rata would not have any adverse effects on equity of access in groundwater in terms of increasing the monopoly power of well owners. This is because the monopoly prices are largely governed by the number of potential water sellers against the number of potential buyers of water in an area. In addition, pro rata pricing has significant impact in reducing groundwater pumpage from every unit of irrigated land, which is disproportionately higher than the reduction in net return from unit of land. Hence, it had a positive impact on improving the sustainability of groundwater use. The empirical evidences further reinforced the fact that introducing pro rata pricing and raising power tariff in agriculture are socio-economically viable, and the arguments against pricing are flawed.

In the fifth chapter, we did a rigorous analysis to see under what conditions micro irrigation system become the "best bet technology", and what benefits it can yield. The aim of the research was to determine the potential benefits from the use of MI systems in India. The overall goal was to assess the potential of MI systems in addressing future water scarcity problems in India. For this, vast amount of existing literature; physical and economic data from primary field research; and macro level data on geo-hydrology, climate and cropping pattern were used. An assessment of potential benefits from MI systems was done through analyzing: (a) the conditions that are favourable for MI system adoption; (b) the field level and aggregate level impacts of the systems on water use; and (c) the yield and economic benefits from adoption. The research also assessed the potential future coverage of MI systems in India, and the potential reduction in aggregate water requirement in crop production.

The findings with regard to constraints in MI system adoption were: (i) lack of independent source of water and pressurizing device for many farmers; (ii) poor quality of groundwater in many semi arid and arid regions; (iii) the mismatch between water delivery schedules and irrigation schedules required in MI systems in surface irrigation systems; (iv) cropping systems that dominate field crops in semi arid regions; (v) dominance of small and marginal farmers, and small plot sizes; (vi) low opportunity costs of pumping groundwater due to lack of well-defined water rights; (vii) negative technical externalities in groundwater use; (viii) poor extension services; and viii] poor administration of subsidies.

The other findings were: (1) the extent of real water-saving and water productivity gains at the field level from adoption of

MI systems varies across crops, climate, geo-hydrology and type of MI devices used; (2) the potential benefits of MI systems in terms of real field level water saving are likely to be realized in semi arid and arid areas with deep water table conditions, for widely spaced row crops; (3) the economics of pressurized MI systems depend on the capital cost of the system, size of the plot, type of crop irrigated, extent of water and energy saving and the market value of the produce; (4) being capital intensive, the economic viability of MI systems is sound for high valued cash crops and orchards, especially in areas where groundwater availability is extremely limited; and (5) in many areas, due to flat rate system of pricing and heavy subsidy in electricity, zero opportunity cost of using groundwater, energy and water saving does not result in cost saving and improved economic returns from MI.

It was argued that the future potential of MI systems to improve basin water productivity is primarily constrained by the physical characteristics of the basins vis-à-vis the opportunities they offer for real water-saving at the field level and basin water productivity improvements, and area under crops that are conducive to MI in those basins. Preliminary analysis showed a very modest potential of MI systems to the tune of 5.6 m. ha, with the impact of drip systems in reducing aggregate water requirement for crop production to the tune of 44.46 BCM. This is far less than the official estimates of 97 m. ha as the ultimate potential of MI systems in India, and the earlier estimates provided by scholars (Narayanamoorthy, 2004 for instance). This shows that the impact of use MI systems in changing the future water scenario of the country would not be remarkable.

A higher scale of adoption of MI systems in well irrigated areas could be encouraged through tariff reforms in electricity and water like those suggested in Chapter 6 are necessary. But to start with, metering of agro wells and provision of incentives for conservative use of electricity could be done. Along with this, changes in subsidy administration; improvement in quality of power supply in agriculture. In canal command areas, improving the quality and reliability of water supplies from canals through provision of intermediate storage systems, and introduction of volumetric pricing are the key. Another important suggestion for policy makers is that providing subsidies for MI systems might require a thorough scrutiny as its use may not result in water saving everywhere so as to provide positive externalities on the society, a major justification for subsidies.

In chapter 6, we examined the validity of a dominant argument that economies that face acute water scarcity problems can and should meet their water demand for food production through cereal imports from water-rich countries. This was done by analyzing whether the virtues of global water use efficiency and "distribution of scarcity", as claimed by the proponents of "virtual water trade", are achieved really through virtual water trade between countries and between regions within countries.

For this, we analyzed country level data on renewable freshwater availability and net virtual water trade of 146 nations across the world. The analysis showed that a country's virtual water trade is not determined by its water situation. Some countries have the advantage of high "economic efficiency" in food production and have surplus water, but resort to food import, whereas some water scarce countries achieve high virtual water trade balances. Further analysis with a set of 131 countries showed that virtual water trade increased with increase in gross cropped area. This is because of two reasons. First: when access to arable land increases, the ability to utilize available blue water for irrigation increases. Second: increasing access to arable land improves the access to water held in the soil profile as "free good", a factor not taken into account in assessing water availability. Many of the humid, water-rich countries will not be in a position to produce surplus food and feed the water scarce nations; and virtual water often flows out of water-poor, land rich countries to land-poor water-rich countries. This means that "distribution of scarcity" and "global water use efficiency", are goals that are difficult to achieve through virtual water trade in a practical sense.

There are two important policy inferences emerging from the analyses. First: assessing the food security challenges posed to nations in future purely from a water resource perspective provides a distorted view of the food security scenario. National policies on food security should take into account "access to arable land" apart from water availability. Second: analysis of water challenges posed by nations purely from the point of view of renewable water availability and aggregate demands will be dangerous. Access to water in the soil profile, which is determined by access to arable land, would be an important determinant of effective water availability.

Virtual water transfer is the dominant water management paradigm suggested for water scarce countries that are characterized by major regional variations in the resource endowment and still relying on food imports. But, this could spell doom if arable land is limited in the "well endowed" area. Such situations exist in India wherein the eastern India is well endowed in water resources, but has limited arable land, while north western India and south Indian peninsula have large amount of arable land, but with extremely limited native freshwater resources. In such cases, physical transfer of water could be attempted thereby enabling productive use of both land and water for crop production at the country level. Studies from eastern UP and western Punjab showed that there is significant incremental economic value of water realized from its use in water-scarce regions over a water-rich region. Transfer of water in addition to the "volumetric surplus" available in the water-rich region also might be justified under two conditions: the cost of water transfer is lower than the incremental economic value realized; and the region which is deprived of the resource is adequately compensated.

In chapter 7, we confronted the larger question of the likely impacts of investments in water sector in developing economies like India. We analyzed the linkage between water security, human development and economic growth, and the role of creating storages. The basic research issue was "whether economic growth drives water security or vice versa". Though scholars have provided robust evidences to the effect that water security catalyses human development and economic growth, the number of regions for which these evidences are available is too limited for evolving a global consensus on this complex issue. Water poverty index, conceived and developed by C. Sullivan (2002), and the international comparisons now available from

Laurence, Meigh and Sullivan (2003) for 147 countries enable us to provide an empirical basis for the argument. A new index called "Sustainable Water Use Index" was derived using four of the five sub-indices of WPI to assess the water situation of a country, vis-à-vis access and use of water, water environment and institutional capabilities in the water sector. Analysis was carried out using data on SWUI, GHI, HDI, per capita GDP and per capita water storage in dams to understand the nature of linkage between water situation of a country and its economic growth.

Findings showed that economically poor countries, which also show very poor indicators of human development, need not wait till the economic conditions improve to address water sector problems. Instead, they should start investing in building water infrastructure, create institutions and introduce policy reforms in water sector that could lead to improved water situation vis-à-vis access to and use of water, water environment and institutional capabilities. Only, this can support progress in human development, and sustain economic growth, through poverty reduction; food security, improved livelihoods and nutrition, with positive effects on productive workforce; and domestic water security with positive effects on health, environmental sanitation, with spin off effects on livelihoods and nutrition, school drop out rates and productive workforce. But, a pre-requisite for hot and arid tropical countries is that they invest in large water resource systems to raise the per capita available storage. This will help them fight hunger and poverty, malnutrition, infant mortality, and reduce the incidence of water-related disasters.

To sum up, it appears that the nation's policy makers need to exercise much more caution while investing in the water sector. While we cannot challenge concepts underlying any of the water management solutions tried by people and governments, certain conditions have to satisfy for them to work and give desired results. Impulsive decisions driven by popular ideas will have to find way for rational decisions based on thorough analysis of the hydrological, socio-economic, political, institutional, and policy environments which would have significant bearing on the success of any solution chosen so as to identify the regions and localities and fix the scale of implementation. Further, more importantly, there need to be greater focus on creating institutions for water management to deal with the new age challenges of ensuring equity in access to and use of water, in the face of increasing competition and conflicts over sharing of scarce water resources.

References

Laurence, Meigh and C. Sullivan (2003) Water Poverty of Nations: International Comparisons, Kellee University, Wallingford, UK.

Narayanamoorthy, A. (2004) Drip irrigation in India: can it solve water scarcity? *Water Policy*, 6 (2004): 117-130.

Shah, Tushaar, Christopher Scott, Avinash Kishore and Abhishek Sharma (2004) *Energy Irrigation Nexus in South Asia: Improving Groundwater Conservation and Power Sector Viability*, IWMI Research Report # 70, Colombo, Sri Lanka.

Sullivan, Caroline (2002) Calculating Water Poverty Index, *World Development*, 30 (7): 1195-1211.

Bibliography

AFPRO (Undated) Manual on Construction and Maintenance of Household Based Rooftop Water Harvesting Systems. Report prepared by AFPRO (Action for Food Production) for UNICEF.

Agarwal, A. and Sunita Narain (eds.) (1997) *Dying Wisdom: Rise, Fall and Potential of Traditional Water Harvesting Systems in India,* 4th Citizen's Report. New Delhi: Centre for Science and Environment.

Ahmad, M. D., I, Masih and H. Turral (2004) Diagnostic analysis of spatial and temporal variations in crop water productivity: A field scale analysis of the rice-wheat cropping system of Punjab, Pakistan, *Journal of Applied Irrigation Science*, 39 (10).

Alagh, Y. K, R. D. Desai, G. S. Guha and S P Kashyap (1995) *Economic Dimensions of Sardar Sarovar Project,* New Delhi: Har-Anand Publications.

Allan, J. A. (1997) Virtual water: A long term solution for water short Middle Eastern economies?' Paper presented at the 1997 British Association Festival of Science, University of Leeds, 9 September 1997.

Allan, J. A. 2003a. Virtual Water Eliminates Water Wars? A Case Study from the Middle East, Virtual water trade, proceedings of the international expert meeting on virtual water trade, edited by Hoekstra, A. Y., Value of water research report series # 12.

Allan, J. A. 2003b. Virtual Water-the Water, Food, Trade Nexus, Useful Concept or Misleading Metaphor?, Discussion paper, *Water International*. 28 (1) pp. 4-10.

Al-Weshah, Radwan A. 2000. Optimal Use of Irrigation Water in the Jordan Valley: A Case Study, *Water Resources Management* 14: 327–338, 2000, pp. 327 -338.

Amarasinghe, U.A.; Sharma, B.R., eds. (2008) *Strategic analyses of the National River Linking Project (NRLP) of India, series 2.* Proceedings of the Workshop on Analyses of Hydrological, Social and Ecological Issues of the NRLP. Colombo, Sri Lanka: International Water Management Institute, 500p.

Amarasinghe, Upali, Bharat R. Sharma, Noel Aloysius, Christopher Scott, Vladimir Smakhtin, Charlotte de Fraiture, A. K. Sinha and A. K. Shukla (2005) *Spatial Variation in Water Supply and Demand across River Basins of India*, IWMI Research Report 83, Colombo, Sri Lanka.

Amarasinghe, Upali, Tushaar Shah and Peter McCornick (2008) Seeking Calm Waters: Exploring policy options for India's Water Future, *Natural Resource Forum*, 32 (4): 305-315.

Ariyabandu, S. de. R. (1999) "Development of Rainwater Harvesting for Domestic Water Use in Rural Sri Lanka," *Asia Pacific Journal of Rural Development*, IX (1), July.

Arlosoroff, Saul (1995) The Water Sector in the Middle East- Potential Conflict Resolutions (Israel and its Neighbours)," The Truman Institute for the Advancement of Peace, Hebrew University, Jerusalem, Israel.

Asian Development Bank (2007) *2007 Benchmarking and Data Book of Water Utilities in India*, a partnership between the Ministry of Urban Development, Government of India and the Asian Development Bank, November.

Athavale, R. N. (2003) *Water Harvesting and Sustainable Supply in India*, Centre for Environment Education, Ahmedabad, Jaipur and New Delhi: Rawat Publications.

Athawale, R. N. (2003) *Water Harvesting and Sustainable Supply in India*, published for Environment and Development Series, Centre for Environment Education, Rawat Publications, Jaipur and New Delhi.

Badiger, S, R. Sakthivadivel, N. Aloysius and H. Sally (2002) Preliminary Assessment of a Traditional Approach to Rainwater Harvesting and Artificial Recharging of Groundwater in Alwar District, Rajasthan, paper presented at the annual partners' meet of IWMI-Tata Water Policy Research Programme, Anand, February 19-20.

Barker, Randolph, David Dawe and Arlene Inocencio (2003) "*Economics of Water Productivity in Managing Water for Agriculture*," in Jacob Kijne and others (Eds.) *Water Productivity in Agriculture: Limits and Opportunities for Improvement*, Comprehensive Assessment of Water Management in Agriculture. UK: CABI Publishing in Association with International Water Management Institute.

Barrios, Salvador, Luisito Bertinelli and Eric Strobl (2004) Rainfall and Africa's Growth Tragedy, research paper.

Bastiaanssen, Wim, Mobin-ud-Din Ahmed and Zubair Tahir (2003) Upscaling Water Productivity in Irrigated Agriculture Using Remote-sensing and GIS Technologies, in Jacob Kijne and others (Eds.) *Water Productivity in Agriculture: Limits and Opportunities for Improvement*, Comprehensive Assessment of Water Management in Agriculture. UK: CABI Publishing in Association with International Water Management Institute.

Bachelor, Charles, Ashok Singh, MS Rama Mohan Rao and Johan Butterworth (2002) Mitigating the Potential Unintended Impacts of Water Harvesting, paper presented at the IWRA International Regional Symposium 'Water for Human Survival', 26-29 November, 2002, Hotel Taj Palace, New Delhi.

Behera, B.P. and N. Sahoo, (1998) Economic evaluation of a drip irrigation system in Orissa. *Environment and Ecology*, Vol. 16(2): 297-299.

Bhattarai, Madhusudan and A. Narayanamoorthy (2003) Impact of irrigation on rural poverty in India: an aggregate panel data analysis, *Water Policy*, 5 (2003): 443-458.

Biswas, Asit K. and Cecilia Tortajada (2001) Development and large Dams: A Global Perspective, *International Journal of Water Resources Development*, 17 (1).

Biswas, Asit. K. (1992) "Water for Sustainable Development: A Global Perspective," *Wasteland News*, 7 (2), November 1991- January 1992.

Boughton, J. C. and J. J. Stone (1985) Variation of Runoff with Watershed Area in a semi arid Location, *Journal of Arid Environment*, Vol. 9, pp. 13-25.

Braga B., O. Rocha and J. Tundisi (1998) Dams and the Environment: The Brazilian Experience, *International Journal of Water Resources Development*, 14 (2).

Brewer, J., Shashi Kolavalli, A.H. Kalro, G. Naik, S. Ramnarayan, K.V. Raju and R. Shakthivadivel (1999) Irrigation Management Transfer in India: Policies, Processes and Performance. New Delhi and Culcutta: Oxford & IBH.

Briscoe, John (2005) "India's Water Economy: Bracing up for a Turbulent Future," key note address at the 4th Annual Partners' Meet of IWMI-Tata Water Policy Research Program, Institute of Rural Management Anand, 26-29 February, 2005.

Carter, Richard, Melvyn Kay and Keith Weatherhead (1999) Water Losses in Smallholder Irrigation Schemes, *Agricultural Water Management*, 40 (1): 15-24.

Central Ground Water Board (1998) Groundwater Problems of Mehsana District. Report, Central Ground Water Board, West-Central region, Ahmedabad.

Central Pollution Control Board (1988) Status of water supply and wastewater collection, treatment and disposal in Class 1 and Class 2 cities, New Delhi: CPCB.

Chapagain A.K. and A.Y. Hoekstra (2003) Virtual water trade: A quantification of virtual water flows between nations in relation to international trade of livestock and livestock products, Virtual water trade, proceedings of the international expert meeting on virtual water trade, edited by Hoekstra, A. Y., Value of water research report series # 12.

Chaturvedi, Mahesh C. (2000) Water for Food and Rural Development, Developing Countries, *Water International*, 25 (1): 40-53.

Chavez, H. and F. Andrew (1974) Drip irrigation increase yields, lowers water costs. *Citrus and Vegetable Magazine*, Vol. 38: 1, 6 and 18.

Cummings Jr. R., S. Rashid and A. Gulati (2006) Grain Price Stabilization Experiences in Asia: What Have We Learned?, *Food Policy*, 31 (4): 302-312.

D'Souza, D. (2002) Narmada Dammed: An Enquiry into the Politics of Development, New Delhi: Penguin Books India.

Dahake, S.G., S. P. Lambe, H.V. Kalpande; D.M. Nikhade and V.V. Kalpande (1998) Utility perception of orange growers about drip irrigation system. *Jouranal of Soils and Crops*, Vol. 8(2): *154-156.*

Datt, G. (1997) *Poverty in India and Indian States*, International Food Policy Research Institute, Washington D.C.

Deepak, and others (2005) Water Demand Management: A Strategy to Deal with Water Scarcity, paper presented at the 4th Annual Partners' Meet of IWMI-Tata Water Policy Research Programme, February

Delgado, Christopher, Mark Rosegrant, Henning Steinfeld, Simeon Ehui and Claude Courbois (2003) Livestock to 2020: The Next Food Revolution, Food, Agriculture and Environment Discussion Paper 28. International Food Policy Research Institute.

Desale, P.G., P.P. Pawar and R.P. Patil (2003) Economics analysis of drip irrigation for banana. *Indian Journal of Agricultural Economics*, July-September, Vol. 58, No. 3, p. 506.

Dharmadhikary, S. (2005) Unraveling Bhakra: Assessing the Temple of Resurgent India, Manthan Adhyayan Kendra, New Delhi.

Dhawan, B. D. (2000) "Drip Irrigation: Evaluating Returns". *Economic and Political Weekly*, pp. 3775-3780, October 14.

Doris, Wiesmann (2006) *Global Hunger Index: A basis for cross country comparison*, International Food Policy Research Institute, Washington D. C.

Down to Earth (1996) "Arsenic Down Under," 5 (10), October 15.

Down to Earth (2004) Water Woes in Wet Kerala, Cover Story, *Down to Earth*, May 31, pp. 26-33.

Earle A. and A. Turton (2003) The virtual water trade amongst countries of the SADC, Virtual water trade, proceedings of the international expert meeting on virtual water trade, edited by Hoekstra, A. Y., Value of water research report series # 12.

Evans, J. P., and A. J. Jakeman (undated) Development of a Simple, Catchment-Scale, Rainfall-Evaporation-Runoff Model, Centre for Resource and Environmental Studies, The Australian National University, Canberra ACT 0200: http://earth.geology.yale.edu/~je84/mystuff/research/ems_paper.pdf.

Evenson, Robert E., Carl E. Pray and Mark W. Rosegrant (1999) *Agricultural Research and Productivity Growth in India*, Research Report 109, International Food Policy Research Institute.

Falkenmark, Malin (2004) Towards Integrated Catchment Management: Opening the Paradigm Locks between Hydrology, Ecology and Policy Making, *International Journal of Water Resources Development*, 20 (3).

Food and Agriculture Organization (2000) FAOAQUASTAT database on line on water and agriculture. http://www.fao.org/ag/agl/aglw/aquastat/dbase/

Food and Agriculture Organization of the United Nations (FAO) (2006) The AQUASTAT database. Rome. [www.fao.org/aq/agl/aglw/aquastat/dbase/index.stm]

Food and Agriculture Organization (2000) FAOSTAT on line database Agricultural. http://apps.fao.org/page/collections

Fox, P., J. Rockström and J. Barron (2002) Risk Analysis and economic viability of water harvesting for supplementary irrigation in semi arid Burkina Faso and Kenya, *Agricultural Systems*, 83 (3): 231-250.

Frederick, K. D. (1993) *Balancing Water Demand with Supplies: The Role of Management in a World of Increasing Scarcity*, Technical Paper 189, Washington D. C: World Bank.

Gallopin, Gilberto C. and Frank R. Rijsberman (2000) Three Global Water Demand Projections, *International Journal of Water*, 1 (2000).

Gaonkar, Rekha and Shashikala Sarmalkar (2003) Policies for sustainable use of water. *Indian Journal of Agricultural Economics*, July-September, Vol. 58, No. 3, p. 508.

Garg, S. K. (1987) *Hydrology and Water Resources Engineering*, Khanna publishers, Delhi, pp.110-181.

Gleick, P. H. (1998) *The World's Water 1998-1999*. Washington D. C: Island Press.

Glieck, P. H. (1997) Human Population and Water: Meeting Basic Needs in the 21st Century. In R. K. Pachauri and Lubina F. Qureshi (Eds.) *Population, Environment and Development*. New Delhi: Tata Energy Research Institute. pp. 105-121.

Government of Gujarat (1994) Integrated Plan of Sabarmati River Basin, Draft Report prepared by Gujarat State Water Resources Planning Group, Gandhinagar, Gujarat.

Government of Gujarat (1996) Water Resource Planning for the State of Gujarat- Phase III, Vol. II, Main Report.

Government of Gujarat (1999) "Report of the Committee on Estimation of Ground Water Resource and Irrigation Potential in Gujarat State: GWRE – 1997", Department of Narmada, Water Resources and Water Supplies, Gandhinagar.

Government of Gujarat (undated) *District-wise classification of land-use in Gujarat – 1998-99*, Department of Agriculture, Government of Gujarat (http://www.indiastat.com/).

Government of India (1994) Drip irrigation in India, Indian National Committee on Irrigation and Drainage, Ministry of Water Resources, Government of India, New Delhi.

Government of India (1999) Integrated Water Resource Development: A Plan for Development, Report of the National Commission for Integrated Water Resources Development Vol. I, Ministry of Water Resources, Government of India, New Delhi.

Government of India (2002) "Annual Report (2001-02) of the Working of State Electricity Boards and Electricity Departments 2001-2002," Planning Commission-Power and Energy Division, May 2002.

Government of India (2005) Dynamic Ground Water Resources of India, Central Ground Water Board, Ministry of Water Resources, Government of India, August.

Government of India (2007) Report of the Expert Group on "Groundwater Management and Ownership," Planning Commission, *Yojana Bhawan*, New Delhi.

Government of India. Undated. *Annual Report 2002-03*, Ministry of Commerce and Industry, Government of India. (http://www.indiastat.com/)

Government of Madhya Pradesh (1972) *Master Plan for Development of Water Resources of The Narmada in Madhya Pradesh*, Volume – II, Statements, Government of Madhya Pradesh.

Government of Rajasthan (1992) Effect of Rainfall and Potential Evapo transpiration on Groundwater Levels of Rajasthan, Groundwater Department, Jodhpur.

Grismer, E. M. (2001) Regional cotton lint yield and water value in Arizona and California. *Agricultural Water Management*, 1710, 1-16.

Gujarat Agriculture University (1997) Agro-climatic Atlas of Gujarat, Department of Agricultural Meteorology, B. A. College of Agriculture, Gujarat Agricultural University, Anand Campus.

Gupta, R. K. (2000) Regional Water Transfer and Human Rights: Some Reflections on Sardar Sarovar Project, *ASIAN Journal* (Formerly Journal of Transportation and Infrastructure, 7 (4) pp: 112-127.

Haddadin, M. J. (2003) Exogenous Water: A Conduit to Globalization of Water Resources, Virtual water trade, proceedings of the international expert meeting on virtual water trade, edited by Hoekstra, A. Y., Value of Water Research Report Series # 12.

Hapase, D.G., A.N. Mankar; A.N. Salunkhe; V.M. Salokhe; Gajendra Singh and S.G. Illangantileke (1992) Techno-economic evaluation of drip irrigation for sugarcane crop. In Proceedings of an International Agricultural Engineering Conference, held in Bangkok, Thailand on 7-10 December, 1992, Vol. III, pp. 897-904.

Hira, G. S. and K. L. Khera (2000) Water Resource Management in Punjab under Rice Wheat Production System, Department of Soils, Punjab Agricultural University, Ludhiana.

Hoekstra A.Y. (2003) Virtual water: An introduction, Virtual water trade, proceedings of the international expert meeting on virtual water trade, edited by Hoekstra, A. Y., Value of Water Research Report Series # 12.

Hoekstra, A.Y. (1998) Perspectives on water: An integrated model-based exploration of the future. International Books, Utrecht, the Netherlands.

Hoekstra, A.Y. and P. Q. Hung (2002) Virtual water trade: A quantification of virtual water flows between nations in relation to international crop trade, Value of Water Research Report Series No.11, IHE, Delft, the Netherlands.

Hoekstra, A.Y. and P.Q. Hung (2003) Virtual water trade: A quantification of virtual water flows between nations in relation to international crop trade, Virtual water trade, proceedings of the international expert meeting on virtual water trade, edited by Hoekstra, A. Y., Value of Water Research Report series # 12.

Howes, S and R. Murugai (2003) Incidence of Agricultural Power Subsidies: An Estimate, *Economic and Political Weekly*, April 19.

http://www.siwi.org/waterweek2003/Workshop%207%20Oral(28).htm

Human Development Report (2006) Human Development Report-2006, New York: United Nations.

Hurd, Brian, Neil Leary, Russell Jones and Joel Smith (1999) Relative Regional Vulnerability of Water Resources to Climate Change, *Journal of the American Water Resources Association*, 35 (6): 1399-1419.

Hussain *et al.* (2003) Land and Water Productivity of Wheat in the Western Indo-Gangetic Plain if India and Pakistan: a Comparative Analysis, in Jacob Kijne and others (Eds.) *Water Productivity in Agriculture: Limits and Opportunities for Improvement*, Comprehensive Assessment of Water Management in Agriculture. UK: CABI Publishing in Association with International Water Management Institute.

Hussain, Intizar and Munir Hanjra (2003) "Does Irrigation Water Matter for Rural Poverty Alleviation? Evidence from South and South East Asia," *Water Policy*, 5(5): 429-442.

Ilyas, S. M. (1999) "Water Harvesting towards Water Demand Management and Sustainable Development," *Journal of Rural Reconstruction*, 32 (2).

Inamdar, P.P., J. R. Pawar and D.L. Sale (1995) Economic efficiency of bi-wall drip irrigation in sugarcane production: a case study in Ankalkhop village in Sangli district of Maharashtra. *Bharatiya Sugar*. Vol. 22(2): 43-48.

Ingle P.O. and N.A. Sagane (1992) Constraints in the use of drip irrigation systems : a case study. *Journal of Maharashtra Agricultural Universities,* Vol. 17(2) :294-297.

IRMA/UNICEF (2001) *White Paper on Water in Gujarat*, report prepared for the government of Gujarat.

Iyer, R. Ramaswamy (2008) Water: A Critique of Three Basic Concepts, *Economic and Political Weekly*, 43 (1): 15-17.

Jadhav S.S., Gutal G.B. and A.A. Chougule (1990) Cost economics of the drip irrigation system for tomato crop. In Proceedings of the 1₁t1~ International Congress on the Use of Plastics in Agriculture, New Delhi, 26th February – 2nd March, 1990.

Jakeman, A. J., David A. Post, and M.B. Beck (1994) From data and theory to environmental models, *Environmetrics*, 5, 297-314.

Kamra, S. K and others (1986) "Water Harvesting for Reclaiming Alkaline Soils," *Agricultural Water Management*, 11.

Keller, A., J. Keller and David Seckler (1996) *Integrated Water Resources Systems: Theory and Policy Implications.* Research Report 3, Colombo: International Water Management Institute.

Kijne, Jacob, Randolph Barker and David Molden (2003) Improving Water Productivity in Agriculture: Editors' Overview, in Jacob Kijne and others (Eds.) *Water Productivity in Agriculture: Limits and Opportunities for Improvement*, Comprehensive Assessment of Water Management in Agriculture. UK: CABI Publishing in Association with International Water Management Institute.

Kolarkar, A. S., K. Murthy and N. Singh (1983) Khadin-a method of harvesting water for agriculture in the Thar desert, *Arid Environment*. 6: 59-66.

Kumar, M. Dinesh (1997) Water Use Study for Coastal Saurashtra and Kachchh, report submitted to the Water Resources Development and Management (WARDEMA) Project, Rajkot, VIKSAT, Ahmedabad.

Kumar, M. Dinesh (2000a) Dug-well Recharging in Saurashtra: Are the Impacts and Benefits Over-stretched? *Journal of Indian Water Resources Society*, July.

Kumar, M. Dinesh (2000b) Institutions for Efficient and Equitable Use of Groundwater: Irrigation Management Institutions and Water Markets in Gujarat, Western India. *Asia-Pacific Journal of Rural Development*, Vol. X (1), July.

Kumar, M. D. Shashikant Chopde, Srinivas Mudrakartha and Anjal Prakash (1999) "Addressing Water Scarcity: Local Strategies for Water Supply and Conservation Management in Sabarmati Basin, Gujarat," in M. Moench, E. Caspari and A. Dixit (eds.)

Rethinking the Mosaic: Investigations into Local Water Management. Kathmandu and Boulder: Nepal Water Conservation Foundation and Institute for Social and Environmental Transition.

Kumar, M. Dinesh (2001) Demand management in the Face of Growing Scarcity and Conflicts: Technological, Institutional and Policy Option, Working Paper 153, Institute of Rural Management Anand.

Kumar, M. D. (2002a) Integrated Water Management in the Face of Growing Scarcity and Threatened Groundwater Ecology: Constraints and Opportunities, discussion paper, IWMI-TATA Water Policy Research programme.

Kumar, M. Dinesh (2002b) Reconciling Water Use and Environment: Water Resource Management in Gujarat, Resource, Problems, Issues, Strategies and Framework for Action, report prepared for State Environmental Action Project supported by the World Bank, Gujarat Ecology Commission.

Kumar, M. Dinesh (2003a) "Demand Management in the Face of Growing Water Scarcity and Conflicts in India: Institutional and Policy Alternatives for Future," In Kanchan Chopra, CH Hanumantha Rao and Ram Prasad Sengupta (Eds.) *Water Resources, Sustainable Livelihoods and Ecosystem Services*. Published by Indian Society for Ecological Economics, New Delhi: Concept Publishing Company.

Kumar, M. Dinesh (2003b) Food Security and Sustainable Agriculture in India: The Water Management Challenge, Working Paper 60, International Water Management Institute, Colombo, Sri Lanka.

Kumar, M. Dinesh (2003c) "Micro Management of Groundwater in North Gujarat, Water Policy Research Highlight # 5: IWMI-Tata Water Policy Programme, Anand.

Kumar, M. Dinesh (2004) Roof Water Harvesting for Domestic Water Security: Who Gains and Who Loses? *Water International*, 39 (1): 43-53.

Kumar, M. Dinesh (2005) Impact of Electricity Prices and Volumetric Water Allocation on Groundwater Demand Management: Analysis from Western India, *Energy Policy*, 33 (1): 39-51

Kumar, M. Dinesh (2007) *Groundwater Management in India: Physical, Institutional and Policy Alternatives*, New Delhi: Sage Publications.

Kumar, M. Dinesh and O.P. Singh (2001) Market Instruments for Demand Management in the Face of Scarcity and Overuse of Water in Gujarat. *Water Policy*, 3 (5): 387-403.

Kumar, M. Dinesh and O. P. Singh (2005) Virtual Water in Global Food and Water Policy Making: Is There a Need for Rethinking? *Water Resources Management*, 19: 759-789.

Kumar, M. Dinesh and P. J. Patel (1995) Depleting buffer and farmers' response: study of villages in Kheralu, Mehsana, Gujarat. In: Moench, M. (Ed.), Electricity Prices: A Tool for Groundwater Management in India?. VIKSAT-Natural Heritage Institute, Ahmedabad.

Kumar, M. Dinesh and Rahul Ranade (2004) Large Water Projects in The Face Of Hydro Ecological and Socioeconomic Changes in Narmada Valley: Future Prospects and Challenges, *Journal of Indian Water Resources Society.*

Kumar, M. Dinesh and Tushaar Shah (2004) Groundwater Contamination and Pollution in India: Emerging Challenges, *Hindu Survey of the Environment 2004*, Kasturi & Sons.

Kumar, M. Dinesh and Vishwa Ballabh (2000) *Water Management Problems and Challenges in India: An Analytical Review*, Working Paper 140, Anand: Institute of Rural Management Anand.

Kumar, M. Dinesh, Ajaya Kumar Malla and Sushanta Kumar Tripathy (2008) Economic value of water in agriculture: comparative analysis of a water-scarce and a water-rich region in India, *Water International*, 33 (2): 214-230.

Kumar, M. Dinesh, Ankit Patel, R. Ravindranath and O. P. Singh (2008) Chasing a Mirage: Water Harvesting and Artificial Recharge in Naturally Water-scarce Regions of India, *Economic and Political Weekly*, 43 (35): 61-71.

Kumar, M. Dinesh, Katar Singh, O.P. Singh and R. L. Shiyani (2004) Impacts of Water Saving and Energy Saving Irrigation Technologies in Gujarat, Research Report 2, India Natural Resources Economics and Management Foundation, Anand.

Kumar, M. Dinesh, OP Singh and Katar Singh (2001) Groundwater Development and Its Socio-economic and Ecological Consequences in Sabarmati River Basin", Monograph-2, Anand: INREM Foundation.

Kumar, M. Dinesh, Shantanu Ghosh, Ankit Patel, O. P. Singh and R. Ravindranath (2006) Rainwater Harvesting in India: Some Critical Issues for Basin Planning and Research, *Land Use and Water Resources Research*, 6 (1): 1-17.

Kumar, M. Dinesh, Vishwa Ballabh and Jayesh Talati (2000) Augmenting or Dividing: Surface water Management in the

Water Scarce River Basin of Sabarmati, IRMA Working Paper 147, Institute of Rural Management, Anand.

Lalljee, B. and S. Facknath (1999) Water Harvesting and Alternative Sources of Water for Agriculture, PROSI Magazine, September 1999.-N 368-Agriculture.

Laurence, Peter, Jeremy Meigh and C. Sullivan (2003) Water Poverty Index: International Comparisons, Keele University, and Centre for Ecology and Hydrology, Wallingford, United Kingdom.

Llamas, M. Ramon (2000), La Inserción De Las Aguas Subterráneas En Los Sistemas De Gestión Integrada, Paper presented at *II Congresso Ibérico Sobre Planeamento E Gestão De Água*, 9-12 November 2000, Oporto.

Luhach, M.S., R.K. Khatkar, and D.P. Malik (2003) Economic viability of sprinkler irrigation: An empirical analysis, *Indian Journal of Agricultural Economics*, July-September, Vol. 58, No. 3, p. 489.

Maroum, M. El-Fadel (2003) The Concept of Virtual Water and Its Applicability in Lebanon, Virtual water trade, proceedings of the international expert meeting on virtual water trade, edited by Hoekstra, A. Y., Value of Water Research Report Series # 12.

Marsden Jacob Associates (2007) The Economics of Rain Water Tanks and Alternative Water Supply Options, a report prepared for Nature Conservation Council of NSW, Australian Conservation Foundation and Environment Victoria.

Mc Cully, Patrick (1996) Climate Change Dooms Dams, *Silenced Rivers: The Ecology and Politics of Large Dam*, Zed Books, London.

Mc Cully, Patrick and Susanne Wong (2004) Powering a Sustainable Future: The Role of Large Hydropower in Sustainable Development, paper prepared for the UN Symposium on Hydropower and Sustainable Development.

Meinzen-Dick, Ruth S. and Bryan Randolph Bruns (2000) Negotiating Water Rights: Introduction, in Bryan Randolph Bruns and Ruth S. Meinzen Dick (Eds.) Negotiating Water Rights, Vistar and Intermediate Technology Publications: IFPRI-ADB Book.

Meissner R. (2003) Regional food security and virtual water: Some environmental, political, and economic considerations, Virtual water trade, proceedings of the international expert meeting on virtual water trade, edited by Hoekstra, A. Y., Value of Water Research Report Series # 12.

Minasia A. N., A.I. Karaghouli and S.K. Habeeb (1994) An economic analysis of drip irrigation systems: A choice among alternatives, Plasti culture, 101: 23-27.

Mishra, Anupam (1999) "Water harvesting here is not a technique, but a culture," Interview, *Down to Earth*, 4 (14) December 1995.

Moench, M. and H. Metzger (1992) *Groundwater Availability for Drinking in Gujarat: Quality, Quantity and Health Dimensions.* Monograph. VIKSAT-Pacific Institute for Studies in Environment, Development and Security, VIKSAT, Ahmedabad.

Moench, M., ed. (1995). *Electricity Pricing: A Tool for Groundwater Management in India?* Ahmedabad: VIKSAT-Natural Heritage Institute.

Moench, Marcus and M. Dinesh Kumar (1993) Local Water Management Initiatives: NGO Activities in Gujarat, VIKSAT-Pacific Institute Monograph, VIKSAT, Ahmedabad.

Molden, D. J., Upali Amarasinghe and I. Hussain (2001) "Water for Rural Development, "Working Paper 32, International Water Management Institute, Colombo.

Molden, David, Hammond Murray-Rust, R. Sakthivadivel and Ian Makin (2003) A Water Productivity Framework for Understanding and Action, in Jacob Kijne and others (Eds.) *Water Productivity in Agriculture: Limits and Opportunities for Improvement*, Comprehensive Assessment of Water Management in Agriculture. UK: CABI Publishing in Association with International Water Management Institute.

Molden, David, R. Sakthivadivel and Zaigham Habib (2001) Basin-*Level Use and Productivity of Water: Examples from South Asia*, IWMI Research Report 49, Colombo: International Water Management Institute.

Molle, Francois, Alireza Mamanpoush and Mokhtar Miranzadeh (2004) *Robbing Yadullah's Water to Irrigate Saeid's Garden Hydrology and Water Rights in a Village of Central Iran*, Research Report 80, International Water Management Institute, Colombo, Sri Lanka.

Mori, K. (2003) Virtual water trade in global governance, Virtual water trade, proceedings of the international expert meeting on virtual water trade, edited by Hoekstra, A. Y., Value of Water Research Report series # 12.

Muralidhara, H. R., D.S. Gundurao, A.M.Sarpeshkar, and R. Ramaiah (1994) Is drip irrigation viable for mulberry cultivation: an economic analysis. *Mysore Journal of Agricultural Sciences*, 28(3): 256-260.

Muralidharan, D. and R. N. Athawale (1998) Artificial Recharge in India, base paper prepared for Rajiv Gandhi National Drinking Water Mission, Ministry of Rural Areas and Development, National Geophysical Research Institute.

Narayanamoorthy, A. (1996) Impact of drip irrigation on consumption of water and electricity. *Asian Economic Review*, 38(3): 350-364.

Narayanamoorthy, A. (1997a) Economic Viability of Drip Irrigation: An Empirical Analysis from Maharashtra. *Indian Journal of Agricultural Economics*, October-December, 52 (4), pp. 728-739.

Narayanamoorthy, A. (1997b) Impact of Electricity Tariff Policies on the Use of Electricity and Groundwater: Arguments and Facts. *Artha Vijnana*, XXXIX (3): 323-340.

Narayanamoorthy, A. (2004a) Impact Assessment of Drip Irrigation in India: The Case of Sugarcane, *Development Policy Review*, 22 (4): 443-462.

Narayanamoorthy, A. (2004b) Drip irrigation in India: can it solve water scarcity? *Water Policy*, 6 (2004): 117-130.

Narayanamurthy, A. and R. S. Deshpande (1997) "Economics of Drip Irrigation: A Comparative Study of Maharashtra and Tamil Nadu". Mimeo, Gokhale Institute of Politics and Economics, No. 47, Pune.

National Geo-physical Research Institute (2000) Geo-hydrological Investigations in M. C. Tanda Watershed, Anantapur District for Formulation of Suitable Artificial Recharge Strategies, interim report, September.

Ohlsson, L. (1998) Water and Social Resource Scarcity - An Issue Paper Commissioned by FAO/AGLW. Presented as a discussion paper for the 2nd FAO E-mail Conference on Managing Water scarcity. WATSCAR 2.

Oweis, T. A. Hachum and J. Kijne (1999) Water Harvesting and Supplementary Irrigation for Improved Water Use Efficiency in Dry Areas. SWIM Paper, Colombo, Sri Lanka.

Palanichamy N.V., K. Palanisamy and T.R. Shanmugam (2002) Economic performance of drip irrigation in coconut farmers in Coimbatore. *Agricultural Economics Research Review*, Conference Issue, pp. 40-48.

Pandey, D. Narayan, Anil K. Gupta and David M. Anderson (2003) Rainwater harvesting as an adaptation to climate change, Review Article, *Current Science*, 85 (1), 10 July.

Parveen, Saila and I. M. Faisal (undated) Trading Virtual Water between India and Bangladesh: A Politico-economic Dilemma.

Patel, A. S. (2002) Impact of Groundwater Recharge Activities in Saurashtra, paper presented at the annual partners' meet of the IWMI-Tata Water Policy Research Programme, Anand, February 19-20.

Pearce, David and Jeremy Warford (1993) *World Without End, Economics, Environment, and Sustainable Development*, published for the World Bank, London and New York: Oxford University Press.

Perry, C. J. (2001) World Commission on Dams: Implications for Food and Irrigation, Irrigation and Drainage, 50: 101-107.

Phadtare, P.N. (1988) Artificial recharge of groundwater, paper submitted in the meeting of the working group on Water Harvesting, NCL, Pune, August 5, 1988.

Phansalkar, Sanjiv and Shilp Verma (2004) "Improved Water Control as a Strategy for Improving Tribal Livelihoods," Review of Agriculture, *Economic and Political Weekly*, XXXIX (12).

Phansalkar, Sanjiv and Shilp Verma (2005) India's Water Future 2025/2050, research highlight, IWMI-Tata water policy research program, Anand, India.

Pisharoty, P. R. (1990) Characteristics of Indian Rainfall, Monograph, Ahmedabad: Physical Research Laboratories.

Postel, Sandra (1996) Dividing the Waters: Food Security, Ecosystem Health, and the New Politics of Scarcity, World Watch Paper No. 132. Washington D.C, World Watch Institute, 1996, cited by Elmusa (1997) pp. 194.

Prinz, D. (2002) The Role of Water Harvesting in Alleviating Water Scarcity in Arid Areas, Keynote Lecture, Proceedings, International Conference on Water Resources Management in Arid Regions. 23-27 March, 2002, Kuwait Institute for Scientific Research, Kuwait (Vol. III. 107-122).

Puranik, R.P., S.R. Khonde and P.L. Ganorkar (1992) Constraints and problems as perceived by non-adopters and adopters of drip irrigation system. *Agricultural Situation in India*, Vol. XLVII, No.1 April, pp. 33-34.

Rangachari, R., Nirmal Sengupta, Ramaswamy R. Iyer, Pranab Banergy, and Shekhar Singh (2000) Large Dams: India's Experience, Final Report, prepared for the World Commission on Dams, Cape Town, South Africa, Secretariat of World Commission on Dams.

Rangachari, R., Nirmal Sengupta, Ramaswamy R. Iyer, Pranab Banergy, and Shekhar Singh (2000) Large Dams: India's Experience, Final Report, prepared for the World Commission on Dams, Cape Town, South Africa, Secretariat of World Commission on Dams.

Rao, P.S. (2003) Study on efficient use of irrigation water device: a case study. *Indian Journal of Agricultural Economics*, July-September, Vol. 58, No. 3, p. 504.

Raskin, P., P. Gleick, P. Kirshen, G. Pontius, and K. Strzepek. 1997. *Water futures: Assessment of long-range patterns and problems*, Comprehensive assessment of the freshwater resources of the world, Stockholm Environment Institute, Stockholm, Sweden.

Rath, N. (2003) Linking rivers: some elementary arithmetic, *Economic and Political Weekly*, 39 (29): 3033.

Reddy, D.V.S. and S. Thimmegowda (1997) Economic analysis of different drip irrigation systems of main and ratoon hybrid cotton. *Mysore Journal of Agricultural Sciences*, Vol. 3 1(1):17-22.

Rockström, J. and L. Gordon (2001) Assessment of green water flows to sustain major biomes of the world: implications for future eco hydrological landscape management, *Phys. Chem. Earth (B)* 26: 843-851.

Rockström, J., Jennie Barron and Patrick Fox (2002) Rainwater management for improving productivity among small holder farmers in drought prone environments, *Physics and Chemistry of the Earth*, 27 (2002): 949-959.

Rockström, J., Jennie Barron and Patrick Fox (2003) Water productivity in rain-fed agriculture: Challenges and opportunities for smallholder farmers in drought-prone tropical ecosystems. In Jacob Kijne and others (Eds.) *Water Productivity in Agriculture: Limits and Opportunities for Improvement*, Comprehensive Assessment of Water Management in Agriculture. UK: CABI Publishing in Association with International Water Management Institute.

Rosegrant, M. W, C. Ringler and R. V. Gerpacio (1999) "Water and Land Resources and Global Food Supply," in G.H. Peters and Joachim Von Braun (eds.) *Food Security, Diversification And Resource Management: Refocusing The Role of Agriculture?* Ashgate.

Sadoff, Claudia and David Grey (2005) "Water Resources, Growth and Development," a Working Paper for Discussion, prepared by The World Bank for the panel of Finance Ministers, the UN Commission for Sustainable Development, 18 April, 2005.

Sahuquillo, Andres (1985) Groundwater in Water Resource Planning: Conjunctive Use, *Water International,* 10 (1985) 57-63.

Sakthivadivel, R. Nihal Fernando and Jeffrey Brewer (1997) *Rehabilitation Planning for Small Tanks in Cascades: A Methodology Based on Rapid Assessment*, Research Report 13, International Irrigation Management Institute, Colombo, Sri Lanka.

Saleth, R. Maria (1997) Power Tariff Policy for Groundwater Regulation: Efficiency, Equity and Sustainability. *Artha Vijnana,* XXXIX (3): 312-322.

Seckler David, Upali Amarasinghe, David Molden, Radhika de Silva and Randolph Barker (1998) *World Water Demand and Supply 1990-2025: Scenarios and Issues*, Research Report 19, Colombo, Sri Lanka: International Water Management Institute.

Seckler, David J. (1996) *The New Era of Water Resources Management: From Dry to Wet Water Savings*, Research Report # 1, International Irrigation Management Institute, Colombo, Sri Lanka.

Shah, Tushaar (1993) *Groundwater markets and Irrigation Development: Political Economy and Practical Policy*, Bombay: Oxford University Press.

Shah, Tushaar (2001) Wells and Welfare in Ganga Basin: Public Policy and Private Initiative in Eastern Uttar Pradesh, India, Research Report 54, International Water Management Institute, Colombo, Sri Lanka

Shah, Tushaar (2002) Decentralized Water Harvesting and Groundwater Recharge: Can these Save Saurashtra and Kachchh from Desiccation, paper presented at the annual partners' meet of the IWMI-Tata Water Policy Research Programme, Anand, February 19-20.

Shah, Tushaar and Barbara van Koppen (2006) Is India Ripe for Integrated Water Resources Management? Fitting Water Policy to National Development Context, Special Articles, *Economic and Political Weekly*, August 5, 2006.

Shah, Tushaar, Christopher Scott, Avinash Kishore and Abhishek Sharma (2004) *Energy Irrigation Nexus in South Asia: Improving Groundwater Conservation and Power Sector Viability*, IWMI Research Report # 70, Colombo, Sri Lanka.

Shah, V.I., Desai, N.V. and Joshi S.V. (1997) Control of Brackishness in Drinking Water. A Base Paper presented by Central Salt and Marine Chemicals Research Institute, Bhavnagar.

Shah, Zankhana and M. Dinesh Kumar (2008) In the Midst of the Large Dam Controversy: Objectives, Criteria for Assessing Large Water Storages in the Developing World, *Water Resources Management*, 22: 1799-1824.

Sharma, Abhishek (2002) Does Water Harvesting Help in Water-Scarce Regions? A Case Study of Two Villages in Alwar, Rajasthan, paper presented at the annual partners' meet of the IWMI-Tata Water Policy Research Programme, Anand, February 19-20.

Shiyani R.L., D.B. Kuchhadiya and M.V. Patat (1999) Economic impact of drip irrigation technology on cotton growers of Saurashtra region. *Agricultural Situation in India*, 56 (7): 407-412.

Singh, O. P. (2004) Water-intensity of North Gujarat's Dairy Industry: Why Dairy Industry Should Take a Serious Look at Irrigation?, paper presented at the second International Conference of the Asia Pacific Association of Hydrology and Water Resources (APHW 2004), Singapore, June 5-9, 2004.

Singh, O. P. (2004), Water Productivity of Milk Production in North Gujarat, Western India, Proceedings of the *2nd Asia Pacific Association of Hydrology and Water Resources (APHW) Conference*, Vol. 1: 442-449.

Sivapalan, M. and J. D. Kalma (1995) Scale problems in hydrology: Contributions of the Robertson Workshop, *Hydrological Processes*, 9 (3-4): 1995.

Smakhtin, Vladimir, Carmen Revenda and Petra Doll (2004) "Taking into Account Environmental Water Requirements in Global-Scale Water Resources Assessments," Comprehensive Assessment Report 2, Comprehensive Assessment Secretariat, Colombo.

Sorooshian, Saroosh, Martha P. L. Witaker and Terri S. Hogue (2002) Regional and global hydrology and water resource issues: The role of international and national programmes, water policy article. *Aquatic Sciences*, 64 (2002) 317-327.

Sullivan, Caroline (2002) Calculating Water Poverty Index, *World Development*, 30 (7): 1195-1211.

TERI (1998) *Looking Back to Think Ahead Growth with Resource Enhancement of Environment and Nature,* Tata Energy Research Institute, New Delhi, March.

Todd, David K. (2003) *Groundwater Hydrology*, Second Edition, John Wiley and Sons (Asia) Pte Ltd. Singapore.

Tortajada, (2001) First Meeting of the Club of Tokyo for a Global Water Policy Dialogue, Tokyo, 25-26 September, *Water Policy*, 3 (5): 359-362.

United Nations Development Programme (2006) *Human Development Report- 2006*, New York: United Nations.

United Nations Development Programme (2003) *Human Development Report – 2003*, Oxford university press, New York.

Varghese, B. G. (2002) Water and Energy for Future India, paper presented at the International Regional Symposium on Water for Human Survival, 26-29, November, 2002, Hotel Taj Residency, New Delhi.

Verghese, B. G. (2001) Sardar Sarovar Project Revalidated by Supreme Court, *International Journal of Water Resources Development*, Vol. 17 (1), 79-88.

Verma, Shilp, Stanzin Tsephal and Tony Jose (2005) Pepsee Systems: Farmer Innovations under Groundwater Stress, *Water Policy*, 6:4 (2004): 303-318.

Vora, B. B. (1994) Major and Medium Dams: Myth and the Reality, *Hindu Survey of the Environment*, The Hindu, Chennai.

Warner, J. (2003) Virtual water – virtual benefits? Scarcity, distribution, security and conflict reconsidered, Virtual water trade, proceedings of the international expert meeting on virtual water trade, edited by Hoekstra, A. Y., Value of Water Research Report Series # 12.

Waykar, K.R., B.K. Mali, Y.C. Sale and A.B. Bhosale (2003). Drip irrigation system: A sustainable way for sugar production. *Indian Journal of Agricultural Economics*, July-September, Vol. 58, No. 3, pp. 498-499.

Wichelns, D. (2001) The role of 'virtual water' in efforts to achieve food security and other national goals, with an example from Egypt. *Agricultural Water Management* 49(2):131-151.

Wichelns, D. (2003) The Role of Public Policies in Motivating Virtual Water Trade, With an Example from Egypt, Virtual water trade, proceedings of the international expert meeting on virtual water trade, edited by Hoekstra, A. Y., Value of Water Research Report Series # 12.

Wood, E. F., M. Sivapalan and K. Beven (1990) Similarity and scale in catchment storm response. *Rev. Geophysics*, 28, 1-18.

World Bank (2004) *Towards a Water Secure Kenya: Water Resources Sector Memorandum*, Washington D. C.

World Bank (2005) "Pakistan Water Economy: Running Dry", Report 34081-PK. South Asia Region, Agriculture and Rural Development Unit, Washington D.C.

World Bank (2006a) *Managing Water Resources to Maximize Sustainable Growth: A Country Water Resources Assistance Strategy for Ethiopia*, Washington D. C.

World Bank (2006b) *Hazards of Nature, Risk to Development*, An IEG Evaluation of World Bank Assistance to Natural Disasters, Independent Evaluation Group, Washington D. C.

World Bank/GOI (1997) "Groundwater Regulation and Management," World Bank-Government of India, India Water Resources Management Sector Review, Volume I-Main Report, New Delhi.

World Resources Institute (1995) *World Resources 1994-95: People and the Environment, Report prepared by World Resource Institute in collaboration with United Nations Environment Programme and United Nations Development Programme*. Bombay: Oxford University Press.

Yang, H. (2002) Water, environment and food security: a case study of the Haihe River basin in China. http://www.rioc.org/wwf/Water_in_China_Haihe.pdf

Zehnder, A.lexander J. B. and Armin Reller (2002) Water Issues. *Editorial*. http://www.oekom.de/verlag/german/periodika/gaia/pdf/lese2002_04.pdf

Zhu, Zhongping, Mark Giordano, Ximing Cai and David Molden (2004) Yellow River Basin Water Accounting, International Water Management Institute, Colombo, Sri Lanka.

Index

D